# BLOOD

## STORIES OF LIFE AND DEATH FROM THE CIVIL WAR

# BLOOD

## STORIES OF LIFE AND DEATH FROM THE CIVIL WAR

### EDITED BY PETER KADZIS
**ADRENALINE SERIES EDITOR CLINT WILLIS**

**Thunder's Mouth Press and
Balliett & Fitzgerald Inc.**

**New York**

**An Adrenaline Book™**

Published by
Thunder's Mouth Press
841 Broadway, 4th Floor
New York, NY 10003

and

Balliett & Fitzgerald Inc.
66 West Broadway, Suite 602
New York, NY 10007

Distributed by Publishers Group West

Book design: Sue Canavan

frontispiece photo: © Bettmann/Corbis

Manufactured in the United States of America

ISBN: 1-56025-259-6

Library of Congress Cataloging-in-Publication Data

Blood: stories of life and death from the Civil War / edited by Peter
Kadzis.
       p. cm.
"An Adrenaline book"—T.p.verso
    ISBN 1-56025-259-6
        1. United States—History—Civil War, 1861-1865—Personal
narratives.    2. United States—History—Civil War, 1861-1865—Fiction.
I. Kadzis, Peter.

   E601.B645 2000
   973.7′8—dc21
                                                    00-021768

To my parents

# contents

# p h o t o g r a p h s

# introduction

I must have been nine years old when I first came across the small stand of Union graves that rest on a rise in Cedar Grove Cemetery, a pocket of refined nineteenth century sensibility—fresh lawns, sturdy shade trees, winding paths, a gentle rolling terrain—which lies on the tidal basin of the Neponset River, marking one of Boston's southerly borders.

By the time I discovered the graves, The Civil War had been over for almost one hundred years. Like most boys that age who took an interest in battles and soldiers and generals, I imagined in storybook terms the events I loved to read about. There were heroes (Lee, the noble adversary), mysteries (Grant, the enigma), controversies (Sherman's march to the sea), selfless heroism (Pickett's charge), all imagined and reimagined with cinematic intensity.

My view of the war began to change that day, although I doubt I realized it as I walked among the 41 graves. I recognized none of the names (Issac Bowen, C.H. Richardson, Robert Adams, Lt. G.B. Smith, Sgt. F.T. Prince. . .), but that only made the experience a bit chilling, thus more potent. These were real men, with real lives; they died real deaths. Their simple white headstones, eighteen inches high, one foot wide, spaced not quite two feet apart, stood in stark contrast to the classically inspired faux mausoleums and bulky oblisques which marked so many of the civilian graves. These dead were clearly men apart.

"The real war," Walt Whitman wrote, "will never get in the books." Whitman was, of course, correct. The varieties of experience were too unique, the passions engaged too disparate, the fields of action too far flung, the political and ideological imperatives too diffuse to be neatly captured between any set of covers. That this can be said of most great conflicts in no way detracts from the truth of the poet's observation.

This collection is an attempt to suggest the breadth and depth of the Civil War experience. It is not comprehensive, or even aggressively representational. Rather, it is a mosaic; a collection of shards of testimony— real and fictional. My hope is that each piece reflects enough of the "real" so that by book's end the reader might begin to imagine the whole.

The story begins offstage. The United States Constitution established the context for the debates and disputes that would ultimately spiral into the Civil War. The Constitution sublimated a double helix of conflict: whether slavery could exist in a nation "dedicated to the proposition that all men were created equal," and where ultimate political power was to be vested—with each state, or with a centralized, federal government.

In the 72 years that intervened between ratification of the Constitution and secession these issues rent the nation with an increasingly religious intensity. Reason may have justified belief, but it was faith that animated action.

Thirty years after the close of the war Oliver Wendell Holmes, who was wounded three times in the course of his Union service, captured this sense in his Memorial Day address, "The Soldier's Faith."

"Most men who know battle," said Holmes, "know the cynic force with which the thoughts of common sense will assail them in times of stress; but they know that in their greatest moments faith has trampled those thoughts under foot. . . . [If] you have known the vicissitudes of terror and triumph in war, you know that there is such a thing as the faith I spoke of. You know your own weakness and are modest; but you know that man has in him that unspeakable somewhat which makes him capable of miracle, able to lift himself by the might of his own soul, unaided, able to face annihilation for a blind belief."

These are the words of a man set apart: set apart even from the host of his fellow veterans by the intensity of his thought and feeling. What follows are the stories of others who shared—in one way or another—that intensity.

—Peter Kadzis

from The Killer Angels
by Michael Shaara

*Joshua L. Chamberlain, a soft-spoken college professor from Maine, commanded the Federal line on Little Round Top at Gettysburg in the pivotal engagement of that battle. Michael Shaara (1929–1988) in his Pulitzer Prize-winning novel evoked his calm amid chaos. Chamberlain two years later would receive the first Confederate flag of surrender at Appomattox.*

Chamberlain heard the cannon begin. Sat up. Kilrain sat up. Tom Chamberlain went on sleeping, mouth open, saintly young, at peace.

Chamberlain said, "That's mostly in the west."

Kilrain cocked his head, listening. "I thought the Rebs were all up at Gettysburg." He looked at Chamberlain, eyes dark. 'You don't suppose they're flanking us again."

The cannons were blossoming, filling the air with thunder, far enough away to soften and roll, not angry yet, but growing.

"At Chancellorsville they came in on the right. This time they could be on the left. "

"Do you think they'll ever learn, our goddamn generals?"

Chamberlain shook his head. "Wait."

The men in the field were stirring. Some of the newer men were pulling the tent halves down, but the others, professionals, had rolled over and were staring in the direction of the firing. The corn popper remained asleep.

Chamberlain thought: Alert the men? Some of them were looking to him. One stood up, yawned, stretched, glanced unconcernedly in his direction. Not yet. Chamberlain put the novel away.

Kilrain said, "That's a whole division."

Chamberlain nodded.

"Good thing their artillery aint very good."

A rider had come over the crest of the hill, was loping down through the tall grass among the boulders. Chamberlain stood up. The courier saluted.

"Colonel Vincent's compliments, sir. You are instructed to form your regiment."

Chamberlain did not ask what was going on. He felt a coolness spreading all the way through him. He began buttoning his shirt as the courier rode off—no hurry, why hurry?—and began slipping on the belt and saber. When he was done with that he began smoothing his hair, yawned, grinned, turned to Tozier.

"Sergeant, have the Regiment fall in."

He looked down on Tom, sleeping Tom. Mom's favorite. He'll be all right. Did not want to wake him. Delayed a moment, buttoned his collar. Hot day for that. Shadows growing longer. Cool soon. He nudged Tom with his foot. Tom groaned, licked his lips, groaned again, opened his eyes.

"Hey, Lawrence." He blinked and sat up, heard the thunder. "What's happening?"

"Let's go," Chamberlain said.

"Right." He jumped to his feet. Chamberlain walked out into the sun. Some of the men were in line, forming by companies. The Regiment was bigger now; Chamberlain was glad of the new men. Ellis Spear had come sleepily up, disarranged, eyes wide. Chamberlain told him to bring everybody, cooks and prisoners, sick-call people. Chamberlain took a deep breath, smelled wet grass, hay, felt his heart beating, looked up into God's broad sky, shivered as a thrill passed through him. He looked down through the woods. The whole Brigade was forming.

And nothing happened. The guns thundered beyond the hill. They were in line, waiting. Chamberlain looked at his watch. Not quite four. The men were remarkably quiet, most of them still sleepy. Sergeant Ruel Thomas, an orderly, reported from sick call. Chamberlain nodded formally. Meade had ordered every soldier to action, even the Provost Guards. This was it, the last great effort. Don't think now: rest.

Here, at last, was Vincent, riding at a gallop down the long slope. He reined up, the horse rising and kicking the air. All the faces watched him.

"Colonel, column of fours. Follow me."

Chamberlain gave the order, mounted, feeling weak. No strength in his arms. Vincent gave orders to aides; they galloped away. Vincent said, "They're attacking the left flank. Sickles has got us in one hell of a jam."

They began moving up the slope. The Twentieth Maine came after them, four abreast. Vincent was shaking his handsome head.

"Damn fool. Unbelievable. But I must say, remarkably beautiful thing to see."

They moved up between rocks. The artillery fire was growing, becoming massive. They found a narrow road leading upward: high ground ahead. Vincent spurred his horse, waved to Chamberlain to come on. They galloped across a wooden bridge, a dark creek, then up a narrow farm road. The firing was louder. A shell tore through the trees ahead, smashed a limb, blasted rock. Fragments spattered the air.

Chamberlain turned, saw Tom's white grinning face, saw him flick rock dust from his uniform, blinking it out of his eyes, grinning bleakly. Chamberlain grimaced, gestured. Tom said, "Whee."

Chamberlain said, "Listen, another one a bit closer and it will be a hard day for Mother. You get back to the rear and watch for stragglers. Keep your distance from me."

"Right, fine." Tom touched his cap, a thing he rarely did, and moved off thoughtfully. Chamberlain felt an easing in his chest, a small weight lifted. Vincent trotted coolly into the open, reined his horse. Chamberlain saw through a break in the trees, blue hills very far away, hazy ridges miles to the west, not ridges, mountains; he was on high ground. Vincent paused, looked back, saw the Regiment coming up the road, shook his head violently.

"That damn fool Sickles, you know him?"

"Know of him."

Another shell passed close, fifty yards to the left, clipped a limb, ricocheted up through the leaves. Vincent glanced that way, then back, went on.

"The Bully Boy. You know the one. The politician from New York. Fella shot his wife's lover. The Barton Key affair. You've heard of it?"

Chamberlain nodded.

"Well, the damn fool was supposed to fall in on the left of Hancock, right *there.*" Vincent pointed up the ridge to the right. "He should be right here, as a matter of fact, where we're standing. But he didn't like the ground." Vincent shook his head, amazed. "He didn't like the ground. So he just up and moved his whole Corps forward, hour or so ago. I saw them go. Amazing. Beautiful. Full marching line forward, as if they were going to pass in review. Moved right on out to the road down there. Leaving this hill uncovered. Isn't that amazing?" Vincent grimaced. "Politicians. Well, let's go."

The road turned upward, into dark woods. Shells were falling up there. Chamberlain heard the wicked hum of shrapnel in leaves.

Vincent said, "Don't mean to rush you people, but perhaps we better double-time."

The men began to move, running upward into the dark. Chamberlain followed Vincent up the rise. The artillery was firing at nothing; there was no one ahead at all. They passed massive boulders, the stumps of newly sawed trees, splinters of shattered ones. Chamberlain could begin to see out across the valley: mass of milky smoke below, yellow flashes. Vincent said, raising his voice to be heard, "Whole damn Rebel army hitting Sickles down there, coming up around his flank. Be here any minute. Got to hold this place. This way."

He pointed. They crossed the crown of the hill, had a brief glimpse all the way out across Pennsylvania, woods far away, a line of batteries massed and firing, men moving in the smoke and rocks below.

Chamberlain thought: Bet you could see Gettysburg from here. Look at those rocks, marvelous position.

But they moved down off the hill, down into dark woods. Shells were passing over them, exploding in the dark far away. Vincent led them down and to the left, stopped in the middle of nowhere, rocks and small trees, said to Chamberlain, "All right, I place you here." Chamberlain looked, saw a dark slope before him, rock behind him, ridges of rock to both sides. Vincent said, "You'll hold here. The rest of the Brigade will form on your right. Looks like you're the flank, Colonel."

"Right," Chamberlain said. He looked left and right, taking it all in. A quiet place in the woods. Strange place to fight. Can't see very far. The Regiment was moving up. Chamberlain called in the company commanders, gave them the position. Right by file into line. Vincent walked down into the woods, came back up. An aide found him with a message. He sent to the rest of the Brigade to form around the hill to the right, below the crown. Too much artillery on the crown. Rebs liked to shoot high. Chamberlain strode back and forth, watching the Regiment form along the ridge in the dark. The sun was behind the hill, on the other side of the mountain. Here it was dark, but he had no sense of temperature; he felt neither hot nor cold. He heard Vincent say, "Colonel?"

"Yes." Chamberlain was busy.

Vincent said, "You are the extreme left of the Union line. Do you understand that?"

"Yes," Chamberlain said.

The line runs from here all the way back to Gettysburg. But it stops here. You know what that means."

"Of course."

"You cannot withdraw. Under any conditions. If you go, the line is flanked. If you go, they'll go right up the hilltop and take us in the rear. You must defend this place to the last. "

"Yes," Chamberlain said absently.

Vincent was staring at him.

"I've got to go now."

"Right," Chamberlain said, wishing him gone.

"Now we'll see how professors fight," Vincent said. "I'm a Harvard man myself."

Chamberlain nodded patiently, noting that the artillery fire had slackened. Could mean troops coming this way. Vincent's hand was out. Chamberlain took it, did not notice Vincent's departure. He turned, saw Ruel Thomas standing there with his horse. Chamberlain said, "Take that animal back and tie it some place, Sergeant, then come back."

"You mean leave it, sir?"

"I mean leave it."

Chamberlain turned back. The men were digging in, piling rocks to make a stone wall. The position was more than a hundred yards long, Chamberlain could see the end of it, saw the Eighty-third Pennsylvania forming on his right. On his left there was nothing, nothing at all. Chamberlain called Kilrain, told him to check the flank, to see that the joint between Regiments was secure. Chamberlain took a short walk. Hold to the last. To the last what? Exercise in rhetoric. Last man? Last shell? Last foot of ground? Last Reb?

The hill was shaped like a comma, large and round with a spur leading out and down.

The Twentieth Maine was positioned along the spur, the other regiments curved around to the right. At the end of the spur was a massive boulder. Chamberlain placed the colors there, backed off. To the left of his line there was nothing. Empty ground. Bare rocks. He peered off into the darkness. He was used to fighting with men on each side of him. He felt the emptiness to his left like a pressure, a coolness, the coming of winter. He did not like it.

He moved out in front of his line. Through the trees to his right he could see the dark bulk of a larger hill. If the Rebs get a battery there. What a mess. This could be messy indeed. He kept turning to look to the vacant left, the dark emptiness. No good at all. Morrill's B Company was moving up. Chamberlain signaled. Morrill came up. He was a stocky man with an angular mustache, like a messy inverted U. Sleepy-eyed, he saluted.

"Captain, I want you to take your company out there." Chamberlain pointed to the left. "Go out a ways, but stay within supporting distance. Build up a wall, dig in. I want you there in case somebody tries to flank us. If I hear you fire I'll know the Rebs are trying to get round. Go out a good distance. I have no idea what's out there. Keep me informed."

Company B was fifty men. Alone out in the woods. Chamberlain was sorry. They'd all rather be with the Regiment. Messy detail. Well, he thought philosophically, so it goes. He moved on back up the hill, saw Morrill's men melt into the trees. Have I done all I can? Not yet, not yet.

Artillery was coming in again behind him. All down the line, in front of him, the men were digging, piling rocks. He thought of the stone wall at Fredericksburg. *Never, forever.* This could be a good place to fight. Spirits rose. Left flank of the whole line. Something to tell the grandchildren.

Nothing happening here. He hopped up the rocks, drawn toward the summit for a better look, saw an officer: Colonel Rice of the Forty-fourth New York, with the same idea.

Rice grinned happily. "What a view!"

He gestured. Chamberlain moved forward. Now he could see: masses of gray rock wreathed in smoke, gray men moving. If Sickles had a line down there it had already been flanked. He saw a Union battery firing to the south, saw sprays of men rush out of the woods, the smoke, and envelop it, dying, and then the smoke drifted over it. But now more masses were coming, in clots, broken lines, red battle flags plowing through the smoke, moving this way, drifting to the left, toward the base of the hill.

Rice said, glasses to his eyes, "My God, I can see all of it. Sickles is being overrun." He put the glasses down and smiled a foolish smile. "You know, there are an awful lot of people headin' this way."

Chamberlain saw gleams in the woods to the south. Bayonets? Must get back to the Regiment. Rice moved off, calling a thoughtful "good luck." Chamberlain walked down back into the dark. Awful lot of people coming this way. Sixty rounds per man. Ought to be enough.

"Colonel?"

At his elbow: Glazier Estabrook. Incapable of standing up straight; he *listed*, like a sinking ship. He was chewing a huge plug of tobacco. Chamberlain grinned, happy to see him.

"Colonel, what about these here prisoners?"

Chamberlain looked: six dark forms squatting in the rocks. The hard cases from the Second Maine. He had completely forgotten them.

Glazier said slowly, around the wet plug, "Now I wouldn't complain normal, Colonel, only if there's goin' to be a fight I got to keep an eye on my cousin. You understand, Colonel."

What he meant was that he would under no circumstances tend these prisoners during the coming engagement, and he was saying it as politely as possible. Chamberlain nodded. He strode to the prisoners.

"Any of you fellas care to join us?"

"The Rebs really coming?" The man said it wistfully, cautiously, not quite convinced.

"They're really comin'."

One man, bearded, stretched and yawned. "Well, be kind of dull sittin' up here just a-watchin'."

He stood. The others watched. At that moment a solid shot passed through the trees above them, tore through the leaves, ripped away a branch, caromed out into the dark over the line. A shower of granite dust drifted down. The ball must have grazed a ledge above. Granite dust had salt in it. Or perhaps the salt was from your own lips.

Chamberlain said, "Any man that joins us now, there'll be no charges."

"Well," another one said. He was the youngest; his beard was only a fuzz. "No man will call me a coward," he said.

He rose. Then a third, a man with fat on him. The other three sat mute. Two looked away from his eyes; the last looked back in hate. Chamberlain turned away. He did not understand a man who would pass by this chance. He did not want to be with him. He turned back.

"I'll waste no man to guard you. I'll expect to find you here when this is over."

He walked down the hill with the three men, forgetting the incomprehensible three who would not come. He gave the three volunteers to Ruel Thomas, to post along the line.

There were no rifles available. Chamberlain said, "You men wait just a bit. Rifles will be available after a while."

And now the softer roar of musketry began opening up behind him; the popping wave of an infantry volley came down from above, from the other side of the hill. The Rebs were pressing the front, against Rice's New York boys, the rest of the brigade. Now there was sharper fire, closer to home; the Eighty-third was opening up. The battle moved this way, like a wall of rain moving through the trees. Chamberlain strode down along the line. Tom came up behind him, Kilrain above. Private Foss was on his knees, praying. Chamberlain asked that he put in a kind word. Amos Long was sweating.

"'Tis a hell of a spot to be in, Colonel. I cannot see fifty yards."

Chamberlain laid a hand on his shoulder. "Amos, they'll be a lot closer than that."

Jim and Bill Merrill, two brothers, were standing next to a sapling. Chamberlain frowned.

"Boys, why aren't you dug in?"

Jim, the older, grinned widely, tightly, scared but proud.

"Sir, I can't shoot worth a damn lying down. Never could. Nor Bill either. Like to fight standin', with the Colonel's permission."

"Then I suggest you find a thicker tree."

He moved on. Private George Washington Buck, former sergeant, had a place to himself, wedged between two rocks. His face was cold and gray. Chamberlain asked him how it was going. Buck said, "Keep an eye on me, sir. I'm about to get them stripes back."

A weird sound, a wail, a ghost, high and thin. For a vague second he thought it was the sound of a man in awful pain, many men. Then he knew: the Rebel yell. Here they come.

He drifted back to the center. To Tom he said, "You stay by me. But get down, keep down." Kilrain was sitting calmly, chewing away. He was carrying a cavalry carbine. A great roar of musketry from behind the hill. Full battle now. They must be swarming Sickles under. Kilrain was right. Flank attack. Whole Reb army coming night this way. Wonder who? Longstreet? He it was behind the stone wall at Fredericksburg. Now we have our own stone wall. Chamberlain hopped down along the line, telling men to keep good cover, pile rocks higher, fire slowly and carefully, take their time. Have to keep your eye on some of them; they loaded and loaded and never fired, just went on loading, and some of them came out of a fight with seven or eight bullets rammed home in a barrel, unfired. He looked again to the left, saw the bleak silence, felt a crawling uneasiness. Into his mind came the delayed knowledge: You are the left of the Union. The Army of the Potomac ends here.

He stopped, sat down on a rock.

A flank attack.

Never to withdraw.

He took a deep breath, smelled more granite dust. Never to withdraw. Had never heard the order, nor thought. Never really thought it possible. He looked around at the dark trees, the boulders, the men hunched before him in blue mounds, waiting. Don't like to wait. Let's get on, get on. But his mind said cheerily, coldly: Be patient, friend, be patient. You are not leaving here. Possibly not forever, except, as they say, trailing clouds of glory, if that theory really is true after all and they do send some sort of chariot, possibly presently you will be on it. My, how the mind does chatter at times like this. Stop thinking. Depart in a chariot of fire. I suppose it's possible. That He is waiting. Well. May well find out.

The Eighty-third engaged. Chamberlain moved to the right. He had been hoping to face a solid charge, unleash a full volley, but the Rebs seemed to be coming on like a lapping wave, rolling up the beach. He told the right to fire at will. He remained on the right while the firing began. A man down in E Company began it, but there was nothing there; he had fired at a falling branch, and Chamberlain heard a sergeant swearing, then a flurry of fire broke out to the right and spread down the line and the white smoke bloomed in his eyes. Bullets zipped in the leaves, cracked the rocks. Chamberlain moved down closer to the line. Far to the left he could see Tozier standing by the great boulder, with the colors.

Then he saw the Rebs.

Gray-green-yellow uniforms, rolling up in a mass. His heart seized him. Several companies. More and more. At least a hundred men. More. Coming up out of the green, out of the dark. They seemed to be rising out of the ground. Suddenly the terrible scream, the ripply crawly sound in your skull. A whole regiment. Dissolving in smoke and thunder. They came on. Chamberlain could see nothing but smoke, the blue mounds bobbing in front of him, clang of ramrods, grunts, a high gaunt wail. A bullet thunked into a tree near him. Chamberlain turned, saw white splintered wood. He ducked suddenly, then stood up, moved forward, crouched behind a boulder, looking.

A new wave of firing. A hole in the smoke. Chamberlain saw a man on his knees before him, facing the enemy, arms clutching his stomach. A man was yelling an obscene word. Chamberlain looked, could not see who it was. But the fire from his boys was steady and heavy and they were behind trees and under rocks and pouring it in, and Chamberlain saw gray-yellow forms go down, saw a man come bounding up a rock waving his arms wide like a crazy Indian and take a bullet that doubled him right over so that he fell forward over the rocks and out of sight, and then a whole flood to the right, ten or twelve in a pack, suddenly stopping to kneel and fire, one man in fringed clothes, like buckskin, stopping to prop his rifle against a tree, and then to go down, punched backward, coming all loose and to rubbery pieces and flipping back so one bare foot stood up above a bloody rock. A blast of fire at Chamberlain's ear. He turned: Kilrain reloading the carbine. Said something. Noise too great to hear. Screams and yells of joy and pain and rage. He saw bloodstains spatter against a tree. Turned. Fire slowing. They were moving back. Thought: we've stopped 'em. By God and by Mary, we've stopped 'em.

The firing went on, much slower. Smoke was drifting away. But the din from the right was unceasing; the noise from the other side of the hill was one long huge roar, like the ground opening. Kilrain looked that way.

"Half expect 'em to come in from behind."

Chamberlain said, "Did you hear Morrill's Company?" "No, sir. Couldn't hear nothing in that mess."

"Tom?"

Tom shook his head. He had the look of a man who has just heard a very loud noise and has not yet regained his hearing. Chamberlain felt a sudden moment of wonderful delight. He put out a hand and touched his brother's cheek.

"You stay down, boy."

Tom nodded, wide-eyed. "Damn right," he said.

Chamberlain looked out into the smoke. Morrill might have run into them already, might already be wiped out. He saw: a red flag, down in the smoke and dark. Battle flag. A new burst of firing. He moved down the line, Kilrain following, crouched. Men were down. He saw the first dead: Willard Buxton of K. Neat hole in the forehead. Instantaneous. Merciful. First Sergeant Noyes was with him. Chamberlain touched the dead hand, moved on. He was thinking: with Morrill gone, I have perhaps three hundred men. Few more, few less. What do I do if they flank me?

The emptiness to the left was a vacuum, drawing him back that way. Men were drinking water. He warned them to save it. The new attack broke before he could get to the left.

The attack came all down the line, a full, wild, leaping charge. Three men came inside the low stone wall the boys had built. Two died; the other lay badly wounded, unable to speak. Chamberlain called for a surgeon to treat him. A few feet away he saw a man lying dead, half his face shot away. Vaguely familiar. He turned away, turned back. Half the right jawbone visible, above the bloody leer: face of the one of the Second Maine prisoners who had volunteered just a few moments past— the fat one. Never had time to know his name. He turned to Kilrain. "That was one of the Maine prisoners. Don't let me forget."

Kilrain nodded. Odd look on his face. Chamberlain felt a cool wind. He put a hand out.

"Buster? You all right?"

Bleak gray look. Holding his side.

"Fine, Colonel. Hardly touched me."

He turned, showed his side. Tear just under the right shoulder, blood filling the armpit. Kilrain stuffed white cloth into the hole. "Be fine in a moment. But plays hell with me target practice. Would you care for the carbine?"

He sat down abruptly. Weak from loss of blood. But not a bad wound, surely not a bad wound.

"You stay there," Chamberlain said. Another attack was coming. New firing blossomed around them. Chamberlain knelt.

Kilrain grinned widely. "Hell, Colonel, I feel saintly."

"Tom'll get a surgeon."

"Just a bit of bandage is all I'll be needin'. And a few minutes off me feet. Me brogans are killin' me." Lapse into brogue.

Tom moved off into the smoke. Chamberlain lost him. He stood. Whine of bullets, whisking murder. Leaves were falling around him. Face in the smoke. Chamberlain stepped forward.

Jim Nichols, K Company: "Colonel, something goin' on in our front. Better come see."

Nichols a good man. Chamberlain hopped forward, slipped on a rock, nearly fell, hopped to another boulder, felt an explosion under his right foot, blow knocked his leg away, twirled, fell, caught by Nichols. Damned undignified. Hurt? Damn!

How are you, sir?

Looked at his foot. Hole in the boot? Blood? No. Numb. Oh my, begins to hurt now. But no hole, thank God. He stood up.

Nichols pointed. Chamberlain clambered up on a high boulder. Going to get killed, give 'em a good high target. Saw: they were coming in groups, from rock to rock, tree to tree, not charging wildly as before, firing as they came, going down, killing us. But there, back there: masses of men, flags, two flags, flanking, moving down the line. They're going to turn us. They're going to that hole in the left . . .

He was knocked clean off the rock. Blow in the side like lightning bolt. Must be what it feels like. Dirt and leaves in his mouth. Rolling over. This is ridiculous. Hands pulled him up. He looked down. His scabbard rippled like a spider's leg, stuck out at a ridiculous angle. Blood? No. But the hip, oh my. Damn, damn. He stood up. Becoming quite a target.

What was that now? He steadied his mind. Remembered: they're flanking us.

He moved back behind the boulder from which he had just been knocked. His hands were skinned; he was licking blood out of his mouth. His mind, temporarily sidetracked, oiled itself and ticked and turned and woke up, functioning. To Nichols: "Find my brother. Send all company commanders. Hold your positions."

Extend the line? No.

He brooded. Stood up. Stared to the left, then mounted the rock again, aware of pain but concentrating. To the left the Regiment ended, a high boulder there. Chamberlain thought: What was the phrase in the manual? Muddled brain. Oh yes: refuse the line.

The commanders were arriving. Chamberlain, for the first time, raised his voice. "You men! MOVE!"

The other commanders came in a hurry. Chamberlain said, "We're about to be flanked. Now here's what we do. Keep up a good hot masking fire, you understand? Now let's just make sure the Rebs keep their heads down. And let's keep a tight hold on the Eighty-third, on old Pennsylvania over there. I want no breaks in the line. That's *you*, Captain Clark, understand? No breaks."

Clark nodded. Bullets chipped the tree above him.

"Now here's the move. Keeping up the fire, and keeping a tight hold on the Eighty-third, we *refuse* the line. Men will sidestep to the left, thinning out to twice the present distance. See that boulder? When we reach that point we'll refuse the line, form a new line at right angles. That boulder will be the salient. Let's place the colors there, right? Fine. Now you go on back and move your men in sidestep and form a new line to the boulder, and then back from the boulder like a swinging door. I assume that, ah, F Company will take the point. Clear? Any questions?"

They moved. It was very well done. Chamberlain limped to the boulder, to stand at the colors with Tozier. He grinned at Tozier.

"How are you, Andrew?"

"Fine, sir. And you?"

"Worn." Chamberlain grinned. "A bit worn."

"I tell you this, Colonel. The boys are making a hell of a fight."

"They are indeed."

The fire increased. The Rebs moved up close and began aimed fire, trying to mask their own movement. In a few moments several men died near where Chamberlain was standing. One boy was hit in the head and the wound seemed so bloody it had to be fatal, but the boy sat up and shook his head and bound up the wound himself with a handkerchief and went back to firing. Chamberlain noted: most of our wounds are in the head or hands, bodies protected. Bless the stone wall. Pleasure to be behind it. Pity the men out there. Very good men. Here they come. Whose?

The next charge struck the angle at the boulder, at the colors, lapped around it, ran into the new line, was enfiladed, collapsed. Chamberlain saw Tom come up, whirling through smoke, saw a rip in his coat, thought: no good to have a brother here. Weakens a man. He sent to the Eighty-third to tell them of his move to the left, asking if perhaps they couldn't come a little this way and help him out. He sent Ruel Thomas back up the hill to find out how things were going there, to find Vincent, to tell him that life was getting difficult and we need a little help.

He looked for Kilrain. The old Buster was sitting among some rocks, aiming the carbine, looking chipper. Hat was off. An old man, really. No business here. Kilrain said, "I'm not much good to you, Colonel."

There was a momentary calm. Chamberlain sat.

"Buster, how are you?"

Grin. Stained crooked teeth. All the pores remarkably clear, red bulbous nose. Eyes of an old man. How old? I've never asked.

"How's the ammunition?" Kilrain asked.

"I've sent back."

"They're in a mess on the other side." He frowned, grinned, wiped his mouth with the good hand, the right arm folded across his chest, a bloody rag tucked in his armpit. "Half expect Rebs comin' right over the top of the hill. Nothing much to do then. Be Jesus. Fight makes a thirst. And I've brought nothin' a-tall, would you believe that? Not even my emergency ration against snakebite and bad dreams. Not even a spoonful of Save the Baby."

Aimed fire now. He heard a man crying with pain. He looked down the hill. Darker down there. He saw a boy behind a thick tree, tears running down his face, ramming home a ball, crying, whimpering, aiming fire, jolted shoulders, ball of smoke, then turning back, crying aloud, sobbing, biting the paper cartridge, tears all over his face, wiping his nose with a wet sleeve, ramming home another ball.

Kilrain said, "I can stand now, I think."

Darker down the hill. Sunset soon. How long had this been going on? Longer pause than usual. But . . . the Rebel yell. A rush on the left. He stood up. Pain in the right foot, unmistakable squish of blood in the boot. Didn't know it was bleeding. See them come, bounding up the rocks, hitting the left flank. Kilrain moved by him on the right, knelt, fired. Chamberlain pulled out the pistol. No damn good except at very close range. You couldn't hit anything. He moved to the left flank. Much smoke. Smoke changing now, blowing this way, blinding. He was caught in it, a smothering shroud, hot, white, the bitter smell of burned powder. It broke. He saw a man swinging a black rifle, grunts and yells and weird thick sounds unlike anything he had ever heard before. A Reb came over a rock, bayonet fixed, black thin point forward and poised, face seemed blinded, head twitched. Chamberlain aimed the pistol, fired, hit the man dead center, down he went, folding; smoke swallowed him. Chamberlain moved forward. He expected them to be everywhere, flood of brown bodies, gray bodies. But the smoke cleared and the line was firm. Only a few Rebs had come up, a few come over the stones, all were down. He ran forward to a boulder, ducked, looked out: dead men, ten, fifteen, lumps of gray, blood spattering everywhere, dirty white skin, a clawlike hand, black sightless eyes. Burst of white smoke, again, again. Tom at his shoulder: "Lawrence?"

Chamberlain turned. All right? Boyish face. He smiled.

"They can't send us no help from the Eighty-third. Woodward said they have got their troubles, but they can extend the line a little and help us out."

"Good. Go tell Clarke to shift a bit, strengthen the center."

Kilrain, on hands and knees, squinting: "They keep coming in on the flank."

Chamberlain, grateful for the presence: "What do you think?"

"We've been shooting a lot of rounds."

Chamberlain looked toward the crest of the hill. No Thomas anywhere. Looked down again toward the dark. Motion. They're forming again. Must have made five or six tries already. To Kilrain: "Don't know what else to do."

Looked down the line. Every few feet, a man down. Men sitting facing numbly to the rear. He thought: let's pull back a ways. He gave the order to Spear. The Regiment bent back from the colors, from the boulder, swung back to a new line, tighter, almost a U. The next assault came against both flanks and the center all at once, worst of all. Chamberlain dizzy in the smoke began to lose track of events, saw only blurred images of smoke and death, Tozier with the flag, great black gaps in the line, the left flank giving again, falling back, tightening. Now there was only a few yards between the line on the right and the line on the left, and Chamberlain walked the narrow corridor between, Kilrain at his side, always at a crouch.

Ruel Thomas came back. "Sir? Colonel Vincent is dead."

Chamberlain swung to look him in the face. Thomas nodded jerkily.

"Yes, sir. Got hit a few moments after fight started. We've already been reinforced by Weed's Brigade, up front, but now Weed is dead, and they moved Hazlett's battery in up top and Hazlett's dead."

Chamberlain listened, nodded, took a moment to let it come to focus.

"Can't get no ammunition, sir. Everything's a mess up there. But they're holdin' pretty good. Rebs having trouble coming up the hill. Pretty steep."

"Got to have bullets," Chamberlain said.

Spear came up from the left. "Colonel, half the men are down. If they come again . . ." He shrugged, annoyed, baffled, as if by a problem he could not quite solve, yet ought to, certainly, easily. "Don't know if we can stop 'em."

"Send out word," Chamberlain said. "Take ammunition from the wounded. Make every round count." Tom went off, along with Ruel Thomas. Reports began coming in. Spear was right. But the right flank was better, not so many casualties there. Chamberlain moved, shifting men. And heard the assault coming, up the rocks, clawing up through the bushes, through the shattered trees, the pocked stone, the ripped and bloody earth. It struck the left flank. Chamberlain shot another man, an officer. He fell inside the new rock wall, face a bloody rag. On the left two Maine men went down, side by side, at the same moment, and along that spot there was no one left, no one at all, and yet no Rebs coming, just one moment of emptiness in all the battle, as if in that spot the end had come and there were not enough men left now to fill the earth, that final death was beginning there and spreading like a stain. Chamberlain saw movement below, troops drawn toward the gap as toward a cool place in all the heat, and looking down, saw Tom's face and yelled, but not being heard, pointed and pushed, but his hand stopped in midair, not my own brother, but Tom understood, hopped across to the vacant place and plugged it with his body so that there was no longer a hole but one terribly mortal exposed boy, and smoke cut him off, so that Chamberlain could no longer see, moving forward himself, had to shoot another man, shot him twice, the first ball taking him in the shoulder, and the man was trying to fire a musket with one hand when Chamberlain got him again, taking careful aim this time. Fought off this assault, thinking all the while coldly, calmly, perhaps now we are approaching the end. They can't keep coming. We can't keep stopping them.

Firing faded. Darker now. Old Tom. Where?

Familiar form in familiar position, aiming downhill, firing again. All right. God be praised.

Chamberlain thought: not right, not right at all. If he was hit, I sent him there. What would I tell Mother? What do I feel myself? His duty to go. No, no. Chamberlain blinked. He was becoming tired. Think on all that later, the theology of it.

He limped along the line. Sips of exhaustion. Men down, everywhere. He thought: we cannot hold.

Looked up toward the crest. Fire still hot there, still hot everywhere. Down into the dark. They are damned good men, those Rebs. Rebs, I salute you. I don't think we can hold you.

He gathered with Spear and Kilrain back behind the line. He saw another long gap, sent Ruel Thomas to this one. Spear made a count.

"We've lost a third of the men, Colonel. Over a hundred down. The left is too thin."

"How's the ammunition?"

"I'm checking."

A new face, dirt-stained, bloody: Homan Melcher, Lieutenant, Company F, a gaunt boy with buck teeth.

"Colonel? Request permission to go pick up some of our wounded. We left a few boys out there."

"Wait," Chamberlain said.

Spear came back, shaking his head. "We're out." Alarm stained his face, a grayness in his cheeks.

"Some of the boys have nothing at all."

"Nothing," Chamberlain said.

Officers were coming from the right. Down to a round or two per man. And now there was a silence around him. No man spoke. They stood and looked at him, and then looked down into the dark and then looked back at Chamberlain. One man said, "Sir, I guess we ought to pull out."

Chamberlain said, "Can't do that."

Spear: "We won't hold 'em again. Colonel, you know we can't hold 'em again."

Chamberlain: "If we don't hold, they go right on by and over the hill and the whole flank caves in."

He looked from face to face. The enormity of it, the weight of the line, was a mass too great to express. But he could see it as clearly as in a broad wide vision, a Biblical dream: If the line broke here, then the hill was gone, all these boys from Pennsylvania, New York, hit from behind, above. Once the hill went, the flank of the army went. Good God! He could see troops running; he could see the blue flood, the bloody tide.

Kilrain: "Colonel, they're coming."

Chamberlain marveled. But we're not so bad ourselves. One recourse: Can't go back. Can't stay where we are. Result: inevitable.

The idea formed.

"Let's fix bayonets," Chamberlain said.

For a moment no one moved.

"We'll have the advantage of moving downhill," he said.

Spear understood. His eyes saw; he nodded automatically.

The men coming up the hill stopped to volley; weak fire came in return. Chamberlain said, "They've got to be tired, those Rebs. They've got to be close to the end. Fix bayonets. Wait. Ellis, you take the left wing. I want a right wheel forward of the whole Regiment."

Lieutenant Melcher said, perplexed, "Sir, excuse me, but what's a 'right wheel forward'?"

Ellis Spear said, "He means 'charge,' Lieutenant, 'charge.'"

Chamberlain nodded. "Not quite. We charge, swinging down to the right. We straighten out our line. Clarke hangs onto the Eighty-third, and we swing like a door, sweeping them down the hill. Understand? Everybody understand? Ellis, you take the wing, and when I yell you go to it, the whole Regiment goes forward, swinging to the right."

"Well," Ellis Spear said. He shook his head. "Well."

"Let's go." Chamberlain raised his saber, bawled at the top of his voice, "Fix bayonets!"

He was thinking: We don't have two hundred men left. Not two hundred. More than that coming at us. He saw Melcher bounding away toward his company, yelling, waving. Bayonets were coming out, clinking, clattering. He heard men beginning to shout, Maine men, strange shouts, hoarse, wordless, animal. He limped to the front, toward the great boulder where Tozier stood with the colors, Kilrain at his side. The Rebs were in plain view, moving, firing. Chamberlain saw clearly a tall man aiming a rifle at him. At me. Saw the smoke, the flash, but did not hear the bullet go by. Missed. Ha! He stepped out into the open, balanced on the gray rock. Tozier had lifted the colors into the clear. The Rebs were thirty yards off. Chamberlain raised his saber, let loose the shout that was the greatest sound he could make, boiling the yell up from his chest: *Fix bayonets! Charge! Fix bayonets! Charge! Fix bayonets! Charge!* He leaped down from the boulder, still screaming, his voice beginning to crack and give, and all around him his men were roaring animal screams, and he saw the whole Regiment rising and pouring over the wall and beginning to bound down through the dark bushes, over the dead and dying and wounded, hats coming off, hair flying, mouths making sounds, one man firing as he ran, the last bullet, last round. Chamberlain saw gray men below stop, freeze, crouch, then quickly turn. The move was so quick he could not believe it. Men were turning and running. Some were stopping to fire. There was the yellow flash and then they turned. Chamberlain saw a man drop a rifle and run. Another. A bullet plucked at Chamberlain's coat, a hard pluck so that he thought he had caught a thorn but looked down and saw the huge gash. But he was not hit. He saw an officer: handsome full-bearded man in gray, sword and revolver. Chamberlain ran toward him, stumbled, cursed the bad foot, looked up and aimed and fired and missed, then held aloft the saber. The officer turned, saw him coming, raised a pistol, and Chamberlain ran toward it downhill, unable to stop, stumbling downhill seeing the black hole of the pistol turning toward him, not anything else but the small hole yards away, feet away, the officer's face a blur behind it and no thought, a moment of gray suspension rushing silently, soundlessly toward the black hole . . . and the gun did not fire; the hammer clicked down on an empty shell, and Chamberlain was at the man's throat with the saber and the man was handing him his sword, all in one motion, and Chamberlain stopped.

"The pistol too," he said.

The officer handed him the gun: a cavalry revolver, Colt.

"Your prisoner, sir." The face of the officer was very white, like old paper. Chamberlain nodded.

He looked up to see an open space. The Rebs had begun to fall back; now they were running. He had never seen them run; he stared, began limping forward to see. Great cries, incredible sounds, firing and yelling. The Regiment was driving in a line, swinging to the fight, into the dark valley. Men were surrendering. He saw masses of gray coats, a hundred or more, moving back up the slope to his front, in good order, the only ones not running, and thought: If they form again we're in trouble, desperate trouble, and he began moving that way, ignoring the officer he had just captured. At that moment a new wave of firing broke out on the other side of the gray mass. He saw a line of white smoke erupt, the gray troops waver and move back this way, stop, rifles begin to fall, men begin to run to the right, trying to get away. Another line of fire—Morrill. B Company. Chamberlain moved that way. A soldier grabbed his Reb officer, grinning, by the arm. Chamberlain passed a man sitting on a rock, holding his stomach. He had been bayoneted. Blood coming from his mouth. Stepped on a dead body, wedged between rocks. Came upon Ellis Spear, grinning crazily, foolishly, face stretched and glowing with a wondrous light.

"By God, Colonel, by God, by God," Spear said. He pointed. Men were running off down the valley. The Regiment was moving across the front of the Eighty-third Pennsylvania. He looked up the hill and saw them waving and cheering. Chamberlain said, aloud, "I'll be damned."

The Regiment had not stopped, was chasing the Rebs down the long valley between the hills. Rebs had stopped everywhere, surrendering. Chamberlain said to Spear, "Go on up and stop the boys. They've gone far enough."

"Yes, sir. But they're on their way to Richmond."

"Not today," Chamberlain said. "They've done enough today."

from Soldier of the South:
General Pickett's War Letters to His Wife

edited by Arthur Crew Inman

*The heroic but tragic charge led by General George Edward Pickett (1825–1875) at Gettysburg is one of the most famous episodes in military history. Three-quarters of Pickett's own division were killed or wounded. Arthur Crew Inman edited the General's deeply affecting letters to his wife. We join Pickett as he marches north, two weeks shy of Gettysburg.*

I never could quite enjoy being a "Conquering Hero." No, my Sallie, there is something radically wrong about my Hurrahism. I can fight for a cause I know to be just, can risk my own life and the lives of those in my keeping without a thought of the consequences; but when we've conquered, when we've downed the enemy and won the victory, I don't want to hurrah. I want to go off all by myself and be sorry for them—want to lie down in the grass, away off in the woods somewhere or in some lone valley on the hillside far from all *human* sound, and rest my soul and put my heart to sleep and get back something—I don't know what—but something I had that is gone from me—something subtle and unexplainable—something I never knew I possessed till I had lost it—till it was gone—gone.

Yesterday my men were marching victoriously through the little town of Greencastle, the bands all playing our glorious, soul inspiring, Southern airs: 'The Bonny Blue Flag,' 'My Maryland,' 'Her Bright Smile Haunts Me Still,' and the soldiers all happy, hopeful, joyously keeping time to the music, many following it with their voices, and making up for the want of the welcome they were receiving in the enemy's country by cheering themselves and giving themselves a welcome. As Floweree's band, playing 'Dixie,' was passing a vine-bowered home, a young girl rushed out on the porch and waved a United States flag. Then, either fearing that it might be taken from her or finding it too large and unwieldy, she fastened it around her as an apron, and taking hold of it on each side, and waving it in defiance, called out with all the strength of her girlish voice and all the courage of her brave young heart:

"Traitors—traitors—traitors, come and take this flag, the man of you who dares!"

Knowing that many of my men were from a section of the country which had been within the enemy's lines, and fearing lest some might forget their manhood, I took off my hat and bowed to her, saluted her flag and then turned, facing the men who felt and saw my unspoken order. And don't you know that they were all Virginians and didn't forget it, and that almost every man lifted his cap and cheered the little maiden who, though she kept on waving her flag, ceased calling us traitors, till, finally, letting it drop in front of her, she cried out:

"Oh, I wish—I wish I had a rebel flag—I'd wave that, too!"

The picture of that little girl in the vine-covered porch, beneath the purple morning glories with their closed lips and bowed heads waiting and saving their prettiness and bloom for the coming morn—of course, I thought of *you*, my beautiful darling. For the time, that little Greencastle Yankee girl with her beloved flag was my own little promised-to-be-wife, my Sallie, receiving from her soldier and her soldier's soldiers the reverence and homage due her.

We left the little girl standing there with the flag gathered up in her arms, as if too sacred to be waved, now that even the enemy had done it reverence.

Forever your devoted

Soldier

*Greencastle, Pa., June 21, 1863*

• • •

We crossed the Potomac on the Keith at Williamsport and went into bivouac on the Maryland side, from which place I sent my Lady-Love a long letter and some flowers gathered on the way. We then went on to Hagerstown, where we met A. P. Hill's Corps, which had crossed the river farther down. From Hagerstown I sent to the same and only Lady-Love another letter, which was not only freighted with all the adoration and devotion of her soldier's heart, but contained messages from the staff and promises to take care of him and bring him safely back to her.

We made no delay at Hagerstown but, passing through in the rear of Hill's Corps, moved on up the Cumberland Valley and bivouacked at Greencastle, where the most homesick letter of all yet written was sent to—well, guess *whom* this time. Why, to the same Lady-Love, the sweetest, loveliest flower that ever blossomed to bless and make fairer a beautiful world—for it is beautiful, betokening in its loveliness nothing of wickedness or woe—nothing of this deadly strife between men who should be brethren of a great and common cause, as they are the inheritors of a great and common country.

The officers and men are all in excellent condition, bright and cheerful, singing songs and telling stories, full of hope and courage, inspired with absolute faith and confidence in our success. There is no straggling, no disorder, no dissatisfaction, no plundering, and there are no desertions. Think of it—an army of sixty thousand men marching through the enemy's country without the *least* opposition. The object of this great movement is, of course, unknown to us. Its purpose, and our destination, are known at present only to the Commanding General and his Chief Lieutenants. The officers and men generally believe that the intention is entirely to surround the Army of the Potomac and to place Washington and Baltimore within our grasp. They think that Marse Robert is merely threatening the Northern cities, with the view of suddenly turning down the Susquehanna, cutting off all railroad connections, destroying all bridges, throwing his army north of Baltimore and cutting off Washington, and that Beauregard is to follow on directly from Richmond via Manassas to Washington, in rear of Hooker, who of course will be in pursuit of Marse Robert.

*Nous verrons.*

We reached here this morning, June 27th, the anniversary of the battle of Gaines's Mill, where your soldier was wounded. We marched
straight through the town of Chambersburg, which was more deserted
than Goldsmith's village. The stores and houses were all closed, with
here and there groups of uncheerful Boers of Deutschland descent,
earnestly talking, more sylvan shadows than smiles wreathing their
faces. I had given orders that the bands were not to play; but as we were
marching through the northeastern part of the city, some young ladies
came out onto the veranda of one of the prettiest homes in the town
and asked:

"Would you mind shooting off the bands a bit?"

So the command was given, and the band played 'Home Sweet
Home,' 'Annie Laurie,' 'Her Bright Smile Haunts Me Still,' 'Nellie Gray,'
and 'Hazel Dell.' The young ladies asked the next band that passed if
they wouldn't play, 'Dixie'. But the band instead struck up 'The Old
Oaken Bucket,' 'The Swanee River,' 'The Old Arm Chair,' 'The Lone Rock
by the Sea,' and, 'Auld Lang Syne'.

"Thought you was rebels. Where'd you come from anyhow? Can't
play 'Dixie', none of you?" they called out. We marched straight on
through the city, and are camped four miles beyond the town, on the
York River road.

Tomorrow, if you'll promise not to divulge it to a human soul, I'll
tell you a great secret. No, my Sallie, I can't wait till tomorrow. I'll tell
you right now. So listen and cross your heart that you won't tell. I love
you—love you—love you, and oh, little one, I want to see you so. That
is the secret.

*A Dios.* With my heart at your feet, and my happiness in your hands,
I am,

Lovingly and forever,

Your

Soldier

*Chambersburg, June 27, 1863*

• • •

I wish, my Sallie, you could see this wonderfully rich and prosperous country, abounding in plenty, with its great, strong, vigorous horses and oxen, its cows and crops and verdantly thriving vegetation—none of the ravages of war, no signs of devastation—all in woeful contrast to the land where we lay dreaming. All the time I break the law 'Thou shalt not covet,' for every fine horse or cow I see I want for my darling, and all the pretty things I see besides. Never mind, she shall have everything some day, and I shall have the universe and heaven's choicest gift when she is my wife—all my very own.

At Chambersburg, Marse Robert preached us a sermon, first instructing us in the meaning of, *'meum'* and *'teum,'* and then taking as his text, 'Vengeance is Mine, saith the Lord.' I observed that the mourners' bench was not overcrowded with seekers for conversion. The poor fellows were thinking of their own despoiled homes, looted of everything, and were not wildly enthusiastic as they obediently acquiesced to our beloved Commander's order. The Yanks have taken into the mountains and across the Susquehanna all the supplies they could, and we pay liberally for those which we are compelled to take, giving them money which is paid to us, our own Confederate script. Some of us have a few pieces of gold with which to purchase some keepsake or token for the dear ones at home. Alas, my little one, how many of us will be blessed with the giving of them? God in His mercy be our Commander-in-Chief.

We have not a wide field for selection here, as we once had at Price's dry goods store or John Tyler's jewelry establishment in Richmond; but it seems quite magnificent to us now, since the Richmond counters are so bare as to offer not even a wedding ring or a yard of calico. We are guying General C——who, after long and grave deliberation, bought three hoop skirts as a present for his betrothed.

All that makes life dear is the thought of seeing you and being with you. And oh, what an eternity it seems since I said good night. Oh, my darling, love me, pray for me, hold me in your thoughts, keep me in your heart.

Our whole army is now in Pennsylvania, north of the river. There were rumors that Richmond was threatened from all sides—Dix from Old Point, Getty from Hanover, Keyes from Bottom's Bridge, and so on—and that we might be recalled. It turned out to be Munchausen, and we are still to march forward. Every tramp—tramp—tramp is a thought—thought—thought of my darling, every halt a blessing invoked, every command a loving caress; and the thought of you and prayer for you make me strong, make me better, give me courage, give me faith. Now, my dearest, let my soul speak to yours. Listen—listen—listen—You hear—I am answered.

Forever and ever,

Your

Soldier

*In Camp, June 29, 1863*

Can my prettice do patchwork? If she can, she must piece together these penciled scraps of soiled paper and make out of them, not a log-cabin quilt, but a wren's nest, cement it with love and fill it with blue and golden and speckled eggs of faith and hope, to hatch out greater love yet for us.

Well, Sallie mine, the long, wearying march from Chambersburg, through dust and heat beyond compare, brought us here yesterday (a few miles from Gettysburg). Though my poor men were almost exhausted by the march in the intense heat, I felt that the exigencies demanded my assuring Marse Robert that we had arrived and that, with a few hours' rest, my men would be equal to anything he might require of them. I sent Walter with my message and rode on myself to Little Round Top to see Old Peter, who, I tell you, was mighty glad to see me. And now, just think of it, though the old warhorse was watching A. P. Hill's attack upon the center and Hood and McLaws of his own corps, who had struck Sickles, he turned, and before referring to the fighting or asking about the march, inquired after *you*, my darling. While we were watching the fight, Walter came back with Marse

Robert's reply to my message, which was in part: "Tell Pickett I'm glad that he has come, that I can always depend upon him and his men, but that I shall not want him this evening."

We have been on the *qui vive*, my Sallie, since midnight; and as early as three o'clock were on the march. About half past three, Gary's pistol signaled the Yankees' attack upon Culp's Hill, and with its echo a wail of regret went up from my very soul that the other two brigades of my old division had been left behind. Oh, God!—if only I had them!—a surety for the honor of Virginia, for I can depend upon them, little one. They know your soldier and would follow him into the very jaws of death, and he will need them right there, too, before he's through.

At early dawn, darkened by the threatening rain, Armistead, Garnett, Kemper and your soldier held a heart-to-heart powwow.

All three sent regards to you, and Old Lewis pulled a ring from his little finger and, making me take it, said, "Give this little token, George, please, to her of the sunset eyes, with my love, and tell her the 'old man' says since he could not be the lucky dog he's mighty glad that you are."

Dear old Lewis—dear old 'Lo,' as Magruder always called him, being short for Lothario. Well, my Sallie, I'll keep the ring for you, and some day I'll take it to John Tyler and have it made into a breast-pin and set around with rubies and diamonds and emeralds. You will be the pearl, the other jewel. Dear old Lewis!

Just as we three separated to go our different ways after silently clasping hands, our fears and prayers voiced in the "Good luck, old man," a summons came from Old Peter, and I immediately rode to the top of the ridge where he and Marse Robert were making a reconnaissance of Meade's position. "Great God!" said Old Peter as I came up. "Look, General Lee, at the insurmountable difficulties between our line and that of the Yankees—the steep hills—the tiers of artillery—the fences—the heavy skirmish line—And then we'll have to fight our infantry against their batteries. Look at the ground we'll have to charge over, nearly a mile of that open ground there under the rain of their canister and shrapnel."

"The enemy is there, General Longstreet, and I am going to strike him," said Marse Robert in his firm, quiet, determined voice.

About eight o'clock I rode with them along our line of prostrate infantry. They had been told to lie down to prevent attracting attention, and though they had been forbidden to cheer they voluntarily arose and lifted in reverential adoration their caps to our beloved commander as we rode slowly along. Oh, the responsibility for the lives of such men as these! Well, my darling, their fate and that of our beloved Southland will be settled ere your glorious brown eyes rest on these scraps of penciled paper—your soldier's last letter, perhaps.

Our line of battle faces Cemetery Ridge. Our detachments have been thrown forward to support our artillery which stretches over a mile along the crests of Oak Ridge and Seminary Ridge. The men are lying in the rear, my darling, and the hot July sun pours its scorching rays almost vertically down upon them. The suffering and waiting are almost unbearable.

Well, my sweetheart, at one o'clock the awful silence was broken by a cannon-shot, and then another, and then more than a hundred guns shook the hills from crest to base, answered by more than another hundred—the whole world a blazing volcano—the whole of heaven a thunderbolt—then darkness and absolute silence—then the grim and gruesome, low-spoken commands—then the forming of the attacking columns. My brave Virginians are to attack in front. Oh, God in mercy help me as He never helped before!

I have ridden up to report to Old Peter. I shall give him this letter to mail to you and a package to give you if—Oh, my darling, do you feel the love of my heart, the prayer, as I write that fatal word 'if?'

Old Peter laid his hand over mine and said: "I know, George, I know— but I can't do it, boy. Alexander has my instructions. He will give you the order." There was silence, and his hand still rested on mine when a courier rode up and handed me a note from Alexander.

Now, I go; but remember always that I love you with all my heart and soul, with every fiber of my being; that now and forever I am yours— yours, my beloved. It is almost three o'clock. My soul reaches out to yours—my prayers. I'll keep up a brave heart for Virginia and for you, my darling.

Your<br>Soldier

*Gettysburg, July 3, 1863*

My letter of yesterday, my darling, written before the battle, was full of hope and cheer; even though it told you of the long hours of waiting from four in the morning, when Gary's pistol rang out from the Federal lines signaling the attack upon Culp's Hill, to the solemn eight o'clock review of my men, who rose and stood silently lifting their hats in loving reverence as Marse Robert, Old Peter and your own soldier reviewed them—on then to the deadly stillness of the five hours following, when the men lay in the tall grass in the rear of the artillery line, the July sun pouring its scorching rays almost vertically down upon them, till one o'clock when the awful silence of the vast battlefield was broken by a cannon-shot which opened the greatest artillery duel of the world. The firing lasted two hours. When it ceased we took advantage of the blackened field and in the glowering darkness formed our attacking column just before the brow of Seminary Ridge.

I closed my letter to you a little before three o'clock and rode up to

Old Peter for orders. I found him like a great lion at bay. I have never seen him so grave and troubled. For several minutes after I had saluted him he looked at me without speaking. Then in an agonized voice, the reserve all gone, he said:

"Pickett, I am being crucified at the thought of the sacrifice of life which this attack will make. I have instructed Alexander to watch the effect of our fire upon the enemy, and when it begins to tell he must take the responsibility and give you your orders, for I can't."

While he was yet speaking a note was brought to me from Alexander. After reading it I handed it to him, asking if I should obey and go forward. He looked at me for a moment, then held out his hand. Presently, clasping his other hand over mine without speaking he bowed his head upon his breast. I shall never forget the look in his face nor the clasp of his hand when I said, "Then, General, I shall lead my Division on." I had ridden only a few paces when I remembered your letter and (forgive me) thoughtlessly scribbled in a corner of the envelope, "If Old Peter's nod means death then good-by and God bless you, little one," turned back and asked the dear old chief if he would be good enough to mail it for me. As he took your letter from me, my darling, I saw tears glistening on his cheeks and beard. The stern old war-horse, God bless him, was weeping for his men and, I know, praying too that this cup might pass from them. I obeyed the silent assent of his bowed head, an assent given against his own convictions, given in anguish and with reluctance.

My brave boys were full of hope and confident of victory as I led them forth, forming them in column of attack, and though officers and men alike knew what was before them—knew the odds against them— they eagerly offered up their lives on the altar of duty, having absolute faith in their ultimate success. Over on Cemetery Ridge the Federals beheld a scene never before witnessed on this continent—a scene which has never previously been enacted and can never take place again—an army forming in line of battle in full view, under their very eyes—charging across a space nearly a mile in length over fields of waving grain and anon of stubble and then a smooth expanse—moving with the steadiness of a dress parade, the pride and glory soon to be crushed by an overwhelming heartbreak.

Well, it is all over now. The battle is lost, and many of us are prisoners, many are dead, many wounded, bleeding and dying. Your soldier lives and mourns and but for you, my darling, he would rather, a million times rather, be back there with his dead, to sleep for all time in an unknown grave.

Your sorrowing

Soldier

*In Camp, July 1, 1863*

On the Fourth—far from a glorious Fourth to us or to any with love for his fellow-men—I wrote you just a line of heartbreak. The sacrifice of life on that blood-soaked field on the fatal third was too awful for the heralding of victory, even for our victorious foe, who, I think, believe as we do, that it decided the fate of our cause. No words can picture the anguish of that roll-call—the breathless waits between the responses. The "Here" of those who, by God's mercy, had miraculously escaped the awful rain of shot and shell was a sob—a gasp—a knell—for the unanswered name of his comrade called before his. There was no tone of thankfulness for having been spared to answer to their names, but rather a toll, and an unvoiced wish that they, too, had been among the missing.

But for the blight to your sweet young life, but for you, only you, my darling, your soldier would rather by far be out there, too, with his brave Virginians dead—

Even now I can hear them cheering as I gave the order, "Forward!" I can feel their faith and trust in me and their love for our cause. I can feel the thrill of their joyous voices as they called out all along the line, "We'll follow you, Marse George. We'll follow you—we'll follow you." Oh, how faithfully they kept their word—following me on—on—to their death, and I, believing in the promised support, led; them on—on—on—Oh, God!

I can't write you a love letter today, my Sallie, for with my great love for you and my gratitude to God for sparing my life to devote to you, comes the overpowering thought of those whose lives were sacrificed— of the broken-hearted widows and mothers and orphans. The moans of my wounded boys, the sight of the dead, upturned faces, flood my soul with grief—and here am I whom they trusted, whom they followed, leaving them on that field of carnage—leaving them to the mercy of —— and guarding four thousand prisoners across the river back to Winchester. Such a duty for men who a few hours ago covered themselves with glory eternal.

Well, my darling, I put the prisoners all on their honor and gave them equal liberties with my own soldier boys. My first command to them was to go and enjoy themselves the best they could, and they have obeyed my order. Today a Dutchman and two of his comrades came up and told me that they were lost and besought me to help them find their commands. They had been with my men and had gotten separated from their own comrades. So I sent old Floyd off on St. Paul to find out where they belonged and deliver them.

This is too gloomy and too poor a letter for so beautiful a sweetheart, but it seems sacrilegious, almost, to say I love you, with the hearts that are stilled to love on the field of battle.

Your

Soldier

*Headquarters, July 6, 1863*

from War Years with Jeb Stuart
by Lieut. Colonel W. W. Blackford

*James Ewell Brown Stuart, a rollicking personality known as "Jeb", distinguished himself early in the war at the first Battle of Bull Run. His hallmark was boldness. He personified a romantic, dashing tradition. W. W. Blackford (1831– 1905) rode with Stuart from the beginning of the war. Blackford's description of Stuart's charge at Bull Run conveys the brio Stuart instilled in his men. Stuart's death in 1864, one year after Stonewall Jackson's, profoundly demoralized the South.*

The duty of cavalry after battle is joined is to cover the flanks to prevent the enemy from turning them. If victorious, it improves the victory by rapid pursuit. If defeated, it covers the rear and makes vigorous charges to delay the advance of the enemy—or in the supreme moment, in the crisis of the battle, when victory is hovering over the field, uncertain upon which standard to alight—when the reserves are brought into action and the death struggle has come, *then* the cavalry comes down like an avalanche, upon the flanks of troops already engaged, with splendid effect.

A skirt of woods hid the battlefield from our view, but occasionally a shell would burst high in air, and sometimes the wind wafted the clouds upward above the trees, the roar of the conflict becoming louder and louder. Stuart was uneasy for fear that he would not be called into action; so every time a body of troops appeared he sent me over to tell the commanding officer that he was there and to ask him to let him know when he could be of service with the cavalry. He also rode over several times to the field to confer with the generals and watch the progress of the action. On one of my trips to a large body of troops moving into action, which one of the men told me was commanded by Colonel Jackson, I pushed on to the head of the column and found Colonel Jackson riding along holding up his hand which was wrapped in a bloody handkerchief, for his finger had just been shot off. This was the man who had just been christened "Stonewall" in the baptism of fire. I gave him Colonel Stuart's message and request, and his stern face lit up with a smile and he said, "That's good! That's good! Tell Stuart I will. That's good!" and rode on into action. "That's good!" was his favorite exclamation at anything which pleased him. Once during the morning, to our horror, we saw a great crowd of fugitives come pouring out of the woods and fleeing across the fields until they were out of sight. My heart seemed to stand still—was the battle lost? But presently they ceased coming—they were some South Carolina troops.

The battle roared louder and louder but still in the same spot. It was about two o'clock: Stuart was striding backwards and forwards in great impatience. Presently we saw a staff officer dash out of the woods and come spurring towards us. The men all sprang to their feet and began tightening their saddle girths, for we had a presentiment he was coming for us. The supreme moment had come at last. Colonel Stuart stepped forward to meet the officer. He reined up his horse and asked if that was Colonel Stuart and then, with a military salute, said, *"Colonel Stuart, General Beauregard directs that you bring your command into action at once and that you attack where the firing is hottest."*

The bugle sounded "boots and saddles" and in a moment more we were moving off at a trot in a column of fours in the direction indicated plainly enough by the firing. It was our fate, however, to pass through a sickening ordeal before reaching the field. Along a shady little valley through which our road lay the surgeons had been plying their vocation all the morning upon the wounded. Tables about breast high had been erected upon which screaming victims were having legs and arms cut off. The surgeons and their assistants, stripped to the waist and all bespattered with blood, stood around, some holding the poor fellows while others, armed with long bloody knives and saws, cut and sawed away with frightful rapidity, throwing the mangled limbs on a pile near by as soon as removed. Many were stretched on the ground awaiting their turn, many more were arriving continually, either limping along or borne on stretchers, while those upon whom operations had already been performed calmly fanned the flies from their wounds. But among these last, alas! some moved not—for them the surgeons' skill had not availed. The battle roared in front—a sound calculated to arouse the sublimest emotions in the breast of the soldier, but the prayers, the curses, the screams, the blood, the flies, the sickening stench of this horrible little valley were too much for the stomachs of the men, and all along the column, leaning over the pommels of their saddles, they could be seen in ecstasies of protest.

Upon reaching the edge of the wood a view of the battle burst upon us, and Stuart halted to take a look. Smoke in dense white clouds lit up by lurid flashes from the cannon wrapped the position of the artillery; while lines of thin, blue, misty vapor floated over infantry, pouring out their deadly hail. At one moment all beneath would be invisible at another the curtain, lifted by a passing breeze, revealed the thousands of busy reapers in the harvest of death. Colonel Stuart and myself were riding at the head of the column as the grand panorama opened before us, and there right in front, about seventy yards distant, and in strong relief against the smoke beyond, stretched a brilliant line of scarlet—a regiment of New York Zouaves in column of fours, marching out of the Sudley road to attack the flank of our line of battle. Dressed in scarlet caps and trousers, blue jackets with quantities of gilt buttons, and white gaiters, with a fringe of bayonets swaying above them as they moved their appearance was indeed magnificent. The Sudley road was here in a deep depression and the rear of the column was still hid from view—there were about five hundred men in sight—they were all looking toward the battlefield and did not see us. Waving his sabre, Stuart ordered a charge, but instantly pulled up and called a halt and turning to me said, "Blackford, are those our men or the enemy?" I said I could not tell, but I had heard that Beauregard had a regiment of Zouaves from New Orleans, dressed, I had been told, like these men. Just then, however, all doubt was removed by the appearance of their colors, emerging from the road—the Stars and Stripes. I shall never forget the feelings with which I regarded this emblem of our country so long beloved, and now seen for the first time in the hands of a mortal foe. But there was no time for sentiment then. The instant the flag appeared, Stuart ordered the charge, and at them we went like an arrow from a bow.

As we were in column of fours it was necessary to deploy, and our gallant Colonel waved his sabre for the rear to oblique to the left, "on right into line," so as to strike the enemy in "echelon" and this they did. While a Lieutenant in my company, I had carried a Sharp's carbine slung to my shoulder and this I still wore; I also had my sabre and a large sized five-shooter. In the occupation of the moment I had not thought which of my weapons to draw until I had started, and as it does not take long for a horse at full speed to pass over seventy yards, I had little time to make the selection. I found in fact that it would be impossible to get either my sabre or pistol in time, and as the carbine hung conveniently under my right hand I seized and cocked that, holding it in my right hand with my thumb on the hammer and finger on the trigger. I thought I would fire it and then use it for a crushing blow, in which it would be almost as effective against a man standing on the ground as a sabre.

Half the distance was passed before they saw the avalanche coming upon them, but then they came to a "front face"—a long line of bright muskets was leveled—a sheet of red flame gleamed, and we could see no more. Capt. Welby Carter's horse sprang forward and rolled over dead, almost in front of Comet, so that a less active animal would have been thrown down, but Comet recovered himself and cleared the struggling horse and his rider. The smoke which wrapped them from our sight also hid us from them, and thinking perhaps that we had been swept away by the volley, they, instead of coming to a "charge bayonet," lowered their pieces to load, and in this position we struck them. The tremendous impetus of horses at full speed broke through and scattered their line like chaff before the wind. As the scarlet line appeared through the smoke, when within a couple of horse's lengths of them, I leaned down with my carbine cocked, thumb on hammer and forefinger on trigger, and fixed my eye on a tall fellow I saw would be the one my course would place in the right position for the carbine, while the man next to him, in front of the horse, I would have to leave to Comet. I then plunged the spurs into Comet's flanks and he evidently thought I wanted him to jump over this strange looking wall I was riding him at, for he rose to make the leap; but he was too close and going too fast to rise higher than the breast of the man, and he struck him full on the chest, rolling him over and over under his hoofs and knocking him about ten feet backwards, depriving him of all further interest in the subsequent proceedings, and knocking the rear rank man to one side. As Comet rose to make the leap, I leaned down from the saddle, rammed the muzzle of the carbine into the stomach of my man and pulled the trigger. I could not help feeling a little sorry for the fellow as he lifted his handsome face to mine while he tried to get his bayonet up to meet me; but he was too slow, for the carbine blew a hole as big as my arm clear through him.

Just beyond their line was a fence, and Comet, exasperated to frenzy by the unusual application of the spur, was almost beyond my control, and entirely beyond the control of one hand; so I had to drop the carbine in its sling, and use both hands to swing him away from the fence which he seemed bent on clearing: the field beyond was filled with their troops and if he had gone over, there would have been small chance for return. With both hands I managed to turn the horse enough to bring him up to the fence so obliquely that even he did not like to attempt it, and he came round.

We now charged back, taking their line in the rear at another place, but they had begun to break and scatter clear down to the Sudley road before we reached them; all order was gone and it became a general melee or rather a chase. I might have put in some effective work with my revolver but it got hung in the case at my belt, and as I wanted to try the effect of a downward blow with the barrel of the carbine when swung high in air, I caught it up again; but the fellows dodged or parried every blow I got close enough to attempt, and I accomplished no more than chasing some of them back into the road where the rear of the regiment stood, and where I had no disposition to follow. This regiment—they say it was the Fire Zouaves—was completely paralyzed by this charge, and though their actual loss in killed and wounded was not very great, their demoralization was complete. The arrest of their dangerous move upon the exposed flank of our main line of battle was a result of the utmost importance and, I shall always think, saved the day. We had only two companies, commanded by Capt. Welby Carter and Capt. J. B. Hogue, actually engaged. Our loss was nine men and eighteen horses killed—the number of wounded is not recorded. It seemed strange that the fire from five hundred muskets, at thirty yards, should not have been more effective, but they had to shoot in a hurry and they were no doubt a little nervous at seeing the dreadful "Black Horse," as they then called all the Southern cavalry, coming down on them in that style, and I don't wonder at it. The mistake they made was in lowering their pieces to load; if they had come to a "charge bayonets," even with only two ranks, they would have given us trouble. But going at the speed we were, we could not have stopped after we got through their smoke, and would certainly have broken through, though with greater loss. The bayonets would have stuck so deep into the first horses that they could not have been recovered in time to meet the others, and the death struggle of the first horses falling into their line would, of itself, have broken it a good deal.

My duty as Adjutant of the regiment was now to reform it, back of the woods from which we had charged. In the charges all formation was of course lost and in the return each man got back as he saw fit. The men had behaved well in attack but when the time came for withdrawal some of them did not want to stop at all, short of Manassas. I rallied about half of them back of the wood, and then found that the other half were going on down the road; so I dashed off after them, calling on all I overtook to return. When I stopped in front of them, they halted, but when I went on after more, they followed. As soon as

I found out this I pushed on as fast as I could until I got ahead of all of them, and then halted them as they came up, until there was a squad of a dozen or so, and these I marched back, sweeping up all we met. When I got back, Colonel Stuart laughed in his jovial way and said as I met him, "Bully for you, Blackford."

He had been a little scandalized at what had happened, but he was so brave a man himself that he never seemed to attribute unworthy motives to his men, and this was one of the secrets of his great influence over them in action. They were ashamed to be anything but brave where he was. I had the names of one or two officers who had refused to return, but he would not let me prefer charges against them, saying they would be all right next time, and with one exception sure enough they were. Colonel Stuart came up to me a little after this and told me he would make my appointment as Adjutant, dated that day—a compliment I felt quite proud of.

It was now all-important that the efforts the enemy were making to extend their lines so as to outflank us should be frustrated until the reinforcements, which were coming from down Bull Run, could arrive. Stuart had secured a couple of guns under Lieut. R. F. Beckham, from a battery attached to the infantry, for at that time we had no horse artillery with the cavalry, and as soon as the men were formed, he moved forward to a hill across, the Sudley road, from which a full view of the field could be had, at a distance of about five hundred yards from their right, and somewhat in their rear. Here he masked the guns behind a clump of pines, the foliage of which so entangled the smoke that they did not find out where we were for a long time; and behind these trees the cavalry support was also bid.

Beckham soon got the range, and then worked his pieces as fast as they could load them, with terrific effect upon the dense masses so near. Their lines were enfiladed by this fire; the fuses were cut long and the shell went skipping along through as round shot as far as we could see, and then did what execution they could in bursting. It was a grand and exciting spectacle. In their passage the shot opened a gap from end to end which remained open for an appreciable instant like the splash produced by striking the surface of water with a stick. This appearance was caused not only by the fall of the men struck by the shot, but from the involuntary dodging of those close to its path in opposite directions on each side. Their batteries were so closely engaged that they took no notice of us whatever, indeed from the way our guns were masked by the pines it is quite probable they never discovered our position at all. The effect of our fire was none the less destructive and materially delayed the extension of their flank at a time when delay was of vital importance. But for our charge and the fire of these guns, there can be no question that the flank of Jackson's "stone wall" would have been turned before Early arrived with his brigade, in which case the day would have been lost.

I now found myself almost perishing from thirst from the intense heat and the violence of my exertions during the charge. It seemed that water I must have or die, and Comet was suffering as much as his master. In rear of the enemy there was a small branch and to this I determined to venture. Its banks were lined with the enemy's wounded who had crawled there to drink, and many had died with their heads in the water, the dark blood flowing into and gradually mingling with the stream. I looked for a clear place in vain, and at last, driven to desperation, had to lie down and watch for the blood stains to pass, then drink until others came, lift my head for them to pass, and drink again. It was a long time before I could get Comet to touch it, but at last, succeeded, and after much snorting, pawing and tossing of head he drank his fill, by following pretty much my plan when the stained water floated by. Then drawing a long breath he turned and looked me full in the face, as much as to say, "Who would have thought, master, that we would ever have had to drink such water as that?" It was, indeed, literally drinking the blood of our enemies, for the clearest of it was suspiciously tinted and flavored. It was now about four o'clock and the battle raged with unabated fury. The lines of blue were unbroken and their fire as vigorous as ever while they surged against the solid walls of gray, standing immovable in their front. It was on that ridge earlier in the day Jackson won the name of Stonewall.

But now the most extraordinary spectacle I have ever witnessed took place. I had been gazing at the numerous well-formed lines as they moved forward to the attack, some fifteen or twenty thousand strong in full view, and for some reason had turned my head in another direction for a moment, when some one exclaimed, pointing to the battle-field, "Look! Look!" I looked, and what a change had taken place in an instant. Where those "well dressed," well-defined lines, with clear spaces between, had been steadily pressing forward, the whole field was a confused swarm of men, like bees, running away as fast as their legs could carry them, with all order and organization abandoned. In a moment more the whole valley was filled with them as far as the eye could reach. They plunged through Bull Run wherever they came to it regardless of fords or bridges, and there many were drowned. Muskets, cartridge boxes, belts, knapsacks, haversacks and blankets were thrown away in their mad race, that nothing might impede their flight. In the reckless haste the artillery drove over every one who did not get out of their way. Ambulance and wagon drivers cut the traces and dashed off on the mules. In crossing Cub Run a shell exploded in a team and blocked the way and twenty-eight pieces of artillery fell into our hands.

By stepping or jumping from one thing to another of what had been thrown away in the stampede, I could have gone long distances without ever letting my foot touch the ground, and this over a belt forty or fifty yards wide on each side of the road. Numbers of gay members of Congress had come out from Washington to witness the battle from the adjacent hills, provided with baskets of champagne and lunches. So there was a regular chariot race when the rout began, with the chariots well in the lead, as was most graphically described by the prisoners I captured and by citizens afterwards. We found, occasionally, along the road, parasols and dainty shawls lost in their flight by the frail, fair ones who had seats in most of the carriages of this excursion. Some of their troops, north of Bull Run, did not participate in the panic, and some did not throw away their arms, but the greater part must have done so, from the quantities we found.

Stuart was uncertain whether this was a general or a partial rout, at the moment, and told me to go as fast as I could to either General Johnston or General Beauregard, report what had happened and ask if he must pursue. He, like everyone else at that period of the war, did not feel the confidence in himself that we did a little later. I gave Comet the rein and struck a bee line to where he said I would probably find the Generals, taking fences, ditches, and worse than all some fearful gullies as they came.

I found General Beauregard, who of course knew what had happened before I got there, for by that time all musketry firing had ceased, though the batteries were still pounding away at long range at the disappearing fugitives. The General was sitting on his horse, his handsome face beaming with pleasure as staff officers came dashing up from every direction with reports and asking for orders. It was the first time I had seen General Beauregard and I looked at him with much interest. He was then looked upon as the "coming man" but his fame never rose higher than it stood after that battle. He was rather a small man and had a good deal of the manner and appearance of a Frenchman. His friends say that Jeff Davis became jealous of him after this battle and never gave him a chance afterwards, which is quite probable: he certainly behaved with great gallantry that day. He returned my salute very politely and told me to tell Colonel Stuart to pursue at once with all speed. I retraced my steps as fast as I had come and though it was not over half a mile, Stuart was gone before I got in sight of our hill. Knowing well enough which direction he would take, I dashed after him and overtook the command before it reached Bull Run and regained my place at its head before it had risen the hill on the other side, though they were moving at a rapid trot. As soon as we appeared on the crest of the hill one of our batteries, mistaking us for the enemy, opened on us. I felt rather queer. It was bad enough to be killed by the enemy, but that could not be helped; but to be bowled over by our own people, and hit in the back at that, was disgusting. There was no way in the world of stopping them in time; so Stuart, with great presence of mind, gave the order "gallop—march" and away we scurried. Our fellows at the battery, seeing this, re-doubled the rapidity of their fire and were getting our range closer and closer, and but for the fact that we had not far to go, would in a moment more have torn us pretty badly. One shot passed between Colonel Stuart's head and mine as we rode together at the head of the column, and burst just beyond.

After crossing the crest of the bill we were safe and resumed the trot. Just then an amusing incident occurred to me. We saw a man run across the road in front of us and take down a little bridle path for dear life. Stuart told me to catch him and find out what made him run so. I went after him; and finding he would not stop by calling and not caring to race Comet who was still panting heavily, I sent a pistol ball over his head which had the desired effect instantly. As I rode up to him, I found a little man in a semimilitary blue dress, scared almost to death. His teeth chattered so that it was a long time, impatient to get off as I was, before he could tell me he was chaplain of some Yankee regiment. I had never taken a prisoner before and I felt him rather an elephant on my hands, small as he was. So I asked him if he was armed. He hurriedly produced a broken-handled pocket knife which I pitched into the bushes, and I then pointed to the road we had come and told him to double quick down it and give himself up to the first of our men he came across, that I would stand there and watch, and if he stopped or looked back I would shoot him dead. When he had gone a little way I turned, and keeping on the grass so he could not hear me, galloped on after the command.

Stuart had taken a road parallel to the line of retreat and about half a mile therefrom, and was pushing along to overtake and strike them in flank. We had gone four or five miles when there appeared, on a hill near the road they were on, some horsemen waving a white flag. Stuart told me to take a dozen men and go over and see what they wanted, and then he rode, on. By the time we had nearly reached the flag, we struck a broad stream of stragglers, extending forty or fifty yards on each side of the road. The main body had just passed and the stream I now struck was the wake. We struck it crossing a meadow and my men went wild. They were like a pack of hounds when they see a fox, and I turned them loose. There were at least a hundred foxes in sight and a most exciting chase began. They were running to get over a very large staked and ridered worm fence on the boundary of the meadow, and over it many escaped. All of these men were fully armed infantry, the disorganized fugitives having all passed by. After the chase began I stopped to watch the scene, but just then saw three Zouaves start to run across the meadow, my men being so much engaged they did not observe them; so I drew my pistol and gave chase, overtaking them as they reached the fence. One, a little in advance, had gotten over, but the other two faced about with their backs to the fence and cocked their muskets. I began to feel a little sheepish, but saw instantly that they were uncertain what to do, and that the only chance was to be prompt and peremptory and at the same time let them see I was cool and would not hurt them if they surrendered. I reined up within ten feet of them and fixing my eye on one of them said, in a quiet but commanding tone, "Throw down your musket, sir." He dropped it like a hot potato. When I turned to the other, he did likewise, to my great relief. In the meantime the fellow over the fence was running as fast as he could, but halted and returned when I threatened to shoot him if he did not. I then found that each one of them, after the fashion of the volunteer foot-soldier of the period, was encumbered with a multiplicity of bloodthirsty weapons, a musket and bayonet, a Colt's five-shooting revolver, and a bowie knife a foot long. I took the pistols, threw the knives away, and stuck the bayonets, with muskets attached, in the ground so our ordnance people could see them, and so they would be saved from rust in the meantime. I wore one of these pistols as a trophy throughout the war and have it still, and gave my own of the same kind to a man in my company.

An Episode of War

by Stephen Crane

*Stephen Crane (1871–1900) is best known for his second novel,* The Red Badge of Courage, *which chronicles the journey of young Henry Fleming through fear and cowardice to a final, quiet heroism. The understanding that war is random and life unfair powers this shorter but equally affecting story. Crane's style—ironic, paradoxical, understated—says much by saying little.*

The lieutenant's rubber blanket lay on the ground, and upon it he had poured the company's supply of coffee. Corporals and other representatives of the grimy and hot-throated men who lined the breast-work had come for each squad's portion.

The lieutenant was frowning and serious at this task of division. His lips pursed as he drew with his sword various crevices in the heap, until brown squares of coffee, astoundingly equal in size, appeared on the blanket. He was on the verge of a great triumph in mathematics, and the corporals were thronging forward, each to reap a little square, when suddenly the lieutenant cried out and looked quickly at a man near him as if he suspected it was a case of personal assault. The others cried out also when they saw blood upon the lieutenant's sleeve.

He had winced like a man stung, swayed dangerously, and then straightened. The sound of his hoarse breathing was plainly audible. He looked sadly, mystically, over the breast-work at the green face of a wood, where now were many little puffs of white smoke. During this moment the men about him gazed statuelike and silent, astonished and awed by this catastrophe which happened when catastrophes were not expected—when they had leisure to observe it.

As the lieutenant stared at the wood, they too swung their heads, so that for another instant all hands, still silent, contemplated the distant forest as if their minds were fixed upon the mystery of a bullet's journey.

The officer had, of course, been compelled to take his sword into his left hand. He did not hold it by the hilt. He gripped it at the middle of the blade, awkwardly. Turning his eyes from the hostile wood, he looked at the sword as he held it there, and seemed puzzled as to what to do with it, where to put it. In short, this weapon had of a sudden become a strange thing to him. He looked at it in a kind of stupefaction, as if he had been endowed with a trident, a sceptre, or a spade.

Finally he tried to sheathe it. To sheathe a sword held by the left hand, at the middle of the blade, in a scabbard hung at the left hip, is a feat worthy of a sawdust ring. This wounded officer engaged in a desperate struggle with the sword and the wobbling scabbard, and during the time of it he breathed like a wrestler.

But at this instant the men, the spectators, awoke from their stonelike poses and crowded forward sympathetically. The orderly-sergeant took the sword and tenderly placed it in the scabbard. At the time, he leaned nervously backward, and did not allow even his finger to brush the body of the lieutenant. A wound gives strange dignity to him who bears it. Well men shy from his new and terrible majesty. It is as if the wounded man's hand is upon the curtain which hangs before the revelations of all existence—the meaning of ants, potentates, wars, cities, sunshine, snow, a feather dropped from a bird's wing; and the power of it sheds radiance upon a bloody form, and makes the other men understand sometimes that they are little. His comrades look at him with large eyes thoughtfully. Moreover, they fear vaguely that the weight of a finger upon him might send him headlong, precipitate the tragedy, hurl him at once into the dim, gray unknown. And so the orderly-sergeant, while sheathing the sword, leaned nervously backward.

There were others who proffered assistance. One timidly presented his shoulder and asked the lieutenant if he cared to lean upon it, but the latter waved him away mournfully. He wore the look of one who knows he is the victim of a terrible disease and understands his helplessness. He again stared over the breast-work at the forest, and then, turning, went slowly rearward. He held his right wrist tenderly in his left hand as if the wounded arm was made of very brittle glass.

And the men in silence stared at the wood, then at the departing lieutenant, then at the wood, then at the lieutenant.

As the wounded officer passed from the line of battle, he was enabled to see many things which as a participant in the fight were unknown to him. He saw a general on a black horse gazing over the lines of blue infantry at the green woods which veiled his problems. An aide galloped furiously, dragged his horse suddenly to a halt, saluted, and presented a paper. It was, for a wonder, precisely like a historical painting.

To the rear of the general and his staff a group, composed of a bugler, two or three orderlies, and the bearer of the corps standard, all upon maniacal horses, were working like slaves to hold their ground, preserve their respectful interval, while the shells boomed in the air about them, and caused their chargers to make furious quivering leaps.

A battery, a tumultuous and shining mass, was swirling toward the right. The wild thud of hoofs, the cries of the riders shouting blame and praise, menace and encouragement, and, last, the roar of the wheels, the slant of the glistening guns, brought the lieutenant to an intent pause. The battery swept in curves that stirred the heart; it made halts as dramatic as the crash of a wave on the rocks, and when it fled onward this aggregation of wheels, levers, motors had a beautiful unity, as if it were a missile. The sound of it was a war-chorus that reached into the depths of man's emotion.

The lieutenant, still holding his arm as if it were of glass, stood watching this battery until all detail of it was lost, save the figures of the riders, which rose and fell and waved lashes over the black mass.

Later, he turned his eyes toward the battle, where the shooting sometimes crackled like bush fires, sometimes sputtered with exasperating irregularity, and sometimes reverberated like the thunder. He saw the smoke rolling upward and saw crowds of men who ran and cheered, or stood and blazed away at the inscrutable distance.

He came upon some stragglers, and they told him how to find the field hospital. They described its exact location. In fact, these men, no longer having part in the battle, knew more of it than others. They told the performance of every corps, every division, the opinion of every general. The lieutenant, carrying his wounded arm rearward, looked upon them with wonder.

At the roadside a brigade was making coffee and buzzing with talk like a girls' boarding school. Several officers came out to him and inquired concerning things of which he knew nothing. One, seeing his arm, began to scold. "Why, man, that's no way to do. You want to fix that thing." He appropriated the lieutenant and the lieutenant's wound. He cut the sleeve and laid bare the arm, every nerve of which softly fluttered under his touch. He bound his handkerchief over the wound, scolding away in the meantime. His tone allowed one to think that he was in the habit of being wounded every day. The lieutenant hung his head, feeling, in this presence, that he did not know how to be correctly wounded.

The low white tents of the hospital were grouped around an old schoolhouse. There was here a singular commotion. In the foreground two ambulances interlocked wheels in the deep mud. The drivers were tossing the blame of it back and forth, gesticulating and berating, while from the ambulances, both crammed with wounded, there came an occasional groan. An interminable crowd of bandaged men were coming and going. Great numbers sat under the trees nursing heads or arms or legs. There was a dispute of some kind raging on the steps of the schoolhouse. Sitting with his back against a tree a man with a face as gray as a new army blanket was serenely smoking a corncob pipe. The lieutenant wished to rush forward and inform him that he was dying.

A busy surgeon was passing near the lieutenant. "Good morning," he said, with a friendly smile. Then he caught sight of the lieutenant's arm, and his face at once changed. "Well, let's have a look at it." He seemed possessed suddenly of a great contempt for the lieutenant. This wound evidently placed the latter on a very low social plane. The doctor cried out impatiently: "What muttonhead tied it up that way anyhow?" The lieutenant answered, "Oh, a man."

When the wound was disclosed the doctor fingered it disdainfully. "Humph," he said, "You come along with me and I'll tend to you." His voice contained the same scorn as if he were saying, "You will have to go to jail."

The lieutenant had been very meek, but now his face flushed, and he looked into the doctor's eyes. "I guess I won't have it amputated," he said.

"Nonsense, man! Nonsense! Nonsense!" cried the doctor. "Come along, now. I won't amputate it. Come along. Don't be a baby."

"Let go of me," said the lieutenant, holding back wrathfully, his glance fixed upon the door of the old schoolhouse, as sinister to him as the portals of death.

And this is the story of how the lieutenant lost his arm. When he reached home, his sisters, his mother, his wife, sobbed for a long time at the sight of the flat. sleeve. "Oh, well," he said, standing shamefaced amid these tears, "I don't suppose it matters so much as all that."

from Army Life in a Black Regiment
by Thomas Wentworth Higginson

*Thomas Wentworth Higginson (1823–1911) in 1862 was made colonel of the First South Carolina Volunteers, one of the first all-black regiments. A fiery advocate of both women's rights and abolition, Higginson campaigned tirelessly—though unsuccessfully—for his soldiers to receive the same pay as their white counterparts. Here he describes a bittersweet respite from the war.*

We were in our winter camp on Port Royal Island. It was a lovely November morning, soft and springlike; the mockingbirds were singing, and the cottonfields still white with fleecy pods. Morning drill was over, the men were cleaning their guns and singing very happily; the officers were in their tents, reading still more happily their letters just arrived from home. Suddenly I heard a knock at my tent-door, and the latch clicked. It was the only latch in camp, and I was very proud of it, and the officers always clicked it as loudly as possible, in order to gratify my feelings. The door opened, and the Quartermaster thrust in the most beaming face I ever saw.

"Colonel," said he, "there are great news for the regiment. My wife and baby are coming by the next steamer!"

"Baby!" said I, in amazement. "Q.M., you are beside yourself." (We always called the Quartermaster Q.M. for shortness.) "There was a pass sent to your wife, but nothing was ever said about a baby. Baby indeed!"

"But the baby was included in the pass," replied the triumphant father-of-a-family. "You don't suppose my wife would come down here without her baby! Besides, the pass itself permits her to bring necessary baggage, and is not a baby six months old necessary baggage?"

"But, my dear fellow," said I, rather anxiously, "how can you make the little thing comfortable in a tent, amidst these rigors of a South Carolina winter, when it is uncomfortably hot for drill at noon, and ice forms by your bedside at night?"

"Trust me for that," said the delighted papa, and went off whistling. I could hear him telling the same news to three others, at least, before he got to his own tent.

That day the preparations began, and soon his abode was a wonder of comfort. There were posts and rafters, and a raised floor, and a great chimney, and a door with hinges,—every luxury except a latch, and that he could not have, for mine was the last that could be purchased. One of the regimental carpenters was employed to make a cradle, and another to make a bedstead high enough for the cradle to go under. Then there must be a bit of red carpet beside the bedstead, and thus the progress of splendor went on. The wife of one of the colored sergeants was engaged to act as nurserymaid. She was a very respectable young woman; the only objection to her being that she smoked a pipe. But we thought that perhaps Baby might not dislike tobacco; and if she did, she would have excellent opportunities to break the pipe in pieces.

In due time the steamer arrived, and Baby and her mother were among the passengers. The little recruit was soon settled in her new cradle, and slept in it as if she had never known any other. The sergeant's wife soon had her on exhibition through the neighborhood, and from that time forward she was quite a queen among us. She had sweet blue eyes and pretty brown hair, with round, dimpled cheeks, and that perfect dignity which is so beautiful in a baby. She hardly ever cried, and was not at all timid. She would go to anybody, and yet did not encourage any romping from any but the most intimate friends. She always wore a warm long-sleeved scarlet cloak with a hood, and in this costume was carried or "toted," as the soldiers said, all about the camp. At "guard-mounting" in the morning, when the men who are to go on guard duty for the day are drawn up to be inspected, Baby was always there, to help inspect them. She did not say much, but she eyed them very closely, and seemed fully to appreciate their bright buttons. Then the Officer-of-the-Day, who appears at guard-mounting with his sword and sash, and comes afterwards to the Colonel's tent for orders, would come and speak to Baby on his way, and receive her orders first. When the time came for drill she was usually present to watch the troops; and when the drum beat for dinner she liked to see the long row of men in each company march up to the cookhouse, in single file, each with tin cup and plate.

During the day, in pleasant weather, she might be seen in her nurse's arms, about the company streets, the center of an admiring circle, her scarlet costume looking very pretty amidst the shining black cheeks and neat blue uniforms of the soldiers. At "dress-parade," just before sunset, she was always an attendant. As I stood before the regiment, I could see the little spot of red out of the corner of my eye, at one end of the long line of men; and I looked with so much interest for her small person, that, instead of saying at the proper time, "Attention, Battalion! Shoulder arms!"—it is a wonder that I did not say, "Shoulder babies!"

Our little lady was very impartial, and distributed her kind looks to everybody. She had not the slightest prejudice against color, and did not care in the least whether her particular friends were black or white. Her especial favorites, I think, were the drummer-boys, who were not my favorites by any means, for they were a roguish set of scamps, and gave more trouble than all the grown men in the regiment. I think Annie liked them because they were small, and made a noise, and had red caps like her hood, and red facings on their jackets, and also because they occasionally stood on their heads for her amusement. After dress-parade the whole drum-corps would march to the great flag-staff, and wait till just sunset-time, when they would beat "the retreat," and then the flag would be hauled down—a great festival for

Annie. Sometimes the Sergeant-Major would wrap her in the great folds of the flag, after it was taken down, and she would peep out very prettily from amidst the stars and stripes, like a newborn Goddess of Liberty.

About once a month, some inspecting officer was sent to the camp by the general in command, to see to the condition of everything in the regiment, from bayonets to buttons. It was usually a long and tiresome process, and, when everything else was done, I used to tell the officer that I had one thing more for him to inspect, which was peculiar to our regiment. Then I would send for Baby to be exhibited, and I never saw an inspecting officer, old or young, who did not look pleased at the sudden appearance of the little, fresh, smiling creature— a flower in the midst of war. And Annie in her turn would look at them, with the true baby dignity in her face—that deep, earnest look which babies often have, and which people think so wonderful when Raphael paints it, although they might often see just the same expression in the faces of their own darlings at home.

Meanwhile Annie seemed to like the camp style of housekeeping very much. Her father's tent was double, and he used the front apartment for his office, and the inner room for parlor and bedroom; while the nurse had a separate tent and washroom behind all. I remember that, the first time I went there in the evening, it was to borrow some writing-paper; and while Baby's mother was hunting for it in the front tent, I heard a great cooing and murmuring in the inner room. I asked if Annie was still awake, and her mother told me to go in and see. Pushing aside the canvas door, I entered. No sign of anybody was to be seen; but a variety of soft little happy noises seemed to come from some unseen corner. Mrs. C. came quietly in, pulled away the counterpane of her own bed, and drew out the rough cradle where lay the little damsel, perfectly happy, and wider awake than anything but a baby possibly can be. She looked as if the seclusion of a dozen family bedsteads would not be enough to discourage her spirits, and I saw that camp life was likely to suit her very well.

A tent can be kept very warm, for it is merely a house with a thinner wall than usual; and I do not think that Baby felt the cold much more than if she had been at home that winter. The great trouble is that a tent-chimney, not being built very high, is apt to smoke when the wind is in a certain direction; and when that happens it is hardly possible to stay inside. So we used to build the chimneys of some tents on the east side, and those of others on the west, and thus some of the tents were always comfortable. I have seen Baby's mother running in a hard rain, with little Red-Riding-Hood in her arms, to take refuge with the Adjutant's wife, when every other abode was full of smoke; and I must admit that there were one or two windy days that season when nobody could really keep warm, and Annie had to remain ignominiously in her cradle, with as many clothes on as possible, for almost the whole time.

The Quartermaster's tent was very attractive to us in the evening. I remember that once, on passing near it after nightfall, I heard our Major's fine voice singing Methodist hymns within, and Mrs. C.'s sweet tones chiming in. So I peeped through the outer door. The fire was burning very pleasantly in the inner tent, and the scrap of new red carpet made the floor look quite magnificent. The Major sat on a box, our surgeon on a stool; Q.M. and his wife, and the Adjutant's wife, and one of the captains, were all sitting on the bed, singing as well as they knew how; and the baby was under the bed. Baby had retired for the night, was overshadowed, suppressed, sat upon; the singing went on, and she had wandered away into her own land of dreams, nearer to heaven, perhaps, than any pitch their voices could attain. I went in, and joined the party. Presently the music stopped, and another officer was sent for, to sing some particular song. At this pause the invisible innocent waked a little, and began to cluck and coo.

"It's the kitten," exclaimed somebody.

"It's my baby!" exclaimed Mrs. C. triumphantly, in that tone of unfailing personal pride which belongs to young mothers.

The people all got up from the bed for a moment, while Annie was pulled from beneath, wide awake and placid as usual; and she sat in one lap or another during the rest of the concert, sometimes winking at the candle, but usually listening to the songs, with a calm and critical expression, as if she could make as much noise as any of them, whenever she saw fit to try. Not a sound did she make, however, except one little soft sneeze, which led to an immediate floodtide of red shawl, covering every part of her but the forehead. But I soon hinted that the concert had better be ended, because I knew from observation that the small damsel had carefully watched a regimental inspection and a brigade drill on that day, and that an interval of repose was certainly necessary.

Annie did not long remain the only baby in camp. One day, on going out to the stables to look at a horse, I heard a sound of baby-talk, addressed by some man to a child nearby, and, looking round the corner of a tent, I saw that one of the hostlers had something black and round, lying on the sloping side of a tent, with which he was playing very eagerly. It proved to be his baby, a plump, shiny thing, younger than Annie; and I never saw a merrier picture than the happy father frolicking with his child, while the mother stood quietly by. This was Baby Number Two, and she stayed in camp several weeks, the two innocents meeting each other every day, in the placid indifference that belonged to their years; both were happy little healthy things, and it never seemed to cross their minds that there was any difference in their complexions. As I said before, Annie was not troubled by any prejudice in regard to color, nor do I suppose that the other little maiden was.

Annie enjoyed the tent-life very much; but when we were sent out on picket soon after, she enjoyed it still more. Our headquarters were at a deserted plantation house, with one large parlor, a dining-room, and a few bedrooms. Baby's father and mother had a room upstairs, with a stove whose pipe went straight out at the window. This was quite comfortable, though half the windows were broken, and there was no glass and no glazier to mend them. The windows of the large parlor were in much the same condition, though we had an immense fireplace, where we had a bright fire whenever it was cold, and always in the evening. The walls of this room were very dirty, and it took our ladies several days to cover all the unsightly places with wreaths and hangings of evergreen. In this performance Baby took an active part.

Her duties consisted in sitting in a great nest of evergreen, pulling and fingering the fragrant leaves, and occasionally giving a little cry of glee when she had accomplished some piece of decided mischief.

There was less entertainment to be found in the camp itself at this time; but the household at headquarters was larger than Baby had been accustomed to. We had a great deal of company, moreover, and she had quite a gay life of it. She usually made her appearance in the large parlor soon after breakfast; and to dance her for a few moments in our arms was one of the first daily duties of each one. Then the morning reports began to arrive from the different outposts—a mounted officer or courier coming in from each place, dismounting at the door, and clattering in with jingling arms and spurs, each a new excitement for Annie. She usually got some attention from any officer who came, receiving with her wonted dignity any daring caress. When the messengers had ceased to be interesting, there were always the horses to look at, held or tethered under the trees beside the sunny piazza. After the various couriers had been received, other messengers would be despatched to the town, seven miles away, and Baby had all the excitement of their mounting and departure. Her father was often one of the riders, and would sometimes seize Annie for a goodby kiss, place her on the saddle before him, gallop her round the house once or twice, and then give her back to her nurse's arms again: She was perfectly fearless, and such boisterous attentions never frightened her, nor did they ever interfere with her sweet, infantine self-possession.

After the riding-parties had gone, there was the piazza still for entertainment, with a sentinel pacing up and down before it; but Annie did not enjoy the sentinel, though his breastplate and buttons shone like gold, so much as the hammock which always hung swinging between the pillars. It was a pretty hammock, with great open meshes; and she delighted to lie in it, and have the netting closed above her, so that she could only be seen through the apertures. I can see her now, the fresh little rosy thing, in her blue and scarlet wrappings, with one round and dimpled arm thrust forth through the netting, and the other grasping an armful of blushing roses and fragrant magnolias. She looked like those pretty French bas-reliefs of Cupids imprisoned in baskets, and peeping through. That hammock was a very useful appendage; it was a couch for us, a cradle for Baby, a nest for the kittens; and we had, moreover, a little hen, which tried to roost there every night.

When the mornings were colder, and the stove upstairs smoked the wrong way, Baby was brought down in a very incomplete state of toilet, and finished her dressing by the great fire. We found her bare shoulders very becoming, and she was very much interested in her own little pink toes. After a very slow dressing, she had a still slower breakfast out of a tin cup of warm milk, of which she generally spilt a good deal, as she had much to do in watching everybody who came into the room, and seeing that there was no mischief done. Then she would be placed on the floor, on our only piece of carpet, and the kittens would be brought in for her to play with.

We had, at different times, a variety of pets, of whom Annie did not take much notice. Sometimes we had young partridges, caught by the drummer-boys in trap-cages. The children called them "Bob and Chloe," because the first notes of the male and female sound like those names. One day I brought home an opossum, with her blind bare little young clinging to the droll pouch where their mothers keep them. Sometimes we had pretty green lizards, their color darkening or deepening, like that of chameleons, in light or shade. But the only pets that took Baby's fancy were the kittens. They perfectly delighted her, from the first moment she saw them; they were the only things younger than herself that she had ever beheld, and the only things softer than themselves that her small hands had grasped. It was astonishing to see how much the kittens would endure from her. They could scarcely be touched by any one else without mewing; but when Annie seized one by the head and the other by the tail, and rubbed them violently together, they did not make a sound. I suppose that a baby's grasp is really soft, even if it seems ferocious, and so it gives less pain than one would think. At any rate, the little animals had the best of it very soon; for they entirely outstripped Annie in learning to walk, and they could soon scramble away beyond her reach, while she sat in a sort of dumb despair, unable to comprehend why anything so much smaller than herself should be so much nimbler. Meanwhile, the kittens would sit up and look at her with the most provoking indifference, just out of arm's length, until some of us would take pity on the young lady, and toss her furry playthings back to her again. "Little baby," she learned to call them; and these were the very first words she spoke.

Baby had evidently a natural turn for war, further cultivated by an intimate knowledge of drills and parades. The nearer she came to actual conflict the better she seemed to like it, peaceful as her own little ways might be. Twice, at least, while she was with us on picket, we had alarms from the Rebel troops, who would bring down cannon to the opposite side of the Ferry, about two miles beyond us, and throw shot and shell over upon our side. Then the officer at the Ferry would think that there was to be an attack made, and couriers would be sent, riding to and fro, and the men would all be called to arms in a hurry, and the ladies at headquarters would all put on their best bonnets and come downstairs, and the ambulance would be made ready to carry them to a place of safety before the expected fight. On such occasions Baby was in all her glory. She shouted with delight at being suddenly uncribbed and thrust into her little scarlet cloak, and brought down stairs, at an utterly unusual and improper hour, to a piazza with lights and people and horses and general excitement. She crowed and gurgled and made gestures with her little fists, and screamed out what seemed to be her advice on the military situation, as freely as if she had been a newspaper editor. Except that it was rather difficult to understand her precise directions, I do not know but the whole Rebel force might have been captured through her plans. And at any rate, I should much rather obey her orders than those of some generals whom I have known; for she at least meant no harm, and would lead one into no mischief.

However, at last the danger, such as it was, would be all over, and the ladies would be induced to go peacefully to bed again; and Annie would retreat with them to her ignoble cradle, very much disappointed, and looking vainly back at the more martial scene below. The next morning she would seem to have forgotten all about it, and would spill her bread and milk by the fire as if nothing had happened.

I suppose we hardly knew, at the time, how large a part of the sunshine of our daily lives was contributed by dear little Annie. Yet, when I now look back on that pleasant Southern home, she seems as essential a part of it as the mockingbirds or the magnolias, and I cannot convince myself that in returning to it I should not find her there. But Annie went back, with the spring, to her Northern birthplace, and then passed away from this earth before her little feet had fairly learned to tread its paths; and when I meet her next it must be in some world where there is triumph without armies, and where innocence is trained in scenes of peace. I know, however, that her little life, short as it seemed, was a blessing to us all, giving a perpetual image of serenity and sweetness, recalling the lovely atmosphere of far-off homes, and holding us by unsuspected ties to whatsoever things were pure.

from A Confederate Girl's Diary
by Sarah Morgan Dawson

*Sarah Morgan Dawson (1842–1909) of Baton Rouge, Louisiana had three brothers in the Confederate army and navy, a fourth brother who supported the Union (though he declined to bear arms against the South) and a brother-in-law who served as a Union officer. This bramble of sympathies enriched the young woman's diary of the war years, as in this account of an incident during the 1862 occupation of her hometown.*

May 11th.

—I am disgusted with myself. No unusual thing, but I am *peculiarly* disgusted this time. Last evening, I went to Mrs. Brunot's, without an idea of going beyond, with my flag flying again. They were all going to the State House, so I went with them; to my great distress, some fifteen or twenty Federal officers were standing on the first terrace, stared at like wild beasts by the curious crowd. I had not expected to meet them, and felt a painful conviction that I was unnecessarily attracting attention, by an unladylike display of defiance, from the crowd gathered there. But what was I to do? I felt humiliated, conspicuous, everything that is painful and disagreeable; but—strike my colors in the face of the enemy? Never! Nettie and Sophie had them, too, but that was no consolation for the shame I suffered by such a display so totally distasteful to me. How I wished myself away, and chafed at my folly, and hated myself for being there, and everyone for seeing me. I hope it will be a lesson to me always to remember a lady can gain nothing by such display.

I was not ashamed of the flag of my country, I proved that by never attempting to remove it in spite of my mortification—but I was ashamed of my position; for these are evidently gentlemen, not the Billy Wilson's crew we were threatened with. Fine, noble-looking men they were, showing refinement and gentlemanly bearing in every motion. One cannot help but admire such foes! They set us an example worthy of our imitation, and one we would be benefited by following. They come as visitors without either pretensions to superiority, or the insolence of conquerors; they walk quietly their way, offering no annoyance to the citizens, though they themselves are stared at most unmercifully, and pursued by crowds of ragged little boys, while even men gape at them with open mouths. They prove themselves gentlemen, while many of our citizens have proved themselves boors, and I admire them for their conduct. With a conviction that I had allowed myself to be influenced by bigoted, narrow-minded people, in believing them to be unworthy of respect or regard, I came home wonderfully changed in all my newly acquired sentiments, resolved never more to wound their feelings, who were so careful of ours, by such unnecessary display. And I hung my flag on the parlor mantel, there to wave, if it will, in the shades of private life; but to make a show, make me conspicuous and ill at ease, as I was yesterday—never again!

There was a dozen officers in church this morning, and the psalms for the 11th day seemed so singularly appropriate to the feelings of the people, that I felt uncomfortable for them. They answered with us, though.

May 14th.

I am beginning to believe that we are even of more importance in Baton Rouge than we thought we were. It is laughable to hear the things a certain set of people, who know they can't visit us, say about the whole family. . . . When father was alive, they dared not talk about us aloud, beyond calling us the "Proud Morgans" and the "Aristocracy of Baton Rouge" . . . But now father is gone, the people imagine we are public property, to be criticized, vilified, and abused to their hearts' content. . . .

And now, because they find absurdities don't succeed, they try improbabilities. So yesterday the town was in a ferment because it was reported the Federal officers had called on the Miss Morgans, and all the gentlemen were anxious to hear how they had been received. One had the grace to say, "If they did, they received the best lesson there that they could get in town; those young ladies would meet them with the true Southern spirit." The rest did not know; they would like to find out.

I suppose the story originated from the fact that we were unwilling to blackguard—yes, that is the word—the Federal officers here, and would not agree with many of our friends in saying they were liars, thieves, murderers, scoundrels, the scum of the earth, etc. Such epithets are unworthy of ladies, I say, and do harm, rather than advance our cause. Let them be what they will, it shall not make me less the lady; I say it is unworthy of anything except low newspaper war, such abuse, and I will not join in.

I have a brother-in-law in the Federal army whom I love and respect as much as any one in the world, and shall not readily agree that his being a Northerner would give him an irresistible desire to pick my pockets, and take from him all power of telling the truth. No! There are few men I admire more than Major Drum, and I honor him for his independence in doing what he believes right. Let us have liberty of speech and action in our land, I say, but not gross abuse and calumny. Shall I acknowledge that the people we so recently called our brothers are unworthy of consideration, and are liars, cowards, dogs? Not I! If they conquer us, I acknowledge them as a superior race; I will not say that we were conquered by cowards, for where would that place us? It will take a brave people to gain us, and that the Northerners undoubtedly are. I would scorn to have an inferior foe; I fight only my equals. These women may acknowledge that *cowards* have won battles in which their brothers were engaged, but I, I will ever say *mine* fought against brave men, and won the day. Which is most honorable?

I was never a Secessionist, for I quietly adopted father's views on political subjects without meddling with them. But even father went over with his State, and when so many outrages were committed by the fanatical leaders of the North, though he regretted the Union, said, "Fight to the death for our liberty." I say so, too. I want to fight until we win the cause so many have died for. I don't believe in Secession, but I do in Liberty. I want the South to conquer, dictate its own terms, and go back to the Union, for I believe that, apart, inevitable ruin awaits both. It is a rope of sand, this Confederacy, founded on the doctrine of Secession, and will not last many years—not five. The North cannot subdue us. We are too determined to be free. They have no right to confiscate our property to pay debts they themselves have incurred. Death as a nation, rather than Union on such terms. We will have our rights secured on so firm a basis that it can never be shaken. If by power of overwhelming numbers they conquer us, it will be a barren victory over a desolate land.

We, the natives of this loved soil, will be beggars in a foreign land; we will not submit to despotism under the garb of Liberty. The North will find herself burdened with an unparalleled debt, with nothing to show for it except deserted towns, burning homes, a standing army which will govern with no small caprice, and an impoverished land.

If that be treason, make the best of it!

from "Co. Aytch"
by Sam R. Watkins

*Former Confederate footsoldier Sam R. Watkins (1839–1901) published his raw and riveting novel of the war in 1882. His local newspaper noted: "In big, gilt-edged books, the General, the President, and the Vice President tell about their plans, their battles, their retreats, their measures . . . and not a word about what the poor, sore-footed, hungry, and naked soldier felt." Watkins righted that wrong.*

The First and Twenty-seventh Tennessee Regiments will ever remember the battle of "Dead Angle," which was fought June 27th, on the Kennesaw line, near Marietta, Georgia. It was one of the hottest and longest days of the year, and one of the most desperate and determinedly resisted battles fought during the whole war. Our regiment was stationed on an angle, a little spur of the mountain, or rather promontory of a range of hills, extending far out beyond the main line of battle, and was subject to the enfilading fire of forty pieces of artillery of the Federal batteries. It seemed fun for the guns of the whole Yankee army to play upon this point. We would work hard every night to strengthen our breastworks, and the very next day they would be torn down smooth with the ground by solid shots and shells from the guns of the enemy. Even the little trees and bushes, which had been left for shade, were cut down as so much stubble. For more than a week this constant tiring had been kept up against this salient point. In the meantime, the skirmishing in the valley below resembled the sounds made by ten thousand wood-choppers.

Well, on the fatal morning of June 27th, the sun rose clear and cloudless, the heavens seemed made of brass and the earth of iron, and as the sun began to mount toward the zenith, everything became quiet, and no sound was heard save a peckerwood on a neighboring tree, tapping on its old trunk, trying to find a worm for his dinner. We all knew it was but the dead calm that precedes the storm. On the distant hills we could plainly see officers dashing about hither and thither, and the Stars and Stripes moving to and fro, and we knew the Federals were making preparations for the mighty contest. We could hear but the rumbling sound of heavy guns, and the distant tread of a marching army, as a faint roar of the coming storm, which was soon to break the ominous silence with the sound of conflict, such as was scarcely ever before heard on this earth. It seemed that the arch-angel of Death stood and looked on with outstretched wings, while all the earth was silent, when all at once a hundred guns from the Federal line opened upon us, and for more than an hour they poured their solid and chain shot, grape and shrapnel right upon this salient point, defended by our regiment alone, when, all of a sudden, our pickets jumped into our works and reported the Yankees advancing, and almost at the same time a solid line of blue coats came up the hill. I discharged my gun, and happening to look up, there was the beautiful flag of the Stars and Stripes flaunting right in my face, and I heard John Branch, of the Rock City Guards, commanded by Captain W. D. Kelley, who were next to Company H, say, "Look at that Yankee flag; shoot that fellow; snatch that flag out of his hand!" My pen is unable to describe the scene of carnage and death that ensued in the next two hours. Column after column of Federal soldiers were crowded upon that line, and by referring to the history of the war you will find they were massed in column forty columns deep; in fact, the whole force of the Yankee army was hurled against this point, but no sooner would a regiment mount our works than they were shot down or surrendered, and soon we had every "gopher hole" full of Yankee prisoners. Yet still the

Yankees came. It seemed impossible to check the onslaught, but every man was true to his trust, and seemed to think that at that moment the whole responsibility of the Confederate government was rested upon his shoulders. Talk about other battles, victories, shouts, cheers, and triumphs, but in comparison with this day's fight, all others dwarf into insignificance. The sun beaming down on our uncovered heads, the thermometer being one hundred and ten degrees in the shade, and a solid line of blazing fire right from the muzzles of the Yankee guns being poured right into our very faces, singeing our hair and clothes, the hot blood of our dead and wounded spurting on us, the blinding smoke and stifling atmosphere filling our eyes and mouths, and the awful concussion causing the blood to gash out of our noses and ears, and above all, the roar of battle, made it a perfect pandemonium. Afterward I heard a soldier express himself by saying that he thought "Hell had broke loose in Georgia, sure enough."

I have heard men say that if they ever killed a Yankee during the war they were not aware of it. I am satisfied that on this memorable day, every man in our regiment killed from one score to four score, yea, five score men. I mean from twenty to one hundred each. All that was necessary was to load and shoot. In fact, I will ever think that the reason they did not capture our works was the impossibility of their living men passing over the bodies of their dead. The ground was piled up with one solid mass of dead and wounded Yankees. I learned afterwards from the burying squad that in some places they were piled up like cord wood, twelve deep.

After they were time and time again beaten back, they at last were enabled to fortify a line under the crest of the hill, only thirty yards from us, and they immediately commenced to excavate the earth with the purpose of blowing up our line.

We remained here three days after the battle. In the meantime the woods had taken fire, and during the nights and days of all that time continued to burn, and at all times, every hour of day and night, you could hear the shrieks and screams of the poor fellows who were left on the field, and a stench, so sickening as to nauseate the whole of both armies, arose from the decaying bodies of the dead left lying on the field.

On the third morning the Yankees raised a white flag, asked an armistice to bury the dead, not for any respect either army had for the dead, but to get rid of the sickening stench. I get sick now when I happen to think about it. Long and deep trenches were dug, and hooks made from bayonets crooked for the purpose, and all the dead were dragged and thrown pell mell into these trenches. Nothing was allowed to be taken off the dead, and finely dressed officers, with gold watch chains dangling over their vests, were thrown into the ditches. During the whole day both armies were hard at work, burying the Federal dead.

Every member of the First and Twenty-seventh Tennessee Regiments deserves a wreath of imperishable fame, and a warm place in the hearts of their countrymen, for their gallant and heroic valor at the battle of Dead Angle. No man distinguished himself above another. All did their duty, and the glory of one is but the glory and just tribute of the others.

After we had abandoned the line, and on coming to a little stream of water, I undressed for the purpose of bathing, and after undressing found my arm all battered and bruised and bloodshot from my wrist to my shoulder, and as sore as a blister. I had shot one hundred and twenty times that day. My gun became so hot that frequently the powder would flash before I could ram home the ball, and I had frequently to exchange my gun for that of a dead comrade.

Colonel H. R. Field was loading and shooting the same as any private in the ranks when he fell off the skid from which he was shooting right over my shoulder, shot through the head. I laid him down in the trench, and he said, "Well, they have got me at last, but I have killed fifteen of them; turn about is fair play, I reckon." But Colonel Field was not killed—only wounded, and one side paralyzed. Captain Joe P. Lee, Captain Mack Campbell, Lieutenant T. H. Maney, and other officers of the regiment, threw rocks and beat them in their faces with sticks. The Yankees did the same. The rocks came in upon us like a perfect hail storm, and the Yankees seemed very obstinate, and in no hurry to get away from our front, and we had to keep up the firing and shooting them down in self-defense. They seemed to walk up and take death as coolly as if they were automatic or wooden men, and our boys did not shoot for the fun of the thing. It was, verily, a life and death grapple, and the least flicker on our part would have been sure death to all. We could not be reinforced on account of our position, and we had to stand up to the rack, fodder or no fodder. When the Yankees fell back, and the firing ceased, I never saw so many broken down and exhausted men in my life. I was as sick as a horse, and as wet with blood and sweat as I could be, and many of our men were vomiting with excessive fatigue, overexhaustion, and sunstroke; our tongues were parched and cracked for water, and our faces blackened with powder and smoke, and our dead and wounded were piled indiscriminately in the trenches. There was not a single man in the company who was not wounded, or had holes shot through his hat and clothing. Captain Beasley was killed, and nearly all his company killed and wounded. The Rock City Guards were almost piled in heaps, and so was our company. Captain Joe P. Lee was badly wounded. Poor Walter Hood and Jim Brandon were lying there among us, while their spirits were in heaven; also, William A. Hughes, my old messmate and friend, who had clerked with me for S. F. & J. M. Mayes, and had slept with me for lo! these many years, and was a boy who loved me more than any other person on earth has ever done. I had just discharged the contents of my gun into the bosoms of two men, one right behind the other, killing them both, and was reloading, when a Yankee rushed upon me, having me at a disadvantage, and said, "You have killed my two brothers, and now I've got you." Everything I had ever done rushed through my mind. I heard the roar, and felt the flash of fire, and saw my more than friend, William A. Hughes, grab the muzzle of the gun, and receive the whole contents in his hand and arm, mortally wounding him. Reader, he died for me. In saving my life, he lost his own. When the infirmary corps carried him off, all mutilated and bleeding he told them to give me "Florence Fleming" (that was the name of his gun, which he had put on it in silver letters), and to give me his blanket and clothing. He gave his life for me, and everything that he had. It was the last time that I ever saw him, but I know that away up yonder, beyond the clouds, blackness, tempest and night, and away above the blue vault of heaven, where the stars keep their ceaseless vigils, away up yonder in the golden city of the New Jerusalem, where God and Jesus Christ, our Savior, ever reign, we will sometime meet at the marriage supper of the Son of God, who gave His life for the redemption of the whole world.

For several nights they made attacks upon our lines, but in every attempt, they were driven back with great slaughter. They would ignite the tape of bomb shells, and throw them over in our lines, but, if the shell did not immediately explode, they were thrown back. They had a little shell called *hand grenade,* but they would either stop short of us, or go over our heads, and were harmless. General Joseph E. Johnston sent us a couple of *chevaux-de-frise.* When they came, a detail of three men had to roll them over the works. Those three men were heroes. Their names were Edmund Brandon, T. C. Dornin, and Arnold Zellner. Although it was a solemn occasion, every one of us was convulsed with laughter at the ridiculous appearance and actions of the detail. Every one of them made their wills and said their prayers truthfully and honestly, before they undertook the task. I laugh now every time I think of the ridiculous appearance of the detail, but to them it was no laughing matter. I will say that they were men who feared not, nor faltered in their duty. They were men, and today deserve the thanks of the people of the South. That night about midnight, an alarm was given that the Yankees were advancing. They would only have to run about twenty yards before they would be in our works. We were ordered to "shoot." Every man was hallooing at the, top of his voice, "Shoot, shoot, tee, shoot, shootee." On the alarm, both the Confederate and Federal lines opened, with both small arms and artillery, and it seemed that the very heavens and earth were in a grand conflagration, as they will be at the final judgment, after the resurrection. I have since learned that this was a false alarm, and that no attack had been meditated.

Previous to the day of attack, the soldiers had cut down all the trees in our immediate front, throwing the tops downhill and sharpening the limbs of the same, thus making, as we thought, an impenetrable *abattis* of vines and limbs locked together; but nothing stopped or could stop the advance of the Yankee line, but the hot shot and cold steel that we poured into their faces from under our head-logs.

One of the most shameful and cowardly acts of Yankee treachery was committed there that I ever remember to have seen. A wounded Yankee was lying right outside of our works, and begging most piteously for water, when a member of the railroad company (his name was Hog Johnson, and the very man who stood videt with Theodore Sloan and me at the battle of Missionary Ridge, and who killed the three Yankees, one night, from Fort Horsley), got a canteen of water, and gave the dying Yankee a drink, and as he started back, he was killed dead in his tracks by a treacherous Yankee hid behind a tree. It matters not, for somewhere in God's Holy Word, which cannot lie, He says that "He that giveth a cup of cold water in my name, shall not lose his reward." And I have no doubt, reader, in my own mind, that the poor fellow is reaping his reward in Emanuel's land with the good and just. In every instance where we tried to assist their wounded, our men were killed or wounded. A poor wounded and dying boy, not more than six-teen years of age, asked permission to crawl over our works, and when he had crawled to the top, and just as Blair Webster and I reached up to help the poor fellow, he, the Yankee, was killed by his own men. In fact, I have ever thought that is why the slaughter was so great in our front, that nearly, if not as many, Yankees were killed by their own men as by us. The brave ones, who tried to storm and carry our works, were simply between two fires. It is a singular fanaticism, and curious fact, that enters the mind of a soldier, that it is a grand and glorious death— to die on a victorious battlefield. One morning the Sixth and Ninth Regiments came to our assistance—not to relieve us—but only to assist us, and every member of our regiment—First and Twenty-seventh—got "as mad as a wet hen." They felt almost insulted, and I believe we would soon have been in a fine fight, had they not been ordered back. As soon as they came up every one of us began to say, "Go back! go back! we can hold this place, and by the eternal God we are not going to leave it." General Johnston came there to look at the position, and told us that a transverse line was about one hundred yards in our rear, and should they come on us too heavy to fall back to that line, when almost every one of us said, "You go back and look at other lines, this place is safe, and can never be taken." And then when they had dug a tunnel under us to blow us up, we laughed, yea, even rejoiced, at the fact of soon being blown sky high. Yet, not a single man was willing to leave his post. When old Joe sent us the two *chevaux-de-frise,* and kept on sending us water, and rations, and whisky, and tobacco, and word to hold our line, we would invariably send word back to rest easy, and that all is well at Dead Angle. I have ever thought that is one reason why General Johnston fell back from this Kennesaw line, and I will say today, in 1882, that while we appreciated his sympathies and kindness toward us, we did not think hard of old Joe for having so little confidence in us at that time. A perfect hail of minnie balls was being continually poured into our head-logs the whole time we remained here. The Yankees would hold up small looking-glasses, so that our strength and breast-works could be seen in the reflection in the glass; and they also had small mirrors on the butts of their guns, so arranged that they could sight up the barrels of their guns by looking through these glasses, while they themselves would not be exposed to our fire, and they kept up this continual firing day and night, whether they could see us or not. Sometimes a glancing shot from our head-logs would wound someone.

But I cannot describe it as I would wish. I would be pleased to mention the name of every soldier, not only of Company H alone, but every man in the First and Twenty-seventh Tennessee Consolidated Regiments on this occasion, but I cannot now remember their names, and will not mention any one in particular, fearing to do injustice to some whom I might inadvertently omit. Every man and every company did their duty. Company G, commanded by Captain Mack Campbell, stood side by side with us on this occasion, as they ever had during the whole war. But soldiers of the First and Twenty-seventh Regiments, it is with a feeling of pride and satisfaction to me, today, that I was associated with

so many noble and brave men, and who were subsequently compli-
mented by Jeff Davis, then President of the Confederate States of America, in person, who said, "That every member of our regiment was fit to
be a captain"—his very words. I mention Captain W. C. Flournoy, of
Company K, the Martin Guards; Captain Ledbetter, of the Rutherford
Rifles; Captains Kelley and Steele, of the Rock City Guards, and Captain
Adkisson, of the Williamson Grays, and Captain Fulcher, and other
names of brave and heroic men, some of whom live today, but many
have crossed the dark river and are "resting under the shade of the trees"
on the other shore, waiting and watching for us, who are left to do justice to their memory and our cause, and when we old Rebels have
accomplished God's purpose on earth, we, too, will be called to give an
account of our battles, struggles, and triumphs.

from I Rode with Stonewall
by Henry Kyd Douglas

*General Thomas Jonathan Jackson's stand at the First Battle of Bull Run (in the words of General Barnard Bee, Jackson's brigade held their position "like a stonewall") is the stuff of legend. Jackson's death at Chancellorsville deprived Lee of a top-notch tactician and a firm, but respected commander. Henry Kyd Douglas (1838–1903), the youngest member of Jackson's staff, presents an admiring view of Stonewall's command style.*

The question has been asked, what was the limit of Jackson's military capacity? It is not possible to answer it. In him there was exhibited no dangerous precociousness. He never sought promotion, but never expressed a doubt of his ability to manage any command given him. He put forth no useless strength. What was in him we shall never know for he went to the grave with the richness of the mine unexplored. He was equal to each new occasion as it arose, and in his movements there was no monotony, except in success. His development came as required, and he closed his career at Chancellorsville with his greatest stroke and died with fresh honors thick upon him. It has been said of his Valley Campaign and his movements around Pope that he violated all the established rules of war. So be it. So Count Wurmser and Beaulieu, the Austrian generals, said of the young Napoleon in his Mantuan Campaign. Rules of war are like piecrust, made to be broken at the right time. Both of these military culprits knew the rules and knew the right time to violate them; their success must be their apology.

I have already referred to an apparent inconsistency in Jackson's character: his gentleness and tenderness of heart and manner in his personal life, and on the other hand a hardness at times in exacting the performance of military duty which had the flavor of deliberate cruelty. Shortly after the First Manassas, when Jackson was Brigadier General, an officer in his command applied for a short furlough to visit his wife who was sick unto death. The General returned the application disapproved. Not dreaming of such a thing, so early in the war, the officer sought General Jackson and made a personal appeal to him. Seeing that his appeal was having no effect, he cried out, with great emotion,

"General, General, my wife is dying. I must see her!"

A shade of sadness and grief passed over the face of the General but for a moment, and then in cold, merciless tones, he replied, "Man, man, do you love your wife more than your country?" and turned away.

The wife died and that soldier never forgave Stonewall Jackson.

Yes, this was the man who was stopped on the highway by an old woman and raised his cap to her when asked innocently if he could tell her if her son would pass that way. Sharply directing his staff, who had thoughtlessly smiled at the interruption, to move on, except Dr. McGuire, he dismounted and began to question her. Having satisfied himself that her son was in the Fifth Virginia Regiment of his old brigade, he directed a courier to remain with her, find her son and give him leave to remain with her until next morning. Then, taking the old lady's hand, he said kind words to her, mounted his horse, and rode away.

This makes clear the distinction between his natural personal kindliness and his exacting, unyielding sense of public duty.

Thus it may be said of General Jackson that he was a normal human being, not a mythological creation. He was a soldier of great ability, activity, and daring, and not an irresponsible, erratic genius. In manner he was deferential, modest, and retiring, in the presence of women diffident to excess. He never blustered and even on the field of battle was rarely severe except to incompetency and neglect. He judged himself more harshly than anyone else did, but toward the weakness of others he had abundant charity. In religion he was a quiet Christian gentleman, absolutely liberal and nonsectarian: he was a Presbyterian but might just as easily have been a Methodist or an Episcopalian or, perchance, a Catholic. He was too liberal to be a bigot and had none of "the presumptuous fanaticism of Cromwell." Like many another great soldier, he was at first called "crazy," but it was soon found out he was always sober and in his right mind. Eccentric as many of his movements were, they were prompted—as Napoleon said of his own—"not by genius but by thought and meditation." He made war like a soldier of great brain and moral force, not as Blind Tom makes music, guided by whispering no one hears but himself.

Many another great soldier has intoxicated his troops with enthusiasm on the battlefield and led them to the performance of great deeds. No one, when he had gone, ever left behind him among the ranks greater reverence or a more tender memory. The morning after the unveiling of the Lee Statue in Richmond as the sun rose over the city, its first rays fell upon a row of figures, wrapped in gray blankets and sleeping on the grass around the Statue of Jackson in Capitol Square. One by one these sleepers began to unroll themselves—here a grey head, there a grey beard—got up, yawned and stretched themselves in the morning air. Just then a passing citizen said to them in kindly anxiety,

"Heavens, men, could you find no other beds in Richmond last night?"

"Oh, yes, there was plenty of places; all Richmond was open to us," said one, and turning his eyes toward the silent face of his immortal chief he added, "but we were his boys and we wanted to sleep with the old man just once more."

A few years afterwards I was present at Lexington when the Jackson Statue erected at his grave was unveiled. It was a day not to be forgotten. Old Confederates were there from far and near—men who had not seen each other since Appomattox. The Valley of Virginia gathered there, and East Virginia, and Maryland. Old soldiers in grey uniforms, all the old soldiers in grey hair or grey beards, crowded the streets of that historic town. The day was given up to memories, and Jubal Early, the oldest Confederate general living, spoke for us all on that occasion. I need not dwell upon the ceremonies, upon the pathetic scenes at this last reunion. The evening drew near and the departing day seemed to linger like a benediction over the sacred place of the dead. People were moving off and the order was given to the old soldiers to fall into line and march away. With trembling step the grey line moved on, but when it reached the gate one old Confederate turned his face for a last look at the monument and, waving his old grey hat toward the figure of his beloved General, he cried out in a voice, that choked itself with sobs,

"Good-by, old man, good-by! We've done all we can for you!"

from The Civil War Letters of
Joshua K. Callaway
by Joshua K. Callaway

*Joshua K. Callaway (1834-1863), a Confede-rate junior officer, died at Missionary Ridge, shot through the bowels. His comrades tried to move him to the rear, but he asked to be left on the battlefield. His burial place is unknown. He was 29 years old. A husband, father and school-teacher, Callaway was a typical citizen soldier. A reader can sense him trying to lose himself—to commune with his other life—through these simple letters home.*

Picket Camp 8 miles from
Shelbyville Wednesday
June 3rd 1863

My Darling Wife:
I must write you a short letter this evening although I have not a great deal of news. But I may not have the chance to write any more for some time. I can now appreciate your discretion in not coming to see me. We have orders now to keep 3 day's rations cooked all the time and hold ourselves in readiness to move at a moment's notice. Some think we will go to Vicksburg, but I think differently. I think Bragg is meditating an attack on old Rosey. Two brigades passed here this morning going to the front. It is thought that the yankees are very weak now at Murfreesboro and hence it is probable that Bragg will advance.

Of course you have all the news from Vicksburg. I have none of importance from there, but hope it is all well there.

It may be that we will not move from here for some time yet but [I] think the chances are that we will leave tomorrow. If we do advance I expect to be in a fight in a few days, perhaps before you get this. May the God of battles be with us & crown us with victory. Pray for me constantly.

I have not got that ring ready to send to T. yet but will send her one before long. Tell her that Pa has not forgotten her.

I forgot to tell you that I got a letter from Eli the other day. He was well when he wrote. I am glad to get a letter from him. I was uneasy about him, had not heard from him since the battle of Chancellorsville. I will write to him [in] a day or two. I wrote Wes twice at Selma, but I understand that they have gone back to Mobile, and if so he will not get my letter.

Wes has been very lucky as a soldier. He has had a real *"hog killing time"* ever since he became one. I wish it may continue favorable for him.

My Dear, I hope I shall hear from you tomorrow and semi-occasionally. May God bless you all and give us peace. Your own

J. K.


Mrs. D. C.

P. S. My Darling, I must apologize a little for not writing more, but, as I said before, I have no news, more than I have written, and then there is a big game of "Town Ball" going on out here and they are all very jolly and I am about to lose it all, hence I know you will excuse me.

A kiss apiece for you all

J. K.


Camp 28th Ala Near Shelbyville
Monday morning June 8th 1863

My Dear Wife, I looked in vain for a letter from you yesterday. I have not one from you since yesterday was a week ago. I am a little uneasy about you. I fear you or some of the family are very sick. Please don't keep me in suspense so long at a time.

I am not so well just now myself I have been troubled for several days with diarrhoea but have not quit doing duty, and am better now.

I have not got a word of news. Of course you are in possession of all the news from Vicksburg. I heard from some citizens yesterday that Vicksburg had fallen but no one believes it.

Everything is very quiet here. Old Rosey and Bragg both seem to be waiting to see the result of the Vicksburg affair before moving. And if we beat them there as badly as I think [we] will they will certainly be willing to make peace. Though it may bring on a fight here.

I believe I wrote you that I had got a letter from Eli & one from Wes. I wrote to Eli yesterday and shall write to Wes tomorrow. I have not had a letter from anybody from Coffee in some time.

We are still on Picket. We have been out here two weeks already and will remain this week which will make a three week tour of picketing, but some want to stay here all the time from the fact that we have a nice place to camp, but I don't because the guard duty is much heavier.

Tell T. that I have not made that ring yet but still intend to make it. But when I make it if it is a better one than I sent before I want you to keep it and give her the one I sent you.

Yesterday was a very pleasant day but cloudy and the mornings are all very cool here. The fire feels very well until after sun up. This morning is very clear and cool. We have a good deal of rain here lately, and I hope you are not needing rain in Alabama.

The crops all look very well but seem to be late. I have not seen any corn higher than my knees. The wheat will do to cut in a week or so and is very fine. I see some rust but don't think it is doing any harm yet, nor don't think it can. I suppose you are getting some flour. If you have not bought any yet you must buy.

When will your subscription for the paper be out? You renew it.

When you buy flour buy enough to do you the balance of the year.

Well, breakfast will soon be ready and [I] must stop. Give my love to your mother. Kiss the children and remember me kindly to the negroes and enquiring friends. Pray for me constantly, write to me frequently and believe me as ever your devoted

J. K. Callaway

from The Diary of Caroline
Seabury, 1854-1863
by Caroline Seabury

*Massachusetts native Caroline Seabury (1827–*

*1893) lost eight members of her family, includ-*

*ing her parents, to consumption. Left alone, she*

*moved south in 1854 to teach French at the*

*Columbus Female Institute in Columbus, Missi-*

*ssippi. The coming of war made her position*

*precarious. In 1862 the director of her school*

*decided to hire only Southern teachers. By*

*1863 Seabury was eager to return North, and*

*so embarked on the dangerous journey of*

*escape related here.*

April 14th 1863—The intense heat of today and the exciting scenes with which the town is filled—have left me exhausted—too much for sleep, but with no one to share my thoughts save my pen & paper—It is still outside—the moon has risen as calmly as though this earth were only smiling back her soft light. What far different sights we have just left—Agony in every conceivable form, & even worse than positive pain, the dull apathy of hopeless sickness, when all suffering is forever past, & all hope— Crowded together in the new hotel were about 800—needing everything—with the same clothes on in which they fought more than a week ago—haggard—filthy beyond description, utterly repulsive except as suffering humanity must excite our pity, a large proportion of them with vacant expressionless faces—with wounds whose only dressing since the battle has been the blessed rains from heaven—their hollow cheeks, & glaring eyes mutely asking relief—The good face of Dr. Eve was seen here & there, he trying to bring some order out of utter confusion—From the room devoted to surgical operations came shrieks & groans, some faint as from the lips of the dying, others with the strength of intense suffering—up three flights of stairs through crowds of miserable objects—lying along the sides of the halls, we went to the fever ward—which was filled to overflowing. As none of the building had been plastered, we could see through the different rooms—and, who can ever forget it. The ladies were asked to distribute some nourishment—and how the poor wasted hands stretched out for it as we passed along—some were too weak even for that & must be fed like children, here was a mere boy, grasping a piece of bread—in the next cot, a gray-haired withered old man—with nothing but rags for clothing—his glassy eyes told too plainly that death had marked him—Not far along was a man of middle age—large frame with hands which bore the marks of hard labor, he had battled with the world in times of peace & had conquered—war had taken him from home, & now wasting sickness had destroyed the strong man— His dying words my friend could not understand. Knowing how often I had listened for the last whisper she called me, telling him I could hear them. He roused all the strength left & whispered, "I want my body sent to my wife. I promised her—tell her I am willing to go—my pay is due for six months—she'll need it"—["]will you write for me & tell her this"—his voice stopped in half an hour he was in the dead room—I learned the address of his wife from another member of his company—& my promise has tonight been kept—We passed the "bunk" of one tall black eyed young man without speaking to him— He lay perfectly quiet—but the surgeon said there is one of the sickest men—& we turned back—He was a lieutenant in a Louisiana cavalry company—wasted to a skeleton but retained the marks of a true gentleman in his wan face & his manner—I had a rose in my hand & involuntarily laid it on his pillow—he smiled—& turned towards it. The nurse said he had been talking that morning early about the sweet shrubs in his mother's yard & wondering if they had come. I happened to have some in my pocket—handed them to him. He could only say—"thank you, I love them." I told him he should have fresh ones everyday. When we passed his place this evening it was vacant—he lived only six hours after we saw him—but kept hold of the flowers the nurse said even in death—They found quite an amount of gold about his person—he told us—As the surgeon walked on with us—a light-haired sunburnt boy of about 17—raised up, & said, "Dr. don't you know me, I'm so glad to see you"—In vain he tried to think who the boy was—at last when told—he could hardly be made to believe it—that the son of his old friend was there. As we went on—he said, wiping tears from his eyes—"I have known that boy from a baby—His father is a wealthy planter, & he an only child—what would his poor mother say to see him now"—"I thank God no responsibility of this war rests on my shoulders."

Just as we passed into one room—there lay one with the sheet over his face—waiting to be carried out—His companions around were talking as though no one of their number had just left—or any of them might soon follow. In one corner was one giving orders for battle—his eyes glaring wildly about—now & then he would level an imaginary gun—& exclaim—"there's one more —— Yankee gone." He had been three days & nights thus raving—No one knew him—& he had nothing by which he could be identified about his person. In the hurried retreat companies had become divided, many had "straggled"—The poor fellow screamed to Mrs. Long—"there mother, I knew you would come & see me"—then—the most violent exertions to come to her, but his feet were tied—Some poor mother may be grieving now for him, longing for some tidings of her dear boy—and he ere long will fill a grave over which will be placed on a plain board—"Unknown"—A pretty little curly headed drummer boy looked so wishfully at us—I asked the doctor about him—He can't speak a word of English—was his reply—He is a French boy from New Orleans—I said only "Avez-vous une mere" when he sprang up and commenced an autobiography at once—His mother was in France, had sent him to an uncle in N. Orleans for a business education—He had run away—was 15 yrs. old but very delicate—"Oh, mlle" ["]ma pavore mêre" he would often repeat. I told him I would send him a pretty French story to read—&

he would soon get better—His tears dried away soon—& he seemed quite happy as I say—"bon jour je reviens une autre fois"—

*Night July 28tb 1863 Waverley, Lowndes Co. Miss.*

After long dreary months of watching and waiting, trying in vain to get a "pass through the lines" of military rule, listening to the stories of others who have failed in the attempt—an unexpected opportunity has presented itself. Though it seems almost "hope against hope" tomorrow morning I start—leaving a desolate country, breaking associations which have been the result of year's companionship—some of joy— others of the bitterest grief—bidding perhaps a last farewell to the dear spot where I have so often found fresh flowers strewn by unknown hands—I have left it to their kind remembrance—will it be forgotten amid the confusion of constantly recurring death scenes in this terrible war—That has been my only quiet retreat—God only knows the prayers which have gone up from my heart there—He alone tonight sees the secrets which have me thus long to stay here—with no sympathy in the cause of the war—secession—believing the principle—or rather its total lack of it wrong—personal rather than any political reasons—have been the "moving why." Nearly three years have passed away since I saw the land of my birth, and my friends there—none but those whose treasures of friendship are divided, can realize how a woman's heart and judgment are divided with them—I know nothing of the true state of things North—with no father's house, to which I could turn without a thought of doubt, no mother whose arms would be open to recieve me, no sister to give me the kiss of welcome, with only one dear brother far up in the Northwest—I have for years felt homeless everywhere—sometimes almost from my soul, uttering poor Hood's "anywhere, anywhere out of the world"—which has seemed so cold and lonely—Now, Providence seems plainly saying "This is the way, walk ye in it"—Whither it will lead He only knows who holds all issues in His Omnipotent hand—There are no sounds out in the silver

moonlight save the whippoorwill's plaintive cry—As I think of the possibilities which tomorrow may bring with it—I well nigh falter—but—
in this still hour—there comes a consciousness of spiritual presence—
those gone to the other land—seem to be around me—I can almost
hear their gentle whisper, see their radiant faces coming as they have
in so many dark hours, with messages of comfort—and support—
bringing what I so much need—that which will strengthen my weak
faith—assurance of His love whose servants they are—teaching me
ever to recieve

> "All as God wills, who wisely heeds
> To give or to withold
> And knoweth more of all my needs
> Than all my prayers have told"

*Monday morning July 29th 1863*

The message yesterday evening was "have the lady & her baggage at
the meeting house by the cross-roads at 5 tomorrow morning" Long
before that the household of my friends Gen. & Mrs. Gerdine[?] was all
astir—A hasty breakfast was gone through with, the kissing over with
"the white folks," good-bye's to the numerous darker ones who were
crowded around us, as they always do when an event is expected—The
family carriage took "mistress," the two little one & myself, "master" on
horseback, with the baggage going ahead—A few minutes driving
brought us to the trysting place in the "piney woods." The thermometer stood at 85° when we left home. This did not promise to be a cool
undertaking in any sense of the word—Punctuality in this latitude
forms no part of the list of positive virtues—We women had time to say
our "last words"—albeit some tell us such things are only myths—the
reality never being manifest—Many a message to father, and sisters at
home, from the Northern wife whose love was divided from the
Southern husband—"tell the Yankees they haven't whipped us yet, if
they have got Vicksburg and Fort Hudson—and Gettysburg too." Since
his son had come from Vicksburg a paroled prisoner two days before,

barefoot, hungry—and having walked 150 miles, from want of both money and any mode of conveyance, and given glowing accounts of Yankee resources, I thought his courage had recovered a little, as to the end—but, in words at least he was unfaltering—From this beginning of final messages some hostile words might have soon grown, had not we heard the tromping of horses feet up the road, then the lumbering of a wagon—soon there emerged from the underbrush, a stout red-faced jolly specimen of humanity—on a refractory mule—His "good mornin to yes" had brogue from "Sweet Erin"—which we seldom heard—Next behind him rode up a meek jaded, guant [gaunt] individual, who nodded silently, and halted, then 4 independent, care-for-nobody-looking mules trotted up—Then my carriage—drawn by 4 mules. Seated on the back of one was my driver, a "yellow boy," Jack—In the rear came Mr. Stone, my protector, who had come up with his cattle, and now was returning for his family—trying to place them all beyond the reach of Yankees—My trunks were soon deposited in the back of the capacious wagon, my "split bottom" chair next went in, "positively the last" words were said, and then came an operation which at first threatened to prove a "nolle prosequi" to farther operations—getting in the passenger. This must be accomplished by mounting the forward wheel, thence by one long step farther—the top was reached. After sundry failures showing too plainly that I was unused to lofty flights, Dan's brawny Irish arm came to my assistance, he comforting me by saying, "N'ver mind ye'll soon get used to it, shure, an not care a bit for it, like the Irishmen bein hung"—I was landed safely and at half past 6 we started—A survey of my domain showed me as a background my trunks—next the chair & occupant, by my side the box of provisions for the week, thanks to my friends at Waverley I had everything necessary—Next in front of me, were "sundries"—blankets, cooking utensils, ropes, axes, and a gun—strongly suggestive in these war times—An extra saddle did me good service as a footstool —Over half the wagon was stretched a cloth cover—A half hour's ride explained fully the meaning of Mr. Stone's first questions after I had asked him to take me back with him—"did you ever ride in a wagon without springs, could you stand it for six days over poor roads, do you think?" I thought my experiences of the ups and downs in Dixie life in the last two years, had prepared my mind for anything but—being now and then summarily deposited among the "sundries" had not entered into my plans— Picking oneself up under the most favorable circumstances is not a pleasant recreation, when there is every prospect of frequent repetition it becomes less so—After the first few miles—we got into "perares" mind—and here I was not so often called upon to "change my base of operations" as the war phrase goes—There was nothing to be done but drag along through the black road—nothing to be seen to change the current of one's thoughts—A cloudless sky made the world look brighter—in the beginning of what to most would have seemed "a leap in the dark"—It was really "flying from ills we have, to those we know not of."—The refusal of Gen. Ruggles to give me a pass had given him "a place in my memory," and I fervently wished that he might be jolted enough in his future career, to make him repent his obduracy and see that nothing was gained by him, a Yankee born in Massachusetts, by such extra efforts to prove his extreme loyalty to the Southern cause. So many obstacles apparently insurmountable had been overcome, that I had become convinced of the truth of Napoleon's life maxim "To a firm faith and determined will there are no impossibilities["] Providence had pointed out to me this means of reaching Federal lines—A convex mirror seemed before my mind's eye—enlarging all the blessings in my present surroundings—Gradually my novel equipage and outriders began to call forth incipient emotions of pride—when we reached West Point, 10 miles journey at noon I was for the first time conscious of being the ["]observed of all observers," not very pleasantly so to be sure—Here it was necessary to get a pass to Panola. Mr. Stone asking for mine as a friend going to visit his wife, a slight fiction, as a week before I had never heard of him or his wife— [(]though my friends had). On giving my name a gentleman standing by said, "It is a pity Miss S. is going way down there on such a hard journey for she'll not get through to the North she may be sure," Mr. S. coolly replying "I only ask a pass to Panola" stopped further remarks.

Of this unknown sympathizer I at the time knew nothing, but I had become used to the saying "We don't blame you for wanting to go, but you'll never get through the lines" &tc—It only strengthened my woman's resolution. Under cover of my long gray calico sunbonnet I had been "plaiting" palmetto—an accomplishment taught me the day I decided to come this way—this was the fancy work of Southern ladies—now, and I flattered myself it was the finishing touch to my thorough disguise as a country woman—Mr. S. having cautioned me to let him do the talking everywhere—West Point was swarming with soldiers—in all sorts of uniforms & all stages of happiness, all "calvary's" as the negroes say—some dismounting without orders or intention to do so, some charging the zig-zag fences, one officer evidently "conquered not by superior numbers" but very inferior whisky—was being supported by two privates who were trying to get him on his horse— they were all hurrahing & whooping—calling on the —— Yankees to come up—They were under orders to reinforce Gen. Chalmers—who had started in pursuit of a "large body of Yankees" who were "coming down"—Slow travelers these same Yankees must be—for a year they have been coming and we have never seen them yet—It was a relief to plod through the mud—& get outside the town limits, for it seemed to me like a glimpse of Pandemonium—We dragged along through a poor country, inhabited by the same class of people—with no men under the conscript age—45 yrs. at home—except here and there one wounded or otherwise disabled—It was not the region for the "last ditch" men—I had seen their homes, and been in the family of a lieutenant for a year who had an unlimited furlough, and had been a "volunteer aid" to Gen. Price—with his body-servant he had "defended his hearth-stone" sitting by it, when not hunting or fishing—after raising a company of poor men to fight for their native land three rich brothers in law—acting the same parts—I had seen the rich side of this war only—except in the hospitals—The other side of the picture began to show itself—even in this one day's journey—Late in the evening we stopped for corn, at the first comfortable looking house I had seen outside of the few at West Point. I was urged to get out during the operation of loading but, recalling my experience in the morning's climb, preferred remaining—so round to the corn crib we drove—& the business of depositing a day's supply of food for our mules was going on in front of my seat—when to my surprise the head of an old acquaintance appeared—He was owner of the place, & with his wife, came to insist upon my coming to the house—but I told them that would be going back which I did not like to do ever—so they spent the half hour with me—Though a young man, he had the good fortune to half an inch difference in the length of his legs, & was exempt. As he understood my destination—there was no danger in declaring himself "strong Union from the start, never for secession &tc—now for reconstruction"—the grounds of which we had not settled when "all ready master" was the signal for us to be off—a few delicious watermelons being added to our commissary department—Before night we met a long train of people "running from the Yankees"—They were preceded by the wagons, containing the bedding, clothing, & provisions—interspersed promiscuously therein were the children too small to walk—their woolly heads peeping out from under the cover—some of them with pale faces and blue eyes—the most pitiable of all sights in a land of slavery—The oldest men and women being left to take care of themselves at home as we were told "it would not pay to take them away" Behind the wagons came a motley assemblage of all shades of color, their faces expressing little but stolid indifference to their fate—"Master & Mistes["] with their family and the overseer—followed at some distance to prevent "straggling"—A few dogs were with them in case of emergency—It recalled a terrible fright I once had when walking alone in the woods, & hearing a pack of their coming in full chase—their yelling was unlike any other bark I ever heard—I was told on reaching home, that my fears were groundless, as they never attacked white people—These were some "common white folks" not the poor class—yet not the F.F's—The panic had seized them—"Yankees is comin"—and they were going—"Isn't you feerd to go where dey is Mistis,["] one of the old women asked me—all our white folks is—Of course they professed to be so too—One of the men asked me if "dey reely is got horns on em?["] When I told him I was one—his eyes rolled about in blank amazement. After a minute he replied coolly—"I doesn't bleeve dat Mistis, you's jes like our white folks."—He had so long heard the horned head of all evil and the Yankees called by the same epithet, that he believed them identical in species. "You can tell a Yankee as far you can see them" were familiar words—everywhere—he perhaps thought horns were the distinctive mark. failing to discover these—he believed me "playing possum"—their most emphatic way of expressing deceiet—for no other animal is so skilled in its use—When I asked them where they were going, some said, "De Lord knows, we don't,["] & "we's gis runnin away from de Yankees somewhar."—Master done started for Souf Caliny,—or Georgy—They were going from home to avoid the "Manifest Destiny" of the system of slavery—believing that the proclamation of Mr. Lincoln was only a dead letter, hoping yet to sit under their own vine and fig tree as of yore—& "making cotton" again in Miss. Not a very long time hence, the question must be decided if the occasional hints we get of "want of provisions," &tc. in our army mean anything—As twilight came on, we stopped to get a resting-place for the night—once we were answered by a grim hard-faced woman, "we hain't no man here, he's gone to the war, and scacely anything ourselves to eat, let alone feedin rank strangers"—another miserable old man, sitting by his cabin door said, "that ain't nobody but me an the women folks to make a crop, conscrips took 'em all away—an God knows were bad off enough—A barefooted boy about 16 hobbled out on a rude crutch—one leg was gone apparently not long ago—for he was unused to the loss of it. We went on seeing the same thriftless class of "poor white folks" who in ordinary times barely make a living by labor on the sandy soil—in war time even that was hardly possible—At length after the moon had for two hours been giv-ing us the light of her countenance we came to a double log-cabin in the "piney woods" where they "took in strangers"—and, we soon found it literally true. I emerged from my retreat, found as is generally the case, it is much easier to get down than up into high positions in life. We crossed the rail fence of our host's front yard, recieved the usual

salute of yelping curs, and were met by the lord of the manor, with a
"howdye" ["]set down"—The space between the two rooms was filled
nearly by soldiers waiting for supper—purporting to be paroled men
from Fort Hudson, probably deserters from Johnson's Army—They
soon left much to my relief—I was escorted into "the room"—a dim
torch light was flickering in the fire-place. There was one servant about,
who came in with "light wood" now & then, she told me "mistis
couldn't come in now, she's gittin you all's supper in de kitchen"—In
due season, that was accomplished, and the lady appeared—bringing
with here a much needed light—only more pines, for even tallow can-
dles were a tabooed luxury. She loomed up in the glare of light—a genuine Meg Merrills—only lacking the determination of her face—She
reminded of hearing a poor woman once say she "had allers had to rub
up against the world" and this one looked as though all had got
rubbed out but her bones, and few clothes were left to cover them—
Her invitation to "take a bite" I could not muster courage to accept.
Telling her I had provisions, with me, but was very tired & wanted
sleep—made no visible impression on her—With arms akimbo, she
stood asking me all manner of questions as deliberately as though I
were in a prisoner's box. Ain't you jes meeried to this yer man—you
must be to be gwine down there—ain't ye feerd o' the Yankees, till I was
out of patience & told her I was too tired to talk. "Well, I spose likely
you be, I reckon I better fix yet bed"—Leaving me alone for a minute,
I took a survey of things in general—which showed me three beds one
unoccupied, the second contained a woman and child sick with "the
ager"—the third contained a half-grown boy—On the reappearance of
madam the door was shut, which was done by drawing a calico curtain
across the door-way—this had in it not a few holes of divers sizes—not
strange when we think calico now is selling from $2,50 to $4,19 pr.
yard—and money just as hard for the poor to get as it ever was. Next,
the strong sinewy arm was brought to bear upon the lubberly boy—&
the shrill voice sounded out "Jim I say, you git up, an give the lady your
bed,"—but he was snoring too loudly to respond—& not until after a
vigorous application of her bony hand, in a manner with which mater-

nal authority everywhere is wont to enforce itself—in the early years of life, did said Jim realize the situation—An unconditional surrender was the result—he retreated in quick time if not good order into the other room.—Soon, I was informed that the bed was ready—The light was gone—or "tired Nature's sweet restorer," would never have been sought there, for scarcely had my aching head touched the scantily filled pillows when an ominous odor greeted me—with which all travelers are so wofully familiar—A reconnaissance by moonlight was soon made— numberless little mahogany colored spots were changing places in all directions—"Overcome by the force of vastly superior numbers" as our army has so often been in reports, "with which we felt it would be useless to contend the field was abandoned"—A chair leaned against the logs was my substitute, in a few minutes I was wandering to a land where the poets tell us soft music fills the air, and every breeze is freighted with sweet odors. How long this dreaming lasted, I could not tell, but, O, what a wakening was there—strange sounds came up from the corner bed I last saw vacant—at first I thought some one was in terrible agony—and sprang up to relieve it—but—there lay placid as the moonbeams playing over their faces—the host & hostess with open mouths seeming to be vying with each other in "making night hideous"—both by sight and sound—Here ended my sleep—for that was unbroken music till morning. Its first dawning was joyfully welcomed, & improved in getting ready for an exit—The reason given by madam for the status of things was—"we hain't got no water under quarter o'a mile from here,"—Gladly did I emerge from that first night's experience of the indoor life of "poor white folks" in Chickasaw, realizing that they did in very fact—"take in strangers"—

*July, 30th.*

Dan, the Irishman, had our breakfast ready before sunrise—with a log serving for both seat and table, a cup of coffee, some bread and ham were soon disposed of—The mules were quietly eating near us— Our entire cuisine arrangements consisted of a frying pan, & an old tin coffee pot—even genuine Yankee ingenuity could hardly have made the pan serve more purposes in half an hour—The invaluable box was replaced by my side in the wagon, other things all went in front, by 5 the mounting this time had been accomplished much more easily— and we were off—hoping to make 35 miles before bedtime. Jack was unable to rouse any latent ambition in our mules—by his persuasive "git, git" and flourishing the long whip he held over them—Their susceptibility to this argument seems blunted by its frequent use—out of a walk they would not go. Not a little fun was made for us all by Dan— who losing patience with his animal would belabor him in Irish style, notwithstanding Jack's cautious, "masa Dan mules is mules—dey won't go no faster den dey want to, an you can't make em no how"— Twice his efforts resulted in a downfall—and some very emphatic remarks on the nature of mules in general—Poor Dan, the certainty of failure seems never to have taught his race caution—He kept trying— and failing—to conquer the unconquerable—but, before night—Jack's remark that "niggers knows best how to manage 'em,—Jes let em alone"—seemed to carry conviction with it—either that or the falls he had got—for he rode resignedly on as any of us—In a southern summer's day there is a feeling of misusing them even though it is only dragging along—Unflattering though the comparison be, I thought there was a striking similarity between our progress and that of the Yankees in their late victories—slow but sure—I could not read without pain to my eyes—so kept my palmetto turning into braid—A flock of wild turkeys appeared once, and were out of sight in quick time— More trains of people running or being run from Yankees met us—all telling the same story—"they leave nothing alive on the place, steal jewelry—and money"—and worst of all "run off the niggers"—their crops except wheat were yet in the field—they going to States which had had already passed laws forbidding any more slaves to be brought there—"as there is already great scarcity of food." They were reaping the harvest which the originators of secession sowed broad-cast—one which those opposed to it foresaw but could hardly realize its extent— and who can tell where it will end—One hope after another has failed the Confederacy—"foreign intervention," the ignis fatuus which somebody has kept dancing before the eyes of politicians has lost its power in recruiting the wasted armies—Vicksburg was declared impregnable but is gone—It has thrown a pall over everything in the tone of even their boasting now—there is an echo of despair—In these long journeys without even the ordinary comforts of life—many must die—This whole country is groaning under the burdens slavery has brought on it—which can never be taken away until the words of the song which now seem such a mockery here—shall be literally true—["]The star-spangled shall wave o'er the land of the free"—black as well as white—

At our dinner today on a log in the woods, I found my love for the old Union no stronger than had my friend Mr. Stone—but, he frankly said, I could not say as much to a Southerner safely—or to anyone at home—I can not find words to express my hatred of secession from the beginning—

This was a "long, long weary day"—but I did not "pass it in tears away" for I kept plaiting and thinking—tonight we'll pitch our wagon A days march nearer—["]Yankee land"—home I could not say—as does the hymn—The poor woman where we stopped for water at noon—expressed what in these two days had become a conviction with me. "This is the rich folk'es war"—She went on—["]I've got only one child, & I want him to come home and take care o'me—and stop fightin for them—he's got wounded once now—an we've got no niggers to work for us"—This was the other side of a story I had heard one way only—and it was pitiful enough—There was the cold reality of this "war for independence"—at every poor man's home we saw—and there were no others on our route thus far. Just at dark we rode up to a two-story "frame house["] painted white—belonging Mr. Stone told me to "Squire Clayton["]—of Calhoun Co. The look of comfort about everything was refreshing—Dan rode up and echoed my thoughts—"Shure, ye'll not be fightin here as ye did the last night—I'm thinkin Miss, ye'll be the better of a night's rest"—Mr. S.—quietly remarked as we went up the walk—"they're sharp here—let me do the talking—we'll tell the same story—they know me well"—I was introduced as "a friend on a visit"—to four young ladies—Squire C. and wife, and a wounded son a Colonel—just from Vicksburg—As the war question is the only subject of conversation—soon all were engaged—fortunately supper was announced—I was too tired to eat, and very soon excused myself—and retired—not to rest at once, for in came the young ladies one by one, questioning me with a persistency which would have done honor to the far famed inquisitiveness of a Vermonter—Their astonishment at my daring to go to "the bottom" where Yankees were, was boundless, and their expressions of bitterness were choice English to say the least—They asked if I had any brothers in the army, telling me about one killed, and the wounded one, who wasn't going in again for "pa's got him a substitute for the war"—Then they showed me cloths they had spun and woven for themselves—saying "I'll wear homespun as long as I live before I'd depend on Yankees for it—wouldn't you"? Of course, I said I would—Finding that there was plenty of water here, I asked to have a bath, and excused my sleepiness by telling them my last night's encounter—so in process of time, I was left alone—to enjoy two of the greatest luxuries to a traveler—cold water—and sleep— "Now I lay me" was soon said—and the "action suited to the word"—

*July. 31st.* My next conscious minute was when Mr. S. rapped on my door in the morning saying "we're waiting breakfast for you, and want to get an early start"—My gray calico dress & bonnet were soon donned, and before our host & hostesses of the night were up we had breakfasted in camp, & were off—The sun rose with promise of the hottest day we had felt, and we were not disappointed—The way was over a more hilly country—harder traveling—but nothing of interest— in the scenery—Mr. S. and the two others went ahead Jack and I were alone for half the day—He giving me a graphic account of "bein took by de Yankees twice down by de riber, an runnin back to Master"—but I'll tell you jes what I thinks mistis—said he—["]dey'll whip us all clean out fore we done—though white folks says dey dont think so—I seen 'em, I been dar, I know dey can—an dey's never g'wine to giv it up till they do"—About 4 p.m. we came to Coffee-ville where last winter a large depot on the Miss. Central Road, and some other buildings

were burned by a retreating force of Yankees. The field where a skirmish took place was pointed out to us. soon we saw large black patches
on the ground, with fleeces of cotton lying around—it was burned "to
prevent its falling into the hands of our enemy"—Here was the first I
had seen of the savages of war, except on humanity. It seemed like
going back to the past which we read of—in other lands, but no part
of our own—"Military necessity" is the plea for much which seems
utterly useless waste of men and property—The tall black chimneys
stood like so many spectres—hovering about the still village which had
no appearance of life in the streets—I was thankful when "Night let
down her curtain" for the heat had been intensely oppressive, and the
last few hour's scenery no less so to the mind—It was eleven before we
got a resting-place—Everybody was suspicious of strangers—and made
some excuse us shelter. At last, through Dan's diplomacy alas—Irish
fibbing—there was "rest for the weary" found under the roof of an old
lady—she having been told that "a sick lady was behind, and could go
no farther—niver a mile without rest." Ignorant of his fabrication, I
wondered at the woman's hurry in preparing my room, asking me if I
felt better &tc—she, poor soul, trying to imagine it possible for me to
be sick—At last—she said—"la me, that man was just foolin me, to get
in"—and I laughed as heartily as she when she told me the story—The
men and beasts were camped near the house always—We sat down in
the bright moon light and with a trembling voice and tears streaming
down her cheeks this mother told me how two sons had been killed—
the last one was a cripple living with her, and "the old man"—with his
wife and two children—"he's worse than crippled too she said, for he's
learned to drink in the army"—Poor before the war—now helpless and
hopeless they were—In other countries there are avenues open to the
same class of people—here—what can they do—This side of the question has been carefully kept concealed by all who have magniloquently
written and spoken of what "The Sunny South will be when we gain
our Independence"—If that day ever came, of what avail can it be to
the poor? They have unresistingly submitted to being ridden over by
the power of money—so long as there is slavery, they will be only a

grade higher in the social scale than those who are bought and sold legitimately. Southern rulers never have come from this class and never will—until "great change comes oe'r the spirit of their dreams"—My own that night were unbroken after a ride of 16 hours—only resting an hour for dinner—Next morning we were [sentence unfinished]

August 1st. I woke with a new feeling of vigor, for in time, we were half through our "tedious and tasteless" journey—more than half in distance—even with the gait of mules we had gone 100 miles.—Before sunrise we had bid the old folks good bye—breakfasted in the woods, and started on—found a shady road, quite in contrast with the red clay—most of yesterday without trees.—At noon we came to the Yokney [Yocona] river at Greenwood where last winter a fine bridge was burned. We crossed on a flatboat—and dined in a beautiful grove of cottonwood and gum trees. in sight of the ruins—somewhat in contrast with the Greenwood of so many sacred memories—but a pretty spot for even an artist's eye— While we were sitting here, a gentleman rode up—whom Mr. Stone knew—he told us that the Yankees were coming now "sure enough"—A body of them nobody knew how many, had landed three days before, from a gunboat. on the Miss. and were "just taking every-thing before them"—Mr. S. thought it a "fresh scare," but concluded to go ahead as scout—as in case we met them, our mules and provisions would all be taken—if nothing more was done—He left me—only telling me I could do more for him, than he for me—perhaps, if the worst came—Dan—was quite unconcerned. He told me he had in one pocket "a small bit o' paper which would serve him a good turn" if he met them which I understood was the oath of allegiance"—He had been into the country from Memphis selling cotton cards at $30 a pair—and was there a strong secessionist—talking loudly of the fights he was in &tc—but never telling on which side—Having about my person the little all of my own money, and about $700 going to Canada for a friend, I had a strange feeling of dread when I thought of meeting Yankees—as all Union soldiers go by that name, whether they can speak a word of English or not. To a woman alone in a strange country, in wartime, with a negro, an Irishman, and a poor scared individual whose only thought was to keep in the rear and so be protected—the prospect was rather dubious—but, there was no alternative being unable to whistle to keep my courage up as boys do, I had only to—sit still—That after all, is the hardest thing to do in an exciting emergency, and often would be the very best. Towards evening, we met several excited parties but could learn nothing definite—Sometimes there was a big army landed from a boat, then again a squad of "Calvaries"—"making a raid an leavin nothing alive"— ["]except the white folks"—so on we went, half doubting—half believing there must be some foundation—some fire to create all this smoke—We stopped six miles from Panola, at a log cabin which recalled forcibly my first night's exploit—in Chickasaw Co. but Mr. S. thought it more prudent to avoid stopping in towns—A bare-footed yellow-haired man appeared on the porch in answer to our "hallos" and asked us to "fight"—so we lit on the ground, and told him we must stay there some way—He said "Yre lady-'ll find us mighty poor sir"— ["]my ole women'll be out soon though an will try to take care on ye"—Our provision box had held out, so in that line we were independent—"Miss Carson" was soon presented conveying along with her a pair of small twins—resembling strongly their pater—Gradually several more children appeared, of different sizes—but all of the light-long-haired weak eyed type—with as little clothing as could be passed for decent— from oldest to youngest of the family—the father was "six months home on sick furlough" I proposed walking a while before trying to sleep, for a fancy came over me—that "coming events cast their shadows before"—as I glanced round my room—and thought exercise in walking might help to quiet my senses—but the hope was vain—So far as humanity went, I was alone, but—O, the travelers over those logs, over the bed, curtains— myself—were innumerable—Moon light reveries are pretty to talk about, and very enjoyable—sometimes—but under existing circumstances, quite another thing—The only relief—was in the pure bright night—for in a southern rain—what would it have been. I thought of the Spaniard who said he always put on glasses when he ate cherries, to make them look larger, and tried hard to see the best side. Being up all night—I was ready for the day's work before any of our party—

• • •

*August, 2nd.* I had laid my watch on the table, and "mine hostess"
appeared with the dawn, that was something of which she could not
understand the use—having never seen a timepiece—"we allers; goes
by de sun—she told me—an when it rains—we knows any how nigh
enuf for poor folks."—She had breakfast ready in time—and in her
own room—two of the children were asleep—things generally thoroughly disgusting She begged for my faded calico dress, till I started to
walk in advance of the wagon—Her "du eat if yer kin eat our vittels"—
had induced me to make sundry fruitless attempts so to do—and I
tried the Beecher philosophy of fresh air and exercise—to carry off my
uncomfortable feelings—He says many a blue total depravity sermon
has been given to the world because the writer needed to plough it
out—into the ground. When our wagon came up, I had gone a mile to
the top of a steep hill, a strange sight in this sandy country. The vision
of that poor forlorn woman, and the hungry twins—her numberless
questions, and the wretched apology for breakfast for which we had
paid so roundly had faded away in the fresh morning air—when Dan
recalled it in genuine Irish, "An shure miss, since the Lord made me,
did iver I set foot in a place the likes o'that intirely—and may He and
the blissid Vargin forgive me if iver I do agin, and indade I'll niver have
to ask it"—We had but a short ride to Panola, Gen. Chalmer's headquarters—Here our pass must be renewed. Fresh reports of "Yankees
coming" were rife everywhere—the streets of the town were full of soldiers under orders to march none seemed to know where—Mr. Stone
sent the wagon on directly through with my outriders he going to the
Provost Marshal's office to get a new pass—which was soon accomplished—and we hurried down to the Tallahatchie just in time to cross
on the flat-boat before the movement of troops began—Had we been
an hour later we would have probably waited at least three days for
them—In the thick cotton-woods through which our route lay—we
met several small companies of men going to join Gen. C. At any other
time the sudden appearance of a dozen horsemen riding at full speed
through a dense forest would have been startling—but, their non-

descript uniforms told us at once they were not the much dreaded "Yankees" and so, we had less to fear—Our poor rear-guard—Mr Sykes could not conceal his fear—he rode slowly along with a general air of shakiness, his long lank figure adding to the effect of the dolorous expression his face wore—Once when he was far behind, we were passing a country grave-yard in a clearing—Dan suggested to Mr S. "wouldn't ye the bether off to stop and take up a dead man & let him change places with yer Misther who's trimbling so bad"—When we were fairly "out of the woods["] his drooping courage seemed to revive—by noon we reached a large clearing where was a cornfield the best we had seen—poor cotton had all along been scattered by the road—though that crop was interdicted by the Confederate government—"except to supply actual necessities at home" It had been said that large planters had found it necessary to raise great quantities—in locations out of sight—providing for future emergencies—We got here some cream sent to "the lady" by the mistress of the house near—Few nerves in Dixie land have trembled from the effect of pure coffee, but we enjoyed our Mocha unadulterated with rye—sweet potatoes, or burnt molasses the fashionable substitutes—now in vogue—Ours had been smuggled through from Memphis—in return for cotton—We dined hastily—not quite at ease about the "undiscovered future"—We found better land and more cotton as we rode on—Corn was nearly ready for harvesting—It seemed incredible that in a land where "devotion to the good of our country" is the watchword, in every rich man's mouth, that the land should be made to bring forth what most materially strengthened the "sinews of war" of the enemy—but, here were the proofs—growing—When night came on, we were in dense woods again—almost pathless—Dan & Mr. S. went ahead prospecting—leaving the silent man, Jack and myself to plod slowly on—The bright moonlight came down through the tall trees, and the birds were all singing their goodnight song to their mates—all manner of flying things were in the air it seemed to me, as we brushed against the low boughs of undergrowth—At about eleven we came to a clearing—the first we had seen for miles, but—"our corn is all done eat up"—was the reply to our asking for shelter at the house—here was no entertainment for man or beast—a few miles farther on we stopped at some negro cabins—there was no white person on the place. Master was a bachelor an gone to the wars—It was almost midnight when after a survey of the houses, I concluded to stay in the wagon—with my chair leaned against the largest trunk, my bag for a pillow. Mr. S. at the other end of the wagon, Dan on a blanket underneath, to get shelter from the heavy dew—the silent man & Jack on the ground near us with our mules—there was soon silence in the camp—This last night of wagon journeying went swiftly by—I was so much exhausted that any place to lay my head would have seemed a down pillow almost—

*August 3d.* The next thought I had was when Dan put his head under the wagon cover, telling me breakfast was ready—It was of the best the place afforded chickens—fresh eggs & corn cakes—The women came to see me, overjoyed as they said "dat de Lord let em see a white lady's face once more." They had been here two years, most of the time alone—clearing young master's place, One of them a light mulatto, had an air of refinement which showed better "raising"—She had been lady's maid in one of the numberless Southern "first families"—In the division of property at "ole master's" death, she fell to this son, and as she expressed it "though I never worked hard a day in my life before, he fetch me to this wilderness, an I ben in the field ever since," ["]my children's all lef behind, they fell to Master's sister in Alabamy, an I never heard from them since—If they was here, I could work, but now I haint no heart left to do anything—seems like" —I spoke to her of that land where no partings come, with tears she answered—"Yes, mistress, thank the Lord we'll have one home, and one Master there forever." Except the cargo of slaves brought over in the Wanderer nothing I had ever seen of slavery touched me more. Those men were said to have belonged to the higher classes in Africa—these had been accustomed to a life totally different—I gave them my remnant of sugar and cake—the first they had seen in two years they said—I was thankful when the time came to leave, for my sympathies were painfully roused—and I knew how useless it was to feel so—We had 25 miles yet to go—so, we pressed on, Mr. Stone going ahead as scout. Stopping at a cabin for water, we heard loud sobbing and the voice of a young girl in expressions of agony—The old negro woman told us "Miss, Mary's sweetheart was killed more nor four weeks ago at Vicksburg an she just heard of it now"—Sorrow everywhere, not one place had we stopped, where war's marks could not be seen—For every poor man who helps to make up "that human machine called a regiment" there may be sad ones at home who watch and wait his coming—too often watching in vain. "The brave General," or "the gallant Colonel" gains all the honors of victory when it comes, if defeated, the poor drink the bitterest dregs in the cup of suffering. War never seemed half so cruel or useless before—The prices of all the ordinary necessaries of life place them beyond the reach of the families of poor soldiers—and the rich care little for their wants. With domestics at from $2.50 to $4.00 per yd., flour from 50, to 75 $ per barrel. know little of comfort, paid as the men are only common soldiers wages. bare existence is all they seem to expect till the war is over. The groans of the taxed rich are loud and deep. The military holding complete sway know no rule but "might makes right—" About ten this morning we reached the Coldwater—the last point w[h]ere Confederate pickets are posted—There was an unusual number on the scare of "Yankees coming." When Mr. S. presented his pass, they di[s]puted its genuineness—looking back to the wagon very suspiciously—I saw there was trouble, and had vividly recalled an account of a Yankee lady arrested only a few days before I started, and "imprisoned on suspicion of being a spy" ["]In the lower part of the state." We waited quietly till Mr. S. by coolness and determination overcame their scruples—and the flat-boat was brought to our side of the stream. It had been sawed nearly apart—by some "raiders" not long before, and was not the most agreeable means of conveyance being partly under water—but, I went over first, then in small lots—our treasures—mules & all—"Getting through the lines" was at last accomplished. a formidable undertaking it had seemed, because so many things "might have been"—but, they were not for us—Ceasar carried no more exultant heart when the Rubicon was passed than beat in that rough wagon as we came to the cane-brake—for I felt that danger from one side was over—Gen. Ruggles friendly words of advice had often come over me—"Miss S. had better not only stop trying to get a pass, but stop thinking or talking of it, for she couldn't get through our lines now possibly." I had thought of the universal "we told you so' which would greet me on every hand if obliged to go back as so many had been. At the river we gained the first definite information about the Yankee raid—They were yesterday "in the bottom" on the only road through the cane-brake—With our scouts ahead, the dumb man in the rear, we went into the close muddy cart-path, scarcely wide enough for our train, the canes growing high above the wagon top, and as thick as even that rich soil could support—above them immense cotton-wood and gum trees with festoons the most luxuriant vines hanging from their branches. The morning was cloudy, a hotter place is hardly concievable this side of where Dante journeyed in imagination. Musquitoes like misfortunes "come not singly but in battalions["]—always ready for an attack. When we came to impassable mud holes—the only alternative was to turn into the cane, and tread down a new road—then the air was filled with all manner of insects robbed of their home so suddenly—All along the roadside were stray fleeces of cotton—the remains of what had been sent clandestinely to Memphis—generally under cover of the night—It was concealed in the canes to prevent its being burned by the Confederate government officers.—then carried to the Yankee boats in small quantities—Even some army officers—who in the beginning of the war, would "give their last dollar on the altar of their country" had it was said recieved gold from the hands of the detested Yankees—though their touch was thought such defilement—except through that incorruptible medium. These vast thickets have been the hiding-place of runaway negroes ever since the country was settled—since the war deserters from the army have taken their places. Strange turning of Fortune's wheel—the former slaves are now freeing themselves by hundreds—a tyranny not much exceeded by slavery rules those who were once masters—No poor man can escape

conscription except by concealment—When about five miles along—
on this way—we came to the first large clearing—judge Gs plantation—he told us we were in danger any minute of being overtaken by
a party—which rode past his house the day before—coming from the
river on a foraging expedition—He expected a call on their return. The
intense heat, and occasional halts to cut down trees we had run
against—the constant fear of losing our motive powers, and being
compelled to plod out on foot as many a luckless one has done—who
chanced to be met by a "raid"—all combined to make this a "long
drawn out" day of misery—But "despair is never quite despair." "Nil
desperandum" was my motto in starting and now—the journey was
almost over in distance at least—Once, as a bear jumped across the
path, I thought we were doomed—but—Bruin was not after us at all—
Jack and I kept up conversation briskly—we being left in the rear—
with directions to hide in the canes if we heard many horses coming
together—which I had not a doubt he would do—This would leave me
literally to "go it alone"—The poetry which Saxe wrote sounds very
well, when he tells us that in the game of life as in euchre, we may hold
the best cards, "Yet, the game may be lost, with all these for your own,
Unless you've the courage to 'go it alone["]"—I had nothing left but a
Jack, and that was a poor dependence, with which to "follow suit" if
Yankees led—under these circumstances—However I had not even the
privilege of looking like poor renowned Lot's wife—who is now shown
to travelers still looking back—"In status quo"—The canes were too
dense and high to see many yards behind or before us—We and our
mules were walking by faith—through one of the lighter places, a large
buck dashed across our path—not even giving us a look—By three—
the air began to grow heavier, and darker—we could hardly get a
glimpse of the sky through the tall trees—but, knew well that a thunder storm was coming soon—Dan was sleeping heavily in the front of
the wagon, having a high fever after a chill—He had rode back—being
unable to keep on his mule any longer—which added nothing to the
cheerfulness of the hour—The thunder and lightning in half an hour
were incessant, We could see the tree tops twisted about by the fury of

the wind, far above us—and soon down came the rain in torrents—
After much urging Dan changed places with me, for my seat had a
cover—This was our first experience of bad weather—"Some days must
be dark and dreary" we all know—All things considered, I thought it
would be hard to imagine a much darker or drearier time, but, when
one is thoroughly wet, there is a quiet assurance in the fact that we have
seen the worst "the fates can do"—and we settle down determined to
make the best of it—let what will come—one soon learns that "to bear
is to conquer our fate"—At home, even, the grandeur of this form of
nature's works—being always to me more of terror than enjoyment—
for twice I have felt the shock of its striking very near—It was an indescribable relief, when we came to an open space—the storm had not
lessened, but, we seemed to have emerged from a dark prison—and
could see a few rods ahead—We came to a cabin, and being captain
pro-tem, I ordered a halt—as we rode up—found Mr. S. had been anxiously waiting for us, and was mounting his horse to go back, fearing
something had happened—We waded over shoes—to get into the
house—where were a dozen people—the men smoking and drinking
the women "dipping snuff" in which they urged me to join—telling me
I "missed a mighty heap" They asked Mr. S. if "his 'oman never dipped
sure"—and stared incredulously when he told them I never did. We
heard graphic accounts of what "the Yankees done here["]—about sun
up yesterday—the poor "lady of the manor" summing up by saying
"they never lef nary thing with legs on the place ceptin us"—Their
panacea for all the woes of Southern women snuff was left—and I
could not but think what a double energy would be added to the
punches with those althea sticks in their broad mouths—if they only
knew that one of the same Yankee nation was face to face with them—
but,—Mr. Stone did the talking—till we concluded that it was useless
to wait for the rain to be over—It was nearly six, and we had four miles
of black mud to plod through—yet—and what mud—when I remon-
strated with Jack for so unmercifully whipping the jaded mules—his
answer was—"Mistis if I jes lets em stop oncet here, dey'll be standin
here till Gabriel comes down—dey musn't know day kin stop"—

["]dat's de only way to do wid mules"—Mr. S. would ride up occasionally and comfort me by saying he knew every stump now we were almost there—We passed one fine plantation with every building burnt—the effect of a last winter's raid—At dark our six day's journey ended in a cordial welcome at Mr. Stones house—Wet, hungry, worn out—but—with a heart overflowing with gratitude to that Hand which "thus far had led me on["]—feeling as says the old Moravian hymn,

> Through waves, through clouds and storms,
> He gently clears thy way,
> Wait thou His time, so shall the night,
> Soon end in joyous day.—

This night was to me what I imagine the home of a sailor is, when he has just escaped shipwreck. I heard the rain on the roof, swarms of musquitoes outside the bar, I knew there were sharp flashes of lightning, and heavy peals of thunder, but felt protected from them—all sheltered once more—It was late on Sunday morning before I awoke—already the neighbors were gathering in from the country round—to talk over the war news, and detail their exploits with Yankees—I soon saw that there was very little devotion to the Confederacy, perhaps because a Yankee market was too accessible. "The bottom" as it is called, is a tract of very rich land formed entirely from overflows of the Mississippi—It produces immense crops of corn & cotton, chills & musquitoes—is owned almost entirely by planters living elsewhere, and managed by overseers whose only ambition is to "make a big crop"—no matter by what means. Since the Yankee raids—most of the "hands" are gone—have either been carried "Into the hills" for safe keeping, or have taken themselves into a free country—Laugh as they may at the Emancipation Proclamation—it seems to me slavery is doomed—Some of the people spoke of their "protection papers"—got in Memphis by taking the oath—All complained bitterly at the neglect of their own government—Scarcely any horses or mules were to be found they said—either one or the other side had taken them. One gent, a member of the last Confed. Congress came on the back of a worn out mule—which he had borrowed from a neighbor—before the war he was rich—now he had neither house—servant or horse. Yet I shall long remember his kindness in offering to give me a letter of introduction to Judge Venable who had tried the principal cases of political affairs in Memphis since it had been "taken"—["]Were about gone up"—was the expression of to one—to which no one seemed inclined to make any comment—With their business at a stand—no churches—or schools—they seemed only to wish for peace—It was hard to understand what their enjoyments could ever be—beyond the bare accumulation of money—carriages were unknown there—as they would be useless most of the year—Vegetation was grand in variety as well as size—Vines running to the tops of tall trees—sometimes a few feet from the trunk going up for a hundred feet perfectly straight having started with the young tree long years ago—There was an incessant chattering of paroquettes—somewhat after the style in which "they say a woman's right's convention is carried on["]—The birds being green are invisible when among the branches—they are very destructive in a corn field—Walking here was impossible even with my homemade leather shoes—equal to any genuine "brogans". so a week passed away very quietly—except the constant occupation of brushing off the largest musquitoes I ever saw—I found little to do but rest—The story of my pounding about in the wagon was told in sundry and various black spots on my person—as well as a general stiffness and disinclination to move—Mrs. Stone did all in her power to make my stay pleasant. Here, all were told I was going to Memphis—how much more they surmised—mattered not.

*August 12th—Monday morning*—A week of absolute quiet has restored my desire to be "moving on"—towards my journey's end—This is still quite a long way off—bidding my kind hostess and family "good bye" —I started again—this time in a one-horse wagon—Jack for dri'ver— my 'chair for a seat—Dan with my trunks and Mr. Stone following us—we had seven miles to ride to the river where we hoped to get a boat—going to Memphis. Not a quarter of a mile from the house, Jack drove into a mud-hole—into which the wheels on my side sank indefinitely—I perched on a high chair with nothing to hold by—being "unexpectedly called on" like so many patriotic orators—out went chair and its occupant between the wheels—A sudden stopping of the horse prevented more serious trouble, or my friend's predictions about my reaching the North would probably have been verified, and my inglorious career ended here. Though less agreeable, falling in the mud so far as safety goes, is far preferable to a firmer landing-place— Mr. Stone came hurrying up to me insisting on my being hurt, and going back—but, after walking a few steps—I found no injury—and was soon reseated this time not ambitious for a high place, I sat on the bottom of the wagon—We saw an enormous water mocassin gliding away from the bank of a creek we crossed—apparently in great fear of us—The plantations through which we passed were all overgrown with weeds—one on which the ordinary crop was 1,000 bales of cotton, & corn in proportion had not a negro at work—Even the plantation road was so hidden—we could hardly find it—There was only silence and desolation, till we came in sight of the Father of Waters—this was my first view—and rather small it looked to me—compared with my ideas of it. Half a mile farther along the levee, brought us to a place opposite Island No. 40 or Buck Island which was my destination—An old bachelor from Boston originally was the major domo—We were just going into his house, when we saw the boatman landing—Mr. S. soon told him that I wanted to be carried over to his house on the Island and wait for a boat. Down the almost perpendicular bank I clambered, with the help of Mr. S. & Dan both—my trunks followed, and we were all deposited in the little leaky "skift"—This seemed more like "flying from ills we have" &tc than anything before on the journey When Mr. S. & Dan gave me the farewell grasp of hands—and Jack his not less hearty one, I left all behind of whom I had ever heard—They had been to me "friends in need" such as cannot soon be forgotten—The sun was at noon-day height—and scorching heat—Our ride was short, fortunately, we landed at the steep bank & ploughed up through the hot sand to the house—found a cabin—with one room—occupied by a squalid woman & 6 children—This was the only place of shelter on the island. Dinner was prepared, but—my appetite failed—the water was lukewarm, just as it was dipped up from the river—The evening passed in hearing details of a visit they had from a band of Southern guerrillas ten days before—who came across from the "main shore"—robbed them in broad daylight of all the money & clothing they could find—& most of their scanty hard earned stock of provisions—They were infuriated by finding the oath of allegiance to the U.S.—which the man had in his trunk—In reality, they were deserters from Gen. Chalmer's army, and men or brutes rather well known to both this man & his wife for years—the man was away—the band left—telling his wife they would come back & get him soon. Daylight faded away-& no boat came—A sleeping place was improvised for me, on the floor of what was called a piazza—a few boards overhead—no sides or front—This was better than sharing a room with 8 others a small one at that—A large black dog lay by me—I was in no mood for sleep—the bright moonlight was the only ray of comfort—Something would move, & I could see stealthy guerrillas on every side—two contrabands were stalking around like black ghosts till after midnight—They had been left by one gunboat and were watching for another—to get away—Robinson Crusoe seemed truer than ever to me—though I had not read it for years—it came fresh to my memory—The river lay sleeping so quietly below—but even its calmness did not soothe me—Every faculty but reason was wide awake. Two boats came puffing round the bend, and passed on—How my thoughts followed them up many a mile in the river's course, to where my only brother I supposed was still living—After the birds had all sung their good night—& the insects grown more subdued in their music—there was a stillness like death brooding over everything—the pale stars looked down so tenderly-that one's thoughts could not but turn to Him whose handiwork are both they—and poor trembling mortals—'Tis said that "silence is vocal if we listen well"—when the first dawning of morning light came, I had not for an instant ceased to lend a listening ear, never did I more heartily "hail the glorious morn"—At sunrise on the high bank—I watched the beautiful painting of every object—The country being level, wants the grandeur of more varied scenery—but it has a quiet majesty at this hour— beyond description. While there alone, I first saw the old flag—the dear old Stars And Stripes. It looked to me now like the protecting arm of a father stretched out to me—the tears fell thick and fast as it passed on—and my signal was unheeded. I had heard that flag called by every derisive name, seen another for 2 years waving over a distracted coun- try—now, my prayers were answered—and my love for it was stronger than I knew before—Now from the rising place of this grand river in the far Northern Lake, to its last wave as it enters the Gulf, there floats on its bosom no other flag than the old Star Spangled Banner—enough in that thought to swell every American's heart—All day boats were passing up and down, not one of them even slackening their speed for my white signal. Gen. Chalmer's forces had not long before fired on one [of] them from the landing near there—Commerce, which in return was soon after burnt—and strict orders were given from head- quarters that nothing but a gun-boat should stop there—the levee afforded fine protection for sharp shooters—who could take off the pilots.—Of this Mr. S. knew nothing when I came there—he thinking boats stopped as they had before—very often—Here was a new dilemma—which grew into mighty proportions as night came on— With river water to drink, miserable food to eat, and feeling sensibly the general effect of my yesterday's fall from the wagon—added to the hopelessness of escape for some time—this was a gloomy day enough—and a few more drops were added to what I thought my full bucket of misery, in the shape of a thunder storm which drove me into "the room" coming up about bedtime—There was no lack of air—for the logs were not close enough together for that—nor rain— either—but—the night wore away—Wednesday morning was cooler— somewhat—I walked to the bank again—this time almost despairing. There was just breeze enough to rustle the leaves of the cotton-wood trees, with a sound like gentle rain—the creeping mimosa coming up in the sand was waiting the sun's rays to unfold its delicate leaves and flowers—Waiting till the sun had for an hour been shining, I went back—to spend a restless uncomfortable day—feeling much like a prisoner condemned without a trial—When the hot sun was down again—I went to the farther end of the island about half a mile—with the oldest daughter of 14 yrs. Dark purple clouds were piled up in the distance and zig-zag lightning flashed across them—far back seemed like a sheet of flame flickering but never dying out—It was awfully grand—the fear of its coming nearer deprived me of all enjoyment—and I thought too of another night in that room with the whole family—The clouds gradually sank away—that fear was gone—Some good angel must have been at my side just then telling me that this was an omen for me—for a thought came to me—that in my trunk were some pieces of red white & blue silk—remnants of a Union flag—made for the last rally before the war in Columbus—Hurrying back—I made as large a flag as I could with them, cut paper stars out of a blank leaf in my notebook—and soon had a Star Spangl'd—though small sized—national emblem—With a cotton-wood stick for staff, it was tied on—the stars down—in token of distress—It was laid under my scanty pillow, and when I fell asleep—it was with a firm conviction, that These darkest days—wait till tomorrow—would all have passed away—and I be released from Buck Island. The prisoners on both sides who have dragged out long weary months often of unjust confinement were often in my mind in these three days for this was my first experience of a feeling of confinement in close quarters—Of the suffering among Southern men—I have heard stories without end, and often I could not but believe without even the slim "founded on fact" of novel title pages—Of Southern prisons I have seen nothing, except the small number in Columbus—& them only at the windows. At best—the loss of liberty is a bitter thing—without useless severity on either side—That night I slept soundly—The morning sun woke me—for nothing came between me and its first beams—Breakfast was here only an apology for eating, like all the other meals with me, as too much of the "peck" we are all said to have as our alloted portion of dirt in this life—was apparent. An hour passed—two, three—no boat—but, before noon we heard a slow puffing coming up—The family went to the bank with me—my trunks having gone early—My little flag was flung to the breeze—I could see the pilot with his glass watching—what minutes of suspense those were—had it not been for my firm faith in my poor little "Stars & Stripes"—I should have been hopeless of success—but it came for the bell struck twice—the signal to stop—The sound thrilled through my ears—and overpowered me—for it told me—my task was done. It was a welcome back to my native land—With trembling hand, and dim eyes—I bade good-bye to the poor woman and her miserable children—and with my trunks embarked once more in the "skift"—to go out into the middle of the river a short—but not very safe adventure, being nearly drawn under the boat—as we came "alongside" The decks were crowded with furloughed men and officers coming from Vicksburg, With the help of some strong arms—I mounted from the top of my trunk—to the boat's side—in a few minutes we were off—The old captain took me to the pilot-house—where he said that although I did not realize it—the greatest danger in my trip had just passed—He had screamed—"don't bring her out"—which we on shore did not understand—and he said everybody expected to see us swamped in the current—after "perils by land"—this last "peril by water" had seemed less to me—than many others—for I could see the goal—Words poorly express the feeling of security—as I sat looking out on the "dangers passed"—once more there was over me the emblem of a strong government—not the flag of a distracted anarchy—where confusion ruled and reigned—in the struggle for power—That land I had loved—and not less in her sorrow—with pity for the blindness which caused her ruin—and unchanging affection for my friends. Now for the first time I began to hear the Union side of "the Rebellion" a new word to me—New name for "this glorious struggle for our freedom" on which so many changes had been rung.

from *Shiloh*
by **Shelby Foote**

*Shelby Foote (born 1916) is best known for his magisterial three-volume narrative history, titled—with a touch of modesty and more than a dash of ambition—The Civil War. In 1952 he published Shiloh, an elegantly austere novel that embodies the anxiety and the pain of one of the war's bloodiest battles. The all-but-imperceptible tilt of Foote's sympathies toward the South infuses his sensitive account of the Union's "6 Squad, 23d Indiana".*

used to think how strange it was that the twelve of us had been brought together by an event which separated brothers and divided the nation. Each of us had his history and each of the histories was filled with accidental happenings.

Myself for instance: I was born in New England and was taken to Indiana, adopted me out of an orphanage. I was six at the time—I can barely remember. "Your name is Robert," they said; "Robert Winter." It was my first ride on a train. "You are our son Robert. We are taking you home." Then we ate sandwiches out of a paper bag. For years I thought all children came from Boston.

That's what I mean by accidental. I had to be adopted out of a New England orphanage to become part of an Indiana squad. And it was the same all down the line. Every one of the twelve had his own particular story.

This tied in with what Corporal Blake said during one of the halts Sunday while we were marching from Stony Lonesome toward the sound of guns across the creek. He said books about war were written to be read by God Amighty, because no one but God ever saw it that way. A book about war, to be read by men, ought to tell what each of the twelve of us saw in our own little corner. Then it would be the way it was—not to God but to us.

I saw what he meant but it was useless talking. Nobody would do it that way. It would be too jumbled. People when they read, and people when they write, want to be looking out of that big Eye in the sky, playing God.

But the strange thing was that I should think of it now, lying before sunup on the edge of the battlefield. Then again, tired and wrought-up as we were from all the waiting and the bungled march the day before, I suppose almost anything could have come into my mind. We had marched onto the field after dark. The first I saw of it was when daylight filtered through and we were lying there waiting for the shooting to get started again. We werent green—we had seen our share of killing: but this was different to begin with. We had heard so many tales the night before. The army had been wrecked, they told us; we were marching in for the surrender.

Our division, Lew Wallace commanding, was in position on the east side of a hollow. There were woods thick on both sides and a creek down in the draw. Across it, half a mile away, where the opposite slope rose up in a bluff, the rebels were lined up waiting. We could see their battle flags and sunlight sparkling on a battery near the center of their line.

We were the flank division of Grant's army. Snake Creek, which we crossed the night before, was off to our right. When dawn broke and the sun came through the haze, I lay there in the grass, watching it glint on the fieldpieces, and I thought: Oh-oh. If Wallace sends us across that hollow in the face of those guns, he's going to have considerably fewer of us when we reach the other side.

There was a long quiet period, nearly an hour, while the two armies lay and looked across the vacant space like two dogs sizing each other up. Then firing began to sputter over on the left, like growling, nothing much at first but finally a steady clatter, growing louder and louder, swelling along the front toward where we lay.

"Hey, sarge," Winter said. "If they marched up here *look*ing for a fight, why dont they come on?"

I didnt answer. Then Klein: "Maybe they know Buell got in last night." Klein was always ready with some kind of remark.

"Let the generals plan the war," I told him. "All you are paid to do is fight it."

I really thought our time had come. But Wallace had more sense than to send us naked across that draw against those guns. He ordered up two of his batteries, one in front of where we were and another down the line. They tuned up, ranging in on the brassy glints on the bluff. We enjoyed watching them work. Thompson's battery, which was directly to our front, did especially well. We watched the balls rise like black dots, getting smaller, then come down on the rebel guns across the hollow. The cannoneers were lively, proud to be putting on a show, and every now and then we cheered them. It didnt last long. As soon as one of the secesh guns was dismounted by a direct hit, the whole battery limbered and got out. That was what we had been waiting for.

It's not often you see war the way a civilian thinks it is, but it was that way now. We were center brigade, and since our company—G— was just to the right of the brigade center, we saw the whole show. Wallace was directly in our rear, standing beside his horse and watching the artillery duel through his field glasses. Grant rode up with Rawlins and dismounted within six feet of Wallace, but Wallace was so busy with his glasses that he didnt know Grant was there until one of the division staff officers coughed nervously: "General . . ." Then Wallace turned and saw Grant.

There was bad blood between them and our poor showing yesterday hadnt helped matters. Wallace saluted and Grant returned it, touching the brim of his hat with the tips of his fingers. He had the look of a man who has missed his sleep. His uniform was rumpled even worse than usual, and he stood so as to keep the weight off his left ankle, which he had sprained two days ago when his horse fell on him.

I could not hear what they were saying (both batteries were going full blast now) but I saw Grant motion with his arm as he talked and Wallace kept nodding his head in quick, positive jerks. It was clear that Grant was indicating the direction of attack—he pointed toward the bluff, stabbing the air—but it seemed foolish to me, seeing we had been given our orders already.

When the rebel battery fell back, their infantry went with it. Grant mounted, still talking and motioning with his arm. Wallace kept nodding—Yes, I understand: Yes—and Grant rode away, Rawlins jogging beside him.

Wallace passed between us and Company F. He went about a hundred yards out front, then turned his horse and faced us. This must have been some sort of signal to the brigade commanders, for all the battle flags tilted forward at once and the whole division stepped out, advancing with brigades in echelon and not even being fired on. It was pretty as a picture.

Until we struck the scrub oaks halfway down the slope we could see from flank to flank, blue flags uncased, snapping in the breeze, and the rifles of the skirmishers catching sunlight. Wallace sat on his horse, waiting for us to come past. As we opened ranks and flowed around him, we put our caps on the ends of our gun barrels and gave him a cheer. He raised himself in the saddle and lifted his hat as we went by. His mustache was black against his high-colored face and his teeth showed white beneath it. He was thirty-four, the youngest major general in the army.

We went on, tramping through underbrush, walking with our rifles held crossways to keep from getting slapped in the face by limbs. As we crossed the creek I saw the line again for a couple of hundred yards both right and left, the yellow water splashing calf-deep as the men passed over. Then we were climbing. We went on up—the bluff was not as steep as it had looked from across the draw; it wasnt really a bluff at all—then reached the flat where the rebel cannon lay wrecked. Its bronze tube had been thrown sidewise, with a big dent at the breech where the cannonball came down, and both wheels were canted inward toward the broken splinter-bar. Off to one side lay a pinch-faced cannoneer, as dead as dead could be. With his long front teeth and his pooched-out cheeks he looked a little like a chipmunk. The men stood gawking at him.

"All right," I told them. "All right. Let it go."

The ground was high and level here, without so many trees, and we could see toward the left where the supporting division was supposed to have kept up. That was Sherman. But there were no men out there, either Union or Confederate, so we got orders from Captain Tubbs to form a defensive line till the front was restored.

I got the squad organized. So far so good, I thought.

But I was beginning to feel a little jumpy. It was too easy: a walk in the woods on a sunny Monday morning, with nothing to bother us but wet socks from crossing the creek. There were bound to be hard things coming.

Talk about lucky—I never knew what it was. Just when everything was going good and I had organized myself a nice grassy spot to take it easy while the outfit on our left came even with us, I looked up and: spat: a big fat raindrop hit me square in the eye. At first they were few and far between, dropping one by one, plumping against the dead leaves with a sound like a leaky tap, then faster and faster, pattering— a regular summer shower. It had been bad enough trying to sleep in it the night before, with our oilcloths left back at Stony Lonesome. Now we were going to have to fight in it as well. For a while it rained in sunshine (the devil beating his wife) but soon that passed too; there was only the gray rain falling slantwise, shrouding the woods.

We waited and waited, hunched over our cartridge boxes trying to keep the rain out. Sergeant Bonner was next to me, still wearing that coon-dog look on his face. I never knew a man so eager, so conscious of his stripes.

"Rebel weather," I said—to be saying something.

He said, "I reckon they dont like it any better than we do, Klein. It wets their powder just as damp as ours."

Bonner was like that. Either he wouldnt answer you at all or he would say something to catch you up short. Holliday, on my other flank, grinned at me through the rain, winking and jerking his head toward the sergeant. Grissom was on the other side of Holliday; he kept the breech of his rifle under his coat and held the palm of his hand over the muzzle to keep out the rain. Diffenbuch was farther down the line, squatting with his collar hiked up, not paying any mind to anyone.

On the far side of the sergeant, Joyner began to yell: "Come on down, Raymond. More rain more rest." He always called the rain Raymond—I never knew why. Joyner was a card. Once at Donelson, where we nearly froze to death, he kept us warm just laughing at him, till his face went numb with the cold and he couldnt talk.

After a while the rain slacked up and Thompson's battery began to bang away at a column of johnnies coming along a road to the right. That started the trouble. Somewhere out beyond the curtain of steely rain—it was thinner now but we still couldnt see more than a couple of hundred yards in any direction—there began to be a series of muffled sounds, sort of like slapping a mattress with a stick, and right behind the booms came some whistling sounds arching toward us through the trees: artillery. We lay there, hugging the ground, never minding the wet. Every now and then one was low, bopping around and banging against the tree trunks. It was nothing new to us. But it was no fun either.

The rain stopped during the cannonade, almost as quick as it started, and the sun came out again. Everything glistened shiny new. We were at the edge of a big field. Beyond a strip of woods on the right was another field even bigger. In the trees at the other end of the far field, just as the sun came clear, we saw a host of grayback cavalry bearing down on the third brigade with their flashing sabers looking clean and rain-washed too. They rode through the skirmishers, on toward the main line. There they met a volley from massed rifles. It was as if they had run into a trip wire. Men and horses went down in a scramble, all confused, and the column turned, what was left of it, and rode back through the woods. It all happened in a hurry. Except for the wounded skirmishers, walking back with blood running down their faces from the saber hacks, they hadnt hurt us at all.

Lavery said, "Wasnt that pretty, Diff?"

I didnt see anything pretty about it, God forgive him.

Sherman finally caught up and we went forward together, across the first field, through the fringe of trees, and into the second, crossing toward where the cavalry charge had begun. When we were within a hundred yards, still holding our fire, a long deep line of men in gray jackets and brown wide-brim hats stood up from the brush and fired directly in our faces. It was the loudest noise I ever heard, and the brightest flash. There was artillery mixed up in it, too.

I fired one round, not even taking aim, and wheeled off at a run for the rear. Half the secret of being a good soldier is knowing when to stand and when to run—the trouble was, so many got killed before they learned it. But there was no doubt about which to do now.

We stopped in the woods between the two fields. Bonner began to count heads. Klein and Winter were missing. "All right," Bonner said. "Lets form! Lets form!"

Then Klein came walking up. That Klein: he'd stayed out with the skirmishers a while. He said, "I waited to give them a chance to shoot at you birds before I crawled back across that field. I'm nobody's fool."

"Lets form!" Sergeant Bonner was yelling. "Lets form! "

Before too long all three brigades were in line at the fringe of trees between those two fields. The skirmishers—Nebraska boys—stayed out in the open, lying behind hillocks and brush clumps, firing into the woods where the rebels had stood up to blast us. When we went forward this time, passing the skirmishers, we knew what we would meet. That made a difference. Crossing, we stopped from time to time to fall on one knee, fire and reload, and worked our way ahead like that. Fifty yards short of the woods we gave them a final volley and went in with the bayonet. This time it was the johnnies ran.

We took some prisoners there, our first for the day. They were a scraggly lot. Their uniforms were like something out of a ragbag and they needed haircuts worse than any men I ever saw. They had beards of all kinds, done up to make them look ferocious, those that were old enough to grow them, and they had a way of talking—jabber jabber—that I couldnt follow. They were from Louisiana, Frenchies off the New Orleans wharfs. They called themselves the Crescent Regiment and were supposed to be one of the best the Confederates had on the field. They didnt look so capable to me.

That was the first hard fighting of the day. We ran into plenty just like it and some more that was worse, but generally speaking it was nothing like as bad as we expected. To hear the stragglers tell it when we came across Snake Creek the previous night, we were going to be cut to pieces before sunup. It turned out there was plenty of cutting done, but we were the ones who did it, not the rebels. Maybe they were fought to a frazzle the day before, or maybe the news that Buell had come up took the wind out of their sails, or maybe they had already decided to retreat. Anyhow, every time we really pushed them they gave.

So if Wallace was worried about his reputation because of our poor showing on the Sunday march, he could stop fretting now. We more than redeemed ourselves in the Monday fight.

This goes back. Sunday morning we'd waked up hearing firing from the direction of Pittsburg, five miles south. It began like a picket clash but it grew to a regular roar, the heavy booming of cannon coming dull behind the rattle of musketry. It may have been our imagination but we thought we felt the ground tremble. The three brigades of our division were strung out two miles apart on the road running west—the first at Crump's Landing on the Tennessee, the second (ours) at Stony Lonesome, and the third at Adamsville, a little over four miles from Crump's.

Soon after the sound of battle grew heavy we got orders to send our baggage to the Landing for safe keeping. The other brigades marched in from east and west, joining us at our camp. Wallace didnt know whether he was going to have to defend his present position or be prepared to march to the tableland back of Pittsburg. In either case he had to concentrate and Stony Lonesome was the place for that. If there was an attack here, it was best not to receive it with our backs too close to the river. If we were to march to Pittsburg to reinforce Grant's other divisions, there were two roads we could take. They ran from our camp like a V, both crossing Snake Creek on the right flank of the army.

I went to Crump's as corporal in charge of the baggage detail. When I got there I saw Grant's dispatch steamer, the *Tigress*, putting in for bank. Grant was standing on the texas deck. He had pulled his hat down over his eyes, against the morning sun, and his hands were on the railing. Wallace waited on another steamer tied at the wharf. Grant's headquarters were at Savannah in a big brick house overlooking the river; every morning he made the nine-mile trip to Pittsburg to inspect the training. The way they told it later, he had just sat down to the breakfast table this Sunday morning and was lifting his coffee cup when he heard cannons booming from up the river. He put down the cup without taking a sip, went straight to the wharf, boarded the *Tigress*, and ordered the captain to make full steam for Pittsburg.

Passing Crump's, the pilot warped in and Grant leaned over the rail and yelled to Wallace: "General, get your troops under arms and have them ready to move at a moment's notice." Wallace shouted back that he'd already done this. Grant nodded approval and the pilot brought the *Tigress* about in a wide swing (she hadnt even slowed) and took her up the river.

That was about eight o' clock. When I got back to Stony Lonesome all three brigades were there, the troops resting by the side of the road with their packs on the grass and their rifles across their knees. The colonels, expecting march orders any minute, hadnt even allowed them to stack arms. I reported to the first sergeant and he sent me back to the squad.

Sergeant Bonner was arguing with Klein about whether Klein could take his pack off. All the other squads had shed theirs long ago, and

Klein was telling him he was torturing his men just to impress the officers; he was stripe-struck, Klein said, working for a dome on his
chevrons. Bonner was riled—which was what Klein wanted—and just
bull-headed enough to make us keep them on, now that Klein had
made an issue of it. But finally he saw it was no use. "All right," he said.
"Drop them." He didnt look at Klein as he said it. Klein took his pack
off and leaned back smiling.

Youd think twelve men who had been through as much as we had
(and who expected to go through even worse, perhaps, within a very
short time) would make it a point to get along among themselves.
Most of us hated the army anyhow, shoved as we were away down here
in this Rebel wilderness. Youd think we would try to make up for it by
finding some sort of enjoyment in our squad relationships. But no.
Not a waking hour passed that one of us wasnt bickering, nursing a
grudge. I blamed it all on Bonner at one time; morale was one of his
responsibilities. Then I saw it wouldnt be a lot different under anyone
else. We hated the army; we hated the war (except when we were
actually fighting it; *then* you dont have time)—and we took it out on
each other.

We lounged there beside the road, chewing grass stems and sweating. The sun rose higher. From time to time the sound of guns would
swell and then die down. Occasionally they faded to almost nothing, a
mutter, and we would think perhaps it was over; Grant had surrendered. But then it would come up louder than ever. Some said the
sound moved toward the left, which would mean Grant was retreating;
others said it moved toward the right, which would mean he was
advancing. Myself, I couldnt tell. Sometimes it seemed to go one way,
then another.

Wallace and his staff, orderlies holding their horses, were across
the road from our company. That was about the center of the column, the point where the road branched off toward the fighting.
Whenever the sound swelled louder, Wallace would raise his head
and stare in that direction. He would take out his watch, look at it hard
for a moment, then put it back in his pocket and shake his head, fret-

ting under Grant's instructions to hold his troops in position till orders came. He didnt like it.

We stayed there three hours, and it seemed longer. At eleven-thirty a quartermaster captain galloped up on a lathered horse, dismounted, and handed Wallace a folded piece of paper. The general read it hurriedly, then slowly. He asked the captain something, and when the captain answered, Wallace turned to his staff. Within two minutes the couriers passed us on their horses, going fast.

At that time the cooks were passing out grub. It was beans as usual. The orders were, finish eating within half an hour, fall in on the road, and be prepared to march hard. By noon we were under way toward the sound of firing.

Then was when trouble began. From Stony Lonesome two roads ran south to the battlefield, both of them crossing Snake Creek, which was the right boundary. They formed a V with its angle at our starting point. The right arm of the V ran to a bridge connecting us with Sherman's line of camps. Wallace had had this bridge strengthened and the road corduroyed (I was on the detail myself, and a nasty detail it was, too) not only for an emergency such as this, in which Sherman needed us, but also for an emergency in which we would need Sherman—it worked both ways. So when Wallace got orders to join the right flank of Grant's army, he naturally took this road. But that was when trouble began, as I said.

It was five miles to the bridge. We were within a mile of it when a major from Grant's staff passed us with his horse in a lope. Shortly afterwards we were halted. It was hot and the dust was thick. We stood there. Soon we were surprised to see the head of the column coming toward us, off to one side of the road. They had countermarched.

Finally the company ahead peeled off and fell in at the tail and we followed. All the way back, men in ranks on the road yelled at the column, asking what had happened—"Did you forget to remember something?"—but by the time we came abreast (we were center brigade) theyd had enough of shouting and were quiet, standing in the road and breathing the dust we raised as we passed.

What had happened, Grant—after sending the Q.M. captain with the note—had got impatient waiting for us and at two oclock, when we still hadnt come, he sent this major to see what was the delay. The major, surprised at not finding us on the road nearest the river (the left arm of the V) had spurred his horse and caught up with Wallace just in time to prevent our marching directly into the arms of the rebs. That was the first we knew of Grant's being pushed back toward the Landing.

When we got to the turn-around point, within sight of Stony Lonesome again, the sun had dropped almost level with the treetops and we were beginning to fag from the ten-mile hike. But there were six miles left to travel and we went hard, marching up the left arm of the V. Two more of Grant's staff officers were with us by then, Colonel Birdseye McPherson and Captain John Rawlins—I saw them when they doubled back down the column with Wallace. They were egging him and he was chafing under it.

The approach to Snake Creek bridge was through a swamp. By then the sun was all the way gone and we marched in a blue dusk. The boles of trees were pale and the backwater glistened. It was gloomy. Crossing the bridge we saw stragglers wading the creek, in too big a panic to wait for us to clear the bridge; they were in even too big a panic to wait for each other, crowding past with wet feet and flopping pants legs. When we shouted down at them, calling them skulkers and cowards, they yelled back: "Youll see! Youll find out!" and such like. They said Grant was whipped and we were marching in for the surrender.

It could have been true. The firing had died for the past hour, and now it was no more than an occasional sputter. We looked at each other, wondering. But when we were across the bridge, onto the flank of the battlefield, we saw that the army was still there, what was left of it, and Buell's men were coming up from the Landing.

Then the rain began. We were put in line on the right of Sherman, along the road we had marched in on. Sherman's men had tales to tell. Most of these were descriptions of how the johnnies had overrun them, but they told some brave ones too. They said a boy in an Ohio regiment had been wounded and sent to the rear but came back a few minutes later and said to his company commander, "Captain, give me a gun. This damned fight aint got any rear."

The rain came down harder and lightning flashed. It seemed like a year since we first left Stony Lonesome.

When we had scattered that Crescent outfit, taking a batch of prisoners, we stopped to re-form and then went forward again. It was that way from then on. They wouldnt stand; they would just wait to ambush us, and every now and then they would come in a rush, screaming and yelling that wild crazy way they had. Sometimes it would shake us a bit, but generally not. They never really pushed it.

The squad worked in two sections: Sergeant Bonner with Klein and Diffenbuch, Amory, Pope and Holliday; Corporal Blake with myself and Pettigrew, Grissom and Lavery. About four oclock Diffenbuch got hit in the shoulder and we left him leaned against a tree. Diffenbuch was always a quiet one, and he didnt have much to say even then.

Raymond was coming and going but it wasnt like in training, where you could knock off when he came down. Right after Diff got hit it faired off and the sun came through. We were walking in sunlight then, dead men all over the place, some left from yesterday, twisted in ugly positions but washed clean by the rain. At one point I saw a reb and a Union man lying on opposite sides of the road, both in the standard prone position for firing. Their rifles were level and they both had one eye shut. They had the same wound, a near red hole in the forehead, and they were stone dead, still lying there with the sights lined up— they must have fired at the same time. Looking at them I thought of the terrible urgency they both must have felt in the last half-second before they both pulled trigger.

We were approaching the camp where Sherman's tents were standing. They had run from here yesterday morning and now we were back where it started. The rebels had formed a line along the ridge. We charged them, bayonets fixed.

That was where Pettigrew got his.

. . .

I have seen my share of men get hit (at Donelson we were caught in a
tight and lost five out of twelve in less than ten minutes) but I never
saw one catch it as pretty as Pettigrew did. It was quick and hard—not
messy, either.

We had formed in this draw, down the slope from the hogback
where the tents were pitched. The johnnies had formed in front of the
tents, advanced down to what they call the military crest, and we got
set to go up after them. Corporal Blake was on the right, then myself,
then Pettigrew, then Lavery. Sergeant Bonner, with the other five, was
over beyond Lavery.

Captain Tubbs walked up and down, checking the platoons.
Lieutenant McAfee stood fiddling with his sword. Warning came down
from the right to get set. We passed it along. Then we heard Colonel
Sanderson bellering and the company officers picking it up all down
the line: *Charge! Charge!* and we went forward. The underbrush was
thick here, creepers and briery vines twined round the trees. They made
a crashing sound as we tramped through.

Toward the crest they thinned and the going was easier. That was where
they opened on us. The minies came our way, singing that song they sing,
and that stopped us. We hugged the ground. "All right, men!" officers
called. "All right!" We crouched in the bushes waiting for the word.

Corporal Blake looked straight ahead. Pettigrew on my left was half
turned in my direction, the expression on his face no different from
usual. When he saw me looking at him he grinned and said something
I couldnt hear because of the bullets singing and plopping into tree
trunks and the rifles banging away across the draw.

While I was watching him it came: *Charge! Charge!* The whole line
sprang up and started forward. I was still watching Pettigrew—I dont
know why; I certainly didnt have a premonition. As he went into it,
bent forward and holding his rifle across his chest, the minie struck
him low in the throat (I heard it hit, above all that racket; it was like
when you thump a watermelon) and he pitched forward with his arms
flung out, crucified.

When I stopped and leaned over him I saw that he was almost gone already. He knew it, too. He tried to tell me something, but all that came out was three words and a bubble of blood that swelled and broke:

"Tell my wife—"

Grissom was wounded just as they fell back. We had taken the ridge and they were retreating across the swampy hollow, almost out of rifle range, when one of them stopped and kneeled and pinked Grissom in the thigh. He sat down with his hands over the bullet hole and began to laugh and cry at the same time, like crazy. I think he was unnerved from seeing Pettigrew get it the way he did back there in the swale. They came from the same home town, grew up together. Pettigrew saved Grissom's life once by getting the drop on a sniper at Donelson. He sat there with blood oozing between his fingers, laughing and crying, both at once, saying he'd got himself a furlough to go home to Indiana and tell Pettigrew's wife how her husband caught one quick and easy.

It turned out that was the last attack of the day. Wallace sent word to hold up. That was enough, he told us. And if anyone thinks we werent glad to hear it, let him try pushing an army of rebels through three miles of scrub oak and briers. The johnnies formed a line about a mile farther on. Probably, though, they were no more anxious to receive a charge than we were to deliver one. The way it looked to me, they were willing to call it a day if we were.

We sat on the grass along the ridge where Sherman's camp was. There was a creek and a bog in the draw, and all across the valley, both sides of the creek, there were dead rebs so thick you could cross it almost without touching your feet to the ground.

Mostly they had been there since yesterday, and they were plenty high.

We were shifted around some then, being put in a defensive line, but there was no more fighting that day. While we were resting, the burial details went to work. The Union dead were buried by their own outfits, tagged and identified one by one and all together. But they buried the johnnies in groups near where they fell. It was interesting to watch, to see the way they did it. One of these burial trenches was near where we halted and we watched them at work.

They dug a trench about a hundred feet long, so deep that when they were finishing all we could see was flying dirt and the bright tips of their shovels. Fast as the collecting wagons brought the rebel bodies (all with their pockets turned inside-out) they laid them face-up, head-to-foot the length of the trench, each corpse resting its head between the feet of the corpse behind. It wasnt nearly as neat as it sounds, though—most of them had stiffened in awkward positions. I had noticed that many of them out on the field lay on their backs with their knees drawn up like women in labor. The diggers had to stomp the worst ones in.

The next row they laid in the other direction, still face-up but with their heads pointing the opposite way. They put them in like that, row above row, until the top ones were almost level with the grass. Then they threw in dirt—which was a relief; rebels generally rotted faster than our men. They turned blacker, too. Maybe the different rations had something to do with it. Or maybe it was just the meanness in them.

There was a big Irishman doing most of the shovel work. He seemed to enjoy it, and we got a laugh out of watching him. Throwing in dirt and smoothing it over, he would pat a dead reb on the face with the back of his shovel and say in a voice like a preacher, "Now lay there, me bye. Lay there quite till the doomsday trump. And dont ye be fomenting no more rebellions down there where ye're burrning."

Winter and Pettigrew were dead, Diffenbuch and Grissom wounded. Thirty-three and a third percent is high casualties in anybody's battle. But as usual Squad Three had caught the brunt end of the stick. Some squads hadnt lost a man. Out of one dozen hurt in Company G, four were ours, all from one squad. It just goes to show.

Bonner was a glory hunter. Anytime he could make himself look good by pushing us into a hot place, that was just what he did, and the hotter the better. Most squads liked to share the glory work, but not ours—we hogged it. Or Bonner did, which amounts to the same thing. I was talking to Klein and told him I had made up my mind to put in for a transfer.

"What ails you, Amory?" he said. "Aint you happy in your work?"

"Happy, hell," I said. "It's not fair. Thats what."

I knew it sounded foolish because I couldnt express myself very well. But I still wanted that transfer.

Watching the way they buried those rebels didnt help matters. I kept thinking maybe someday it might work out the other way round, so that the johnnies would be the ones doing the burying, and I sure didnt want to be stuffed into any ditch like that, all packed together without a marker or anything, no one to say a prayer when they let me down, no one to tell them back home how bravely I died.

When a man gives his life for his country he wants to get the worth of it, if you see what I mean.

Just before sundown they marched us away. Sherman's men moved into their camps (without even a thank-you for us winning them back) and we went over to the far right and bivouacked near Owl Creek for the night. The mess crew came down from Stony Lonesome with our supper—beans again. Night closed in while we ate. We sat in a big huddle, dirty, dog tired. The moon, in its first quarter, came up early in a cloudy sky. We bedded down.

I was so tired my legs were twitching; I couldnt even relax to go to sleep. We had paired off for warmth—Bonner and Joyner, Blake and Holliday, Klein and Lavery, Amory and myself—all lying on the leeward side of a blackberry clump. Amory had organized himself a strip of blanket from one of the cooks. It wasnt much help to me, though. Soon as he went to sleep he began to roll, wrapping it round and around him. For a while I tugged back, wanting my share, but then I gave it up and just lay there. It wasnt really cool enough for a blanket anyhow, though it probably would be before morning. In this crazy, no-account country a man could never tell what weather the next hour was going to bring.

I thought about Winter and Pettigrew lying out there dead in the woods unless one of the burial squads got to them before nightfall. I thought for a minute: What did those two die for? And the answer came back: *Nothing.* It was like a voice in the night: *They died for nothing.*

This war was so much easier for the Confederates. I could see how they would feel different about the whole thing, thinking they were fighting to form a new nation the way our grandfathers did back in '76 and believing they would go down among the heroes in the books. That was why they were so frantic in their charges, coming against our lines with those wild crazy yells, not minding their losses. With us it was not that way at all. They had dared us to fight and we fought. I thought it must be lots easier to fight for something than it was to fight *against* something.

But that was what the voice said. I also remembered what Corporal Blake said once. It was back in February, after Donelson; we lost six men in that fight, including one that froze to death. Blake said the rebels were really on our side. It sounded crazy but he explained it. He said they wanted the same things we wanted, the right kind of life, the right kind of government—all that—but theyd been misled by bad men. When they learned the truth they would stop fighting, he said.

As usual, though, when I began thinking stuff like that my mind got all confused, mixed up, and everything ran right back to the beginning. Winter and Pettigrew were lying dead out there in the woods and I was not. What right did I have thinking it was up to me to say why?

from Three Years in the Sixth Corps.
by George T. Stevens

*Today's sensibilities are more elastic than those of the 19th century. The physical and psychic dislocations of the war in some instances may have cultivated an appreciation for ambiguity—a tolerance for the other. But the standards for moral conduct were strict on both sides of the Mason-Dixon line, oscillating between the sentimental and the stoic. George T. Stevens (1832–1921), a surgeon with the 77th Regiment, New York Volunteers, was decidedly a man of his time.*

An incident of much interest to Neill's brigade occurred while we were here. A lieutentant, belonging to the Twenty-first New Jersey regiment, had been tried by a court-martial and convicted of cowardice at the battle on May 3d. The whole brigade was brought out at the hour for evening parade, and formed in a hollow square. To the center of the inclosure the culprit was brought. His sentence was then read to him, which was that he be dismissed the service in disgrace. The adjutant-general of the brigade then proceeded to execute the details of the sentence. The sword of the cowardly officer was taken from him and broken over his head; his shoulder-straps and buttons were then cut off, and his pistol broken and thrown away. The sentence, and the manner of its execution, were ordered to be published in the newspapers of the county where the regiment was raised. A similar sentence was executed in the Seventy-seventh regiment on the same evening. Lewis Burke, of Company F, was convicted of cowardice at the same battle. He was brought before the regiment, which stood in line; his sentence read, his buttons and the blue cord on his coat cut off, and a placard marked "COWARD" hung to his back. A guard, with fixed bayonets pointing at his back, then marched him off, the band playing "The Rogues' March." Burke went to serve out his time at the Dry Tortugas at hard labor, without pay or allowance.

As we looked upon the execution of these humiliating sentences, we could not help feeling how much better it would have been to have fallen nobly on that field of battle, honored and lamented, than to live to be thus degraded and despised. It had never been so forcibly impressed upon our minds, how much better it was to die nobly than to live in disgrace. When we thought of the noble Wheeler and his brave companions, who had given their lives for their country on yonder heights, and then turned to the sickening scene before us, we could but exclaim, "How are the dead to be envied!"

from The Diary of
George Templeton Strong
by George Templeton Strong

*Like his 18th century London counterpart, Samuel Pepys, diarist George Templeton Strong (1820–1875)—Columbia College graduate, Wall Street lawyer, and man about Manhattan—had a talent for presenting life as it was lived. Here Strong describes the riots that engulfed New York after Lincoln's 1863 decision to draft immigrants as well as citizens.*

July 13, Monday. A notable day. Stopped at the Sanitary Commission office on my way downtown to endorse a lot of checks that had accumulated during my absence, and heard there of rioting in the upper part of the city. As Charley is at Newport and Bidwell in Berkshire County, I went to Wall Street nevertheless; but the rumors grew more and more unpleasant, so I left it at once and took a Third Avenue car for uptown. At the Park were groups and small crowds in more or less excitement (which found relief afterwards, I hear, in hunting down and maltreating sundry unoffending niggers), but there was nothing to indicate serious trouble. The crowded car went slowly on its way, with its perspiring passengers, for the weather was still of this deadly muggy sort with a muddy sky and lifeless air. At Thirteenth Street the track was blocked by a long line of stationary cars that stretched indefinitely up the Avenue, and I took to the sidewalk. Above Twentieth Street all shops were closed, and many people standing and staring or strolling uptown, not riotously disposed but eager and curious. Here and there a rough could be heard damning the draft. No policemen to be seen anywhere. Reached the seat of war at last, Forty-sixth Street and Third Avenue. Three houses on the Avenue and two or three on the Street were burned down: engines playing on the ruins—more energetically, I'm told, than they did when their efforts would have been useful.

The crowd seemed just what one commonly sees at any fire, but its nucleus of riot was concealed by an outside layer of ordinary peaceable lookers-on. Was told they had beat off a squad of police and another of "regulars" (probably the Twelfth Militia). At last, it opened and out streamed a posse of perhaps five hundred, certainly less than one thousand, of the lowest Irish day laborers. The rabble was perfectly homogeneous. Every brute in the drove was pure Celtic—hod-carrier or loafer. They were unarmed. A few carried pieces of fence-paling and the like. They turned off west into Forty-fifth Street and gradually collected in front of two three-story dwelling houses on Lexington Avenue, just below that street, that stand alone together on a nearly vacant block. Nobody could tell why these houses were singled out. Some said a drafting officer lived in one of them, others that a damaged policeman had taken refuge there. The mob was in no hurry; they had no need to be; there was no one to molest them or make them afraid. The beastly ruffians were masters of the situation and of the city. After a while sporadic paving-stones began to fly at the windows, ladies and children emerged from the rear and had a rather hard scramble over a high board fence, and then scudded off across the open, Heaven knows whither. Then men and small boys appeared at rear windows and began smashing the sashes and the blinds and shied out light articles, such as books and crockery, and dropped chairs and mirrors into the back yard; the rear fence was demolished and loafers were seen marching off with portable articles of furniture. And at last a light smoke began to float out of the windows and I came away. I could endure the disgraceful, sickening sight no longer, and what could I do?

The fury of the low Irish women in that region was noteworthy.

Stalwart young vixens and withered old hags were swarming everywhere, all cursing the "bloody draft" and egging on their men to mischief.

Omnibussed down to No. 823, where is news that the Colored Half Orphan Asylum on Fifth Avenue, just above the reservoir, is burned. "*Tribune* office to be burned tonight." Railroad rails torn up, telegraph wires cut, and so on. If a quarter one hears be true, this is an organized insurrection in the interest of the rebellion and Jefferson Davis rules New York today.

Attended to business. Then with Wolcott Gibbs to dinner at Maison Dorée. During our symposium, there was an alarm of a coming mob, and we went to the window to see. The "mob" was moving down Fourteenth Street and consisted of just thirty-four lousy, blackguardly Irishmen with a tail of small boys. Whither they went, I cannot say, nor can I guess what mischief the handful of *canaille* chose to do. A dozen policemen would have been more than a match for the whole crew, but there were no policemen in sight.

Walked uptown with Wolcott Gibbs. Large fire on Broadway and Twenty-eighth Street. Signs of another to the east, said to be on Second Avenue. Stopped awhile at Gibbs's in Twenty-ninth Street, where was madame, frightened nearly to death, and then to St. Nicholas Hotel to see the mayor and General Wool. We found a lot of people with them. There were John Jay and George W. Blunt and Colonel Howe and John Austin Stevens, Jr., all urging strong measures. But the substantial and weighty and influential men were not represented; out of town, I suppose.

Their absence emboldened Gibbs and myself to make pressure for instant action, but it was vain. We begged that martial law might be declared. Opdyke said that was Wool's business, and Wool said it was Opdyke's, and neither would act. "Then, Mr. Mayor, issue a proclamation calling on all loyal and law-abiding citizens to enroll themselves as a volunteer force for defense of life and property." "Why," quoth Opdyke, "that is civil war at once." Long talk with Colonel Cram, Wool's chief of staff, who professes to believe that everything is as it should be and sufficient force on the ground to prevent further mischief. Don't believe it. Neither Opdyke nor General Wool is nearly equal to this crisis. Came off disgusted. Went to Union League Club awhile. No comfort there. Much talk, but no one ready to do anything whatever, not even to telegraph to Washington.

We telegraphed, two or three of us, from General Wool's rooms, to the President, begging that troops be sent on and stringent measures taken. The great misfortune is that nearly all our militia regiments have been despatched to Pennsylvania. All the military force I have seen or heard of today were in Fifth Avenue at about seven p.m. There were two or three feeble companies of infantry, a couple of howitzers, and a squadron or two of unhappy-looking "dragoons."

These wretched rioters have been plundering freely, I hear. Their outbreak will either destroy the city or damage the Copperhead cause fatally. Could we but catch the scoundrels who have stirred them up, what a blessing it would be! God knows what tonight or tomorrow may bring forth. We may be thankful that it is now (quarter past twelve) raining briskly. Mobs have no taste for the effusion of cold water. I'm thankful, moreover, that Ellie and the children are out of town. I sent Johnny off to Cornwall this afternoon in charge of John the waiter.

*July 14.* Eleven p.m. Fire bells clanking, as they have clanked at intervals through the evening. Plenty of rumors throughout the day and evening, but nothing very precise or authentic. There have been sundry collisions between the rabble and the authorities, civil and military. Mob fired upon. It generally runs, but on one occasion appears to have rallied, charged the police and militia, and forced them back in disorder. The people are waking up, and by tomorrow there will be adequate organization to protect property and life. Many details come in of yesterday's brutal, cowardly ruffianism and plunder. Shops were cleaned out and a black man hanged in Carmine Street, for no offence but that of Nigritude. Opdyke's house again attacked this morning by a roaming handful of Irish blackguards. Two or three gentlemen who chanced to be passing saved it from sack by a vigorous charge and dispersed the popular uprising (as the *Herald, World,* and *News* call it), with their walking sticks and their fists.

Walked uptown perforce, for no cars and few omnibi were running. They are suppressed by threats of burning railroad and omnibus stables, the drivers being wanted to reinforce the mob. Tiffany's shop, Ball & Black's, and a few other Broadway establishments are closed. (Here I am interrupted by report of a fire near at hand, and a great glare on the houses across the Park. Sally forth, and find the Eighteenth Ward station house, Twenty-second Street, near First Avenue, in full blaze. A splendid blaze it made, but I did not venture below Second Avenue, finding myself in a crowd of Celtic spectators disgorged by the circumjacent tenement houses. They were exulting over the damage to "them bloody police," and so on. I thought discretion the better part of curiosity. Distance lent enchantment to that view.)

At 823 with Bellows four to six; then home. At eight to Union League Club. Rumor it's to be attacked tonight. Some say there is to be great mischief tonight and that the rabble is getting the upper hand. Home at ten and sent for by Dudley Field, Jr., to confer about an expected attack on his house and his father's, which adjoin each other in this street just below Lexington Avenue. He has a party there with muskets and talks of fearful trouble before morning, but he is always a blower and a very poor devil. Fire bells again at twelve-fifteen. No light of conflagration is visible.

Bellows's report from Gettysburg and from Meade's headquarters very interesting. Thinks highly of Meade. Thinks the battle around Williamsport will be tolerably evenly matched, Lee having been decidedly beaten a week ago, but not at all demoralized. But there's a despatch at the Union League Club tonight that Lee has moved his whole army safely across, except his rear guard, which we captured.

A good deal of yelling to the eastward just now. The Fields and their near neighbour, Colonel Frank Howe, are as likely to be attacked by this traitor-guided mob as any people I know. If they are, we shall see trouble in this quarter, and Gramercy Park will acquire historical associations. O, how tired I am! But I feel reluctant to go to bed. I believe I dozed off a minute or two. There came something like two reports of artillery, perhaps only falling walls. There go two jolly Celts along the street, singing a genuine Celtic howl, something about "Tim O'Laggerty," with a refrain of pure Erse. Long live the sovereigns of New York, Brian Boroo *redivivus* and multiplied. Paddy has left his Egypt—Connaught—and reigns in this promised land of milk and honey and perfect freedom. Hurrah, there goes a strong squad of police marching, eastward down this street, followed by a company of infantry with gleaming bayonets. One a.m. Fire bells again, southeastward, Swinging slow with sullen roar." Now they are silent, and I shall go to bed, at least for a season.

*July 15.* Wednesday begins with heavy showers, and now (ten a.m.) cloudy, hot, and steaming. Morning papers report nothing specially grave as occurring since midnight. But there will be much trouble today. Rabbledom is not yet dethroned any more than its ally and instigator, Rebeldom.

News from the South is consolatory. Port Hudson surrendered. Sherman said to have beaten Joseph Johnston somewhere near Vicksburg. Operations commencing against Charleston. Bragg seems to be abandoning Chattanooga and retiring on Atlanta. *Per contra*, Lee has got safely off. I thought he would. . . . Lots of talk and rumors about attacks on the New York Custom-house (*ci-devant* Merchants' Exchange) and the Treasury (late Custom-house). Went to see [John J.] Cisco and found his establishment in military occupation—sentinels pacing, windows barricaded, and so on. He was as serene and bland as the loveliest May morning ("so cool, so calm, so bright") and showed me the live shell ready to throw out of the window and the "battery" to project Assay Office oil-of-vitriol and the like. He's all right. Then called on Collector Barney and had another long talk with him. Find him well prepared with shells, grenades, muskets, and men, but a little timid and anxious, "wanting counsel," doubtful about his right to fire on the mob, and generally flaccid and tremulous—poor devil!

Walked uptown with Charley Strong and Hoppin, and after my cup of coffee, went to Union League Club. A delegation returned from police headquarters, having vainly asked for a squad of men to garrison the clubhouse. *None can be spared.* What is worse, we were badly repulsed in an attack on the mob in First Avenue, near Nineteenth Street, at about six p.m. Fired upon from houses, and had to leave sixteen wounded men and a Lieutenant Colonel Jardine in the bands of these brutes and devils. This is very bad indeed. But tonight is quieter than the last, though there seems to be a large fire downtown, and we hear occasional gun-shots.

At the club was George Biggs, full of the loudest and most emphatic jawing. "General Frémont's house and Craven's to be attacked tonight, Croton mains to be cut, and gas works destroyed," and so on. By way of precaution, I had had the bathtubs filled, and also all the pots, kettles, and pails in the house. . . . Twelve-thirty: Light as of a large fire to the south.

*July 16.* Rather quiet downtown. No trustworthy accounts of riot on any large scale during the day. General talk downtown is that the trouble is over. We shall see. It will be as it pleases the scoundrels who are privily engineering the outbreak—agents of Jefferson Davis, permitted to work here in New York.

Omnibusses and railroad cars in full career again. Coming uptown tonight I find Gramercy Park in military occupation. Strong parties drawn up across Twentieth Street and Twenty-first Streets at the east end of the Square, by the G[ramercy] House, each with a flanking squad, forming an L. Occasional shots fired at them from the region of Second or First Avenue, which were replied to by volleys that seem to have done little execution. An unlucky cart-horse was knocked over, I hear. This force was relieved at seven by a company of regulars and a party of the Seventh with a couple of howitzers, and there has been but a stray shot or two since dark. The regulars do not look like steady men. I have just gone over to the hotel with John Robertson and ordered a pail of strong coffee to put a little life into them.

Never knew exasperation so intense, unqualified, and general as that which prevails against these rioters and the politic knaves who are supposed to have set them going, Governor Seymour not excepted. Men who voted for him mention the fact with contrition and self-abasement, and the Democratic Party is at a discount with all the people I meet.

(Apropos of discount, gold fell to one hundred and twenty-six today, with the city in insurrection, a gunboat at the foot of Wall Street, the Custom-house and Treasury full of soldiers and live shells, and two howitzers in position to rake Nassau Street from Wall to Fulton!!!!)

Every impression that's made on our people passes away so soon, almost as if stamped on the sand of the sea-beach. Were our moods a little less fleeting, I should have great hope of permanent good from the general wrath these outrages have provoked, and should put some faith in people's prophesyings that Fernando Wood and McCunn, and the New York *Herald,* and the Brookses and others, are doomed hence-forth to obscurity and contempt. But we shall forget all about it before next November. Perhaps the lesson of the last four days is to be taught us still more emphatically, and we have got to be worse before we are better. It is not clear that the resources of the conspiracy are yet exhausted. The rioters of yesterday were better armed and organized than those of Monday, and their inaction today may possibly be meant to throw us off our guard, or their time may be employed perfecting plans for a campaign of plundering and brutality in yet greater force. They are in full possession of the western and the eastern sides of the city, from Tenth Street upward, and of a good many districts beside. I could not walk four blocks eastward from this house this minute with-out peril. The outbreak is spreading by concerted action in many quar-ters. Albany, Troy, Yonkers, Hartford, Boston, and other cities have each their Irish anti-conscription nigger-murdering mob, of the same type with ours. It is a grave business, a *jacquerie* that must be put down by heroic doses of lead and steel.

Dr. Peters and Charley Strong called at eleven p.m. They have been exploring and report things quiet except on First Avenue from Nineteenth to Thirtieth Street, where there is said to be trouble. A detachment of the Seventh Regiment, five hundred or six hundred strong, marched to that quarter from their armory an hour ago.

*July 17.* The Army of Gramercy Park has advanced its headquarters to Third Avenue, leaving only a picket guard in sight. Rain will keep the rabble quiet tonight. We are said to have fifteen thousand men under arms, and I incline to hope that this movement in aid of the rebellion is played out.

> The draft riots, which had filled four days with tumult and terror, were indeed ended. General Wool had thrown into the city about eight hundred United States troops, drawn from the forts in the harbor, the Navy Yard, and West Point. Though Governor Horatio Seymour played a dubious part in the affair, making a speech on Tuesday the 14th from the City Hall steps which was altogether too conciliatory and pacific, he cooperated with Wool by ordering all the militia within reach (commanded by General Sandford) to turn out and help maintain order. About two thousand policemen were brought into action and behaved with energy and courage. Moreover, as Strong reports, bodies of citizens organized themselves, obtained arms from the authorities, and with the aid of returned veterans took a hand in restoring order. Pitched battles occurred in Broadway, on Forty-second Street, and along the West Side avenues uptown. A strong set of barricades in Twenty-ninth Street had to be carried by storm. Many of the mob were slain—how many no one knew, for the Evening Post recorded that many of the rioters were buried secretly at night, clandestine parties carrying the bodies across the East River. Some estimates of the total casualties on both sides ran as high as one thousand, while about $1,500,000 worth of private property was destroyed. The last sharp fighting took place near Gramercy Park, where on the evening of Thursday, the 16th, United States forces dealt severely with a body of rioters who were looting residences. Next day New York was quiet; and in August the drafting of men was resumed without difficulty.

*July 19, Sunday.* Have been out seeking information and getting none that is to be trusted. Colonel Frank Howe talks darkly and predicts an outbreak on the east side of the town tonight, but that's his way. I think this Celtic beast with many heads is driven back to his hole for the present. When government begins enforcing the draft, we shall have more trouble, but not till then.

Not half the history of this memorable week has been written. I could put down pages of incidents that the newspapers have omitted, any one of which would in ordinary times be the town's talk. Men and ladies attacked and plundered by daylight in the streets; private houses suddenly invaded by gangs of a dozen ruffians and sacked, while the women and children run off for their lives. Then there is the unspeakable infamy of the nigger persecution. They are the most peaceable, sober, and inoffensive of our poor, and the outrages they have suffered during this last week are less excusable—are founded on worse pretext and less provocation—than St. Bartholomew's or the Jew-hunting of the Middle Ages. This is a nice town to call itself a center of civilization! Life and personal property less safe than in Tipperary, and the "people" (as the *Herald* calls them) burning orphan asylums and conducting a massacre. How this infernal slavery system has corrupted our blood, North as well as South! There should be terrible vengeance for these atrocities, but McCunn, Barnard & Co. are our judges and the disgrace will rest upon us without atonement.

I am sorry to find that England is right about the lower class of Irish. They are brutal, base, cruel, cowards, and as insolent as base. Choate (at the Union League Club) tells me he heard this proposition put forth by one of their political philosophers in conversation with a knot of his brethren last Monday: "Sure and if them dam Dutch would jine us we'd drive the dam Yankees out of New York entirely!" These caitiffs have a trick, I hear, of posting themselves at the window of a tenement house with a musket, while a woman with a baby in her arms squats at their feet. Paddy fires on the police and instantly squats to reload, while Mrs. Paddy rises and looks out. Of course, one can't fire at a window where there is a woman with a child!! But how is one to deal with women who assemble around the lamp-post to which a negro had been hanged and cut off certain parts of his body to keep as souvenirs? Have they any womanly privilege, immunity, or sanctity?

No wonder St. Patrick drove all the venomous vermin out of

Ireland! Its biped mammalia supply that island its full average share of creatures that crawl and eat dirt and poison every community they infest. Vipers were superfluous. But my own theory is that St. Patrick's campaign against the snakes is a Popish delusion. They perished of biting the Irish people.

# Letter To James C. Conkling
## by Abraham Lincoln

*Eight months after the Emancipation Proclamation and three months before his Gettysburg Address, Abraham Lincoln (1809–1865) wrote to James C. Conkling, an old friend and Illinois political leader. The President declined to speak before a pro-Union rally, but asked Conkling to read his letter to the crowd. "Read it very slowly," he instructed. The document was one of the purest expressions of Lincoln's war aims.*

Hon. James C. Conkling    Executive Mansion,
My Dear Sir.    Washington, August 26, 1863.

Your letter inviting me to attend a mass-meeting of unconditional Union-men, to be held at the Capital of Illinois, on the
3d day of September, has been received.

It would be very agreeable to me, to thus meet my old
friends, at my own home; but I can not, just now, be absent from here,
so long as a visit there, would require.

The meeting is to be of all those who maintain unconditional devotion to the Union; and I am sure my old political friends will thank me
for tendering, as I do, the nation's gratitude to those other noble men,
whom no partizan malice, or partizan hope, can make false to the
nation's life.

There are those who are dissatisfied with me. To such I would say:
You desire peace; and you blame me that we do not have it. But how

can we attain it? There are but three conceivable ways. First, to suppress the rebellion by force of arms. This, I am trying to do. Are you for it? If you are, so far we are agreed. If you are not for it, a second way is, to give up the Union. I am against this. Are you for it? If you are, you should say so plainly. If you are not for *force*, nor yet for *dissolution*, there only remains some imaginable *compromise*. I do not believe any compromise, embracing the maintenance of the Union, is now possible. All I learn, leads to a directly opposite belief. The strength of the rebellion, is its military—its army. That army dominates all the country, and all the people, within its range. Any offer of terms made by any man or men within that range, in opposition to that army, is simply nothing for the present; because such man or men, have no power whatever to enforce their side of a compromise, if one were made with them. To illustrate—Suppose refugees from the South, and peace men of the North, get together in convention, and frame and proclaim a compromise embracing a restoration of the Union; in what way can that compromise be used to keep Lee's army out of Pennsylvania? Meade's army can keep Lee's army out of Pennsylvania; and, I think, can ultimately drive it out of existence. But no paper compromise, to which the controllers of Lee's army are not agreed, can, at all, affect that army. In an effort at such compromise we should waste time, which the enemy would improve to our disadvantage; and that would be all. A compromise, to be effective, must be made either with those who control the rebel army, or with the people first liberated from the domination of that army, by the success of our own army. Now allow me to assure you, that no word or intimation, from that rebel army, or from any of the men controlling it, in relation to any peace compromise, has ever come to my knowledge or belief. All charges and insinuations to the contrary, are deceptive and groundless. And I promise you, that if any such proposition shall hereafter come, it shall not be rejected, and kept a secret from you. I freely acknowledge myself the servant of the people, according to the bond of service—the United States constitution; and that, as such, I am responsible to them.

But, to be plain, you are dissatisfied with me about the negro. Quite likely there is a difference of opinion between you and myself upon that subject. I certainly wish that all men could be free, while I suppose you do not. Yet I have neither adopted, nor proposed any measure, which is not consistent with even your view, provided you are for the Union. I suggested compensated emancipation; to which you replied you wished not to be taxed to buy negroes. But I had not asked you to be taxed to buy negroes, except in such way, as to save you from greater taxation to save the Union exclusively by other means.

You dislike the emancipation proclamation; and, perhaps, would have it retracted. You say it is unconstitutional—I think differently. I think the constitution invests its commander-in-chief, with the law of war, in time of war. The most that can be said, if so much, is, that slaves are property. Is there—has there ever been—any question that by the law of war, property, both of enemies and friends, may be taken when needed? And is it not needed whenever taking it, helps us, or hurts the enemy? Armies, the world over, destroy enemies' property when they can not use it; and even destroy their own to keep it from the enemy. Civilized belligerents do all in their power to help themselves, or hurt the enemy, except a few things regarded as barbarous or cruel. Among the exceptions are the massacre of vanquished foes, and noncombatants, male and female.

But the proclamation, as law, either is valid, or is not valid. If it is not valid, it needs no retraction. If it is valid, it can not be retracted, any more than the dead can be brought to life. Some of you profess to think its retraction would operate favorably for the Union. Why better *after* the retraction, than *before* the issue? There was more than a year and a half of trial to suppress the rebellion before the proclamation issued, the last one hundred days of which passed under an explicit notice that it was coming, unless averted by those in revolt, returning to their allegiance. The war has certainly progressed as favorably for us, since the issue of the proclamation as before. I know as fully as one can know the opinions of others, that some of the commanders of our armies in the field who have given us our most important successes, believe the emancipation policy, and the use of colored troops, constitute the heaviest blow yet dealt to the rebellion; and that, at least one of those important successes, could not have been achieved when it was, but for the aid of black soldiers. Among the commanders holding these views are some who have never had any affinity with what is called abolitionism, or with republican party politics; but who hold them purely as military opinions. I submit these opinions as being entitled to some weight against the objections, often urged, that emancipation, and arming the blacks, are unwise as military measures, and were not adopted, as such, in good faith.

You say you will not fight to free negroes. Some of them seem willing to fight for you; but, no matter. Fight you, then, exclusively to save the Union. I issued the proclamation on purpose to aid you in saving the Union. Whenever you shall have conquered all resistance to the Union, if I shall urge you to continue fighting, it will be an apt time, then, for you to declare you will not fight to free negroes.

I thought that in your struggle for the Union, to whatever extent the negroes should cease helping the enemy, to that extent it weakened the enemy in his resistance to you. Do you think differently? I thought that whatever negroes can be got to do as soldiers, leaves just so much less for white soldiers to do, in saving the Union. Does it appear otherwise to you? But negroes, like other people, act upon motives. Why should they do any thing for us, if we will do nothing for them? If they stake their lives for us, they must be prompted by the strongest motive—even the promise of freedom. And the promise being made, must be kept.

The signs look better. The Father of Waters again goes unvexed to the sea. Thanks to the great North-West for it. Nor yet wholly to them. Three hundred miles up, they met New-England, Empire, Key-Stone, and Jersey, hewing their way right and left. The Sunny South too, in more colors than one, also lent a hand. On the spot, their part of the history was jotted down in black and white. The job was a great national one; and let none be banned who bore an honorable part in it. And while those who have cleared the great river may well be proud, even that is not all. It is hard to say that anything has been more bravely, and well done, than at Antietam, Murfreesboro, Gettysburg, and on many fields of lesser note. Nor must Uncle Sam's Web-feet be forgotten. At all the watery margins they have been present. Not only on the deep sea, the broad bay, and the rapid river, but also up the narrow muddy bayou, and wherever the ground was a little damp, they have been, and made their tracks. Thanks to all. For the great republic—for the principle it lives by, and keeps alive—for man's vast future,—thanks to all.

Peace does not appear so distant as it did. I hope it will come soon, and come to stay; and so come as to be worth the keeping in all future time. It will then have been proved that, among free men, there can be no successful appeal from the ballot to the bullet; and that they who take such appeal are sure to lose their case, and pay the cost. And then, there will be some black men who can remember that, with silent tongue, and clenched teeth, and steady eye, and well-poised bayonet, they have helped mankind on to this great consummation; while, I fear, there will be some white ones, unable to forget that, with malignant heart, and deceitful speech, they have strove to hinder it.

Still let us not be over-sanguine of a speedy final triumph. Let us be quite sober. Let us diligently apply the means, never doubting that a just God, in his own good time, will give us the rightful result. Yours very truly

—A. Lincoln

from Specimen Days
by Walt Whitman

*Forty-two years old when the Civil War broke out, Walt Whitman (1819–1892) served as a volunteer nurse in the Union hospitals in and around Washington. That brought him closer to the battlefields than other writers of military age at the time, such as Henry James, William Dean Howells and Mark Twain. The poet's great humanity shines on almost every page of his record of those years.*

## DOWN AT THE FRONT

FALMOUTH, VA., *opposite Fredericksburgh, December 21, 1862.*— Begin my visits among the camp hospitals in the army of the Potomac. Spend a good part of the day in a large brick mansion on the banks of the Rappahannock, used as a hospital since the battle—seems to have receiv'd only the worst cases. Out doors, at the foot of a tree, within ten yards of the front of the house, I notice a heap of amputated feet, legs, arms, hands, &c., a full load for a one-horse cart. Several dead bodies lie near, each cover'd with its brown woolen blanket. In the dooryard, towards the river, are fresh graves, mostly of officers, their names on pieces of barrel-staves or broken boards, stuck in the dirt. (Most of these bodies were subsequently taken up and transported north to their friends.) The large mansion is quite crowded upstairs and down, everything impromptu, no system, all bad enough, but I have no doubt the best that can be done; all the wounds pretty bad, some frightful, the men in their old clothes, unclean and bloody.

Some of the wounded are rebel soldiers and officers, prisoners. One, a Mississippian, a captain, hit badly in leg, I talk'd with some time; he ask'd me for papers, which I gave him. (I saw him three months afterward in Washington, with his leg amputated, doing well.) I went through the rooms, downstairs and up. Some of the men were dying. I had nothing to give at that visit, but wrote a few letters to folks home, mothers, &c. Also talk'd to three or four, who seem'd most susceptible to it, and needing it.

### AFTER FIRST FREDERICKSBURG

*December 23 to 31.*—The results of the late battle are exhibited everywhere about here in thousands of cases, (hundreds die every day,) in the camp, brigade, and division hospitals. These are merely tents, and sometimes very poor ones, the wounded lying on the ground, lucky if their blankets are spread on layers of pine or hemlock twigs, or small leaves. No cots; seldom even a mattress. It is pretty cold. The ground is frozen hard, and there is occasional snow. I go around from one case to another. I do not see that I do much good to these wounded and dying; but I cannot leave them. Once in a while some youngster holds on to me convulsively, and I do what I can for him; at any rate, stop with him and sit near him for hours, if he wishes it.

Besides the hospitals, I also go occasionally on long tours through the camps, talking with the men, &c. Sometimes at night among the groups around the fires, in their shebang enclosures of bushes. These are curious shows, full of characters and groups. I soon get acquainted anywhere in camp, with officers or men, and am always well used. Sometimes I go down on picket with the regiments I know best. As to rations, the army here at present seems to be tolerably well supplied, and the men have enough, such as it is, mainly salt pork and hard tack. Most of the regiments lodge in the flimsy little shelter-tents. A few have built themselves huts of logs and mud, with fireplaces.

### BACK TO WASHINGTON

*January, '63.*—Left camp at Falmouth, with some wounded, a few days since, and came here by Aquia creek railroad, and so on government steamer up the Potomac. Many wounded were with us on the cars and boat. The cars were just common platform ones. The railroad journey of ten or twelve miles was made mostly before sunrise. The soldiers guarding the road came out from their tents or shebangs of bushes with rumpled hair and half-awake look. Those on duty were walking their posts, some on banks over us, others down far below the level of the track. I saw large cavalry camps off the road. At Aquia creek landing were numbers of wounded going north. While I waited some three hours, I went around among them. Several wanted word sent home to parents, brothers, wives, &c., which I did for them (by mail the next day from Washington.) On the boat I had my hands full. One poor fellow died going up.

I am now remaining in and around Washington, daily visiting the hospitals. Am much in Patent-office, Eighth street, H street, Armory-square, and others. Am now able to do a little good, having money, (as almoner of others home,) and getting experience. Today, Sunday afternoon and till nine in the evening, visited Campbell hospital; attended specially to one case in ward 1, very sick with pleurisy and typhoid fever, young man, farmer's son, D. F. Russell, company E, 60th New York, downhearted and feeble; a long time before he would take any interest; wrote a letter home to his mother, in Malone, Franklin county, N. Y., at his request; gave him some fruit and one or two other gifts; envelop'd and directed his letter, &c. Then went thoroughly through ward 6, observ'd every case in the ward, without, I think, missing one; gave perhaps from twenty to thirty persons, each one some little gift, such as oranges, apples, sweet crackers, figs, &c.

*Thursday, Jan. 21.*—Devoted the main part of the day to Armory-square hospital; went pretty thoroughly through wards F, G, H, and I; some fifty cases in each ward. In ward F supplied the men throughout with writing paper and stamp'd envelope each; distributed in small portions, to proper subjects, a large jar of first-rate preserv'd berries, which had been donated to me by a lady—her own cooking. Found several cases I thought good subjects for small sums of money, which

I furnish'd. (The wounded men often come up broke, and it helps their spirits to have even the small sum I give them.) My paper and envelopes all gone, but distributed a good lot of amusing reading matter; also, as I thought judicious, tobacco, oranges, apples, etc. Interesting cases in ward I; Charles Miller, bed 19, company D, 53d Pennsylvania, is only sixteen years of age, very bright, courageous boy, left leg amputated below the knee; next bed to him, another young lad very sick; gave each appropriate gifts. In the bed above, also, amputation of the left leg; gave him a little jar of raspberries; bed 1, this ward, gave a small sum; also to a soldier on crutches, sitting on his bed near. . . . (I am more and more surprised at the very great proportion of youngsters from fifteen to twenty-one in the army. I afterwards found a still greater proportion among the southerners.)

Evening, same day, went to see D. F. R., before alluded to; found him remarkably changed for the better; up and dress'd—quite a triumph; he afterwards got well, and went back to his regiment. Distributed in the wards a quantity of note-paper, and forty or fifty stamp'd envelopes, of which I had recruited my stock, and the men were much in need.

### FIFTY HOURS LEFT WOUNDED ON THE FIELD

*1863*—Here is a case of a soldier I found among the crowded cots in the Patent-office. He likes to have some one to talk to, and we will listen to him. He got badly hit in his leg and side at Fredericksburgh that eventful Saturday, 13th of December. He lay the succeeding two days and nights helpless on the field, between the city and those grim terraces of batteries; his company and regiment had been compell'd to leave him to his fate. To make matters worse, it happen'd he lay with his head slightly down hill, and could not help himself. At the end of some fifty hours he was brought off, with other wounded, under a flag of truce. I ask him how the rebels treated him as he lay during those two days and nights within reach of them—whether they came to him—whether they abused him? He answers that several of the rebels, soldiers and others, came to him at one time and another. A couple of them, who were together, spoke roughly and sarcastically, but nothing worse. One middle-aged man, however, who seem'd to be moving around the field, among the dead and wounded, for benevolent purposes, came to him in a way he will never forget; treated our soldier kindly, bound up his wounds, cheer'd him, gave him a couple of biscuits and a drink of whiskey and water; asked him if he could eat some beef. This good secesh, however, did not change our soldier's position, for it might have caused the blood to burst from the wounds, clotted and stagnated. Our soldier is from Pennsylvania; has had a pretty severe time; the wounds proved to be bad ones. But he retains a good heart, and is at present on the gain. (It is not uncommon for the men to remain on the this way, one, two, or even four or five days.)

### HOSPITAL SCENES AND PERSONS

*Letter Writing.*—When eligible, I encourage the men to write, and myself, when called upon, write all sorts of letters for them, (including love letters, very tender ones.) Almost as I reel off these memoranda, I write for a new patient to his wife. M.de F., of the 17th Connecticut, company H, has just come up (February 17th) from Windmill point, and is received in ward H, Armory-square. He is an intelligent-looking man, has a foreign accent, black-eyed and hair'd, a Hebraic appearance. Wants a telegraphic message sent to his wife, New Canaan, Conn. I agree to send the message—but to make things sure I also sit down and write the wife a letter, and despatch it to the post-office immediately, as he fears she will come on, and he does not wish her to, as he will surely get well.

*Saturday, January 30th.*—Afternoon, visited Campbell hospital. Scene of cleaning up the ward, and giving the men clean clothes— through the ward (6) the patients dressing or being dress'd—the naked upper half of the bodies—the good-humor and fun—the shirts, drawers, sheets of beds, &c., and the general fixing up for Sunday. Gave J.L. 50 cents.

*Wednesday, February 4th.*—Visited Armory-square hospital, went pretty thoroughly through wards E and D. Supplied paper and

envelopes to all who wish'd—as usual, found plenty of men who
needed those articles. Wrote letters. Saw and talk'd with two or three
members of the Brooklyn 14th regt. A poor fellow in ward D, with a
fearful wound in a fearful condition, was having some loose splinters
of bone taken from the neighborhood of the wound. The operation
was long, and one of great pain—yet, after it was well commenced, the
soldier bore it in silence. He sat up, propp'd—was much wasted—had
lain a long time quiet in one position (not for days only but weeks,) a
bloodless, brown-skinn'd face, with eyes full of determination—
belong'd to a New York regiment. There was an unusual cluster of surgeons, medical cadets, nurses, &c., around his bed—I thought the
whole thing was done with tenderness, and done well. In one case, the
wife sat by the side of her husband, his sickness typhoid fever, pretty
bad. In another, by the side of her son, a mother—she told me she had
seven children, and this was the youngest. (A fine, kind, healthy, gentle mother, goodlooking, not very old, with a cap on her head, and
dress'd like home—what a charm it gave to the whole ward.) I liked the
woman nurse in ward E—I noticed how she sat a long time by a poor
fellow who just had, that morning, in addition to other sickness, bad
hemorrhage—she gently assisted him, reliev'd him of the blood, holding a cloth to his mouth, as he coughed it up—he was so weak he could
only just turn his head over on the pillow.

One young New York man, with a bright, handsome face, had been
lying several months from a most disagreeable wound, receiv'd at Bull
Run. A bullet had shot him right through the bladder, hitting him front,
low in the belly, and coming out back. He had suffer'd much—the water
came out of the wound, by slow but steady quantities, for many
weeks—so that he lay almost constantly in a sort of puddle—there were
other disagreeable circumstances. He was of good heart, however. At
present comparatively comfortable, had a bad throat, was delighted
with a stick of horehound I gave him, with one or two other trifles.

## PATENT-OFFICE HOSPITAL

*February 23.*—I must not let the great hospital at the Patent-office pass away without some mention. A few weeks ago the vast area of the second story of that noblest of Washington buildings was crowded close with rows of sick, badly wounded and dying soldiers. They were placed in three very large apartments. I went there many times. It was a strange, solemn,and, with all its features of suffering and death, a sort of fascinating sight. I go sometimes at night to soothe and relieve particular cases. Two of the immense apartments are fill'd with high and ponderous glass cases, crowded with models in miniature of every kind of utensil, machine or invention it ever enter'd into the mind of man to conceive; and with curiosities and foreign presents. Between these cases are lateral openings, perhaps eight feet wide and quite deep, and in these were placed the sick, besides a great long double row of them up and down through the middle of the hall. Many them were very bad cases, wounds and amputations. Then there was a gallery running above the hall in which there were beds also. It was, indeed, a curious scene, especially at night when lit up. The glass cases, the beds, the forms lying there, the gallery above, and the marble pavement under foot—the suffering, and the fortitude to bear it in various degrees—occasionally, from some, the groan that could not be repress'd—sometimes a poor fellow dying, with emaciated face and glassy eye, the nurse by his side, the doctor also there, but no friend, no relative—such were the sights but lately in the Patent-office. (The wounded have since been removed from there, and it is now vacant again.)

### THE WHITE HOUSE BY MOONLIGHT

*February 24th.*—A spell of fine soft weather. I wander about a good deal, sometimes at night under the moon. Tonight took a long look at the President's house. The white portico—the palace-like, tall, round columns, spotless as snow—the walls also—the tender and soft moonlight, flooding the pale marble, and making peculiar faint languishing shades, not shadows—everywhere a soft transparent hazy, thin, blue moon—lace, hanging in the air—the brilliant and extra-plentiful clusters of gas, on and around the facade, columns, portico, &c.—everything so white, so marbly pure and dazzling, yet soft—the White

House of future poems, and of dreams and dramas, there in the soft and copious moon—the gorgeous front, in the trees, under the lustrous flooding moon, full of reality, full of illusion—the forms of the trees, leafless, silent, in trunk and myriad—angles of branches, under the stars and sky—the White House of the land, and of beauty night—sentries at the gates, and by the portico, silent, pacing there in blue overcoats—stopping you not at all, but eyeing you with sharp eyes, whichever way you move.

## AN ARMY HOSPITAL WARD

Let me specialize a visit I made to the collection of barracklike one-story edifices, Campbell hospital, out on the flats, at the end of the then horse railway route, on Seventh street. There is a long building appropriated to each ward. Let us go into ward 6. It contains today, I should judge, eighty or a hundred patients, half sick, half wounded. The edifice is nothing but boards, well whitewash'd inside, and the usual slender-framed iron bedsteads, narrow and plain. You walk down the central passage, with a row on either side, their feet towards you, and their heads to the wall. There are fires in large stoves, and the prevailing white of the walls is reliev'd by some ornaments, stars, circles, &c., made of evergreens. The view of the whole edifice and occupants can be taken at once, for there is no partition. You may hear groans or other sounds of unendurable suffering from two or three of the cots, but in the main there is quiet—almost a painful absence of demonstration; but the pallid face, the dull eye, and the moisture on the lip, are demonstration enough. Most of these sick or hurt are evidently young fellows from the country, farmers' sons, and such like. Look at the fine large frames, the bright and broad countenances, and the many yet lingering proofs of strong constitution and physique. Look at the patient and mute manner of our American wounded as they lie in such a sad collection; representatives from all New England, and from New York, and New Jersey, and Pennsylvania—indeed from all the States and all the cities—largely from the west. Most of them are entirely without friends or acquaintances here—no familiar face, and hardly a word of judicious sympathy or cheer, through their sometimes long and tedious sickness, or the pangs of aggravated wounds.

## A CONNECTICUT CASE

This young man in bed 25 is H. D. B., of the 27th Connecticut, company B. His folks live at Northford, near New Haven. Though not more than twenty-one, or thereabouts, he has knock'd much around the world, on sea and land, and has seen some fighting on both. When I first saw him he was very sick, with no appetite. He declined offers of money—said he did not need anything. As I was quite anxious to do something, he confess'd that he had a hankering for a good home-made rice pudding—thought he could relish it better than anything. At this time his stomach was very weak. (The doctor, whom I consulted, said nourishment would do him more good than anything; but things in the hospital, though better than usual, revolted him.) I soon procured B. his rice pudding. A Washington lady, (Mrs. O'C.), hearing his wish, made the pudding herself, and I took it up to him the next day. He subsequently told me he lived upon it for three or four days. This B. is a good sample of the American eastern young man—the typical Yankee. I took a fancy to him, and gave him a nice pipe, for a keepsake. He receiv'd afterwards a box of things from home, and nothing would do but I must take dinner with him, which I did, and a very good one it was.

## TWO BROOKLYN BOYS

Here in this same ward are two young men from Brooklyn, members of the 51st New York. I had known both the two a young lads at home, so they seem near to me. One of them, J. L., lies there with an amputated arm, the stump healing pretty well. (I saw him lying on the ground at Fredericksburgh last December, all bloody, just after the arm was taken off. He was very phlegmatic about it, munching away at a cracker in the remaining hand—made no fuss.) He will recover, and thinks and talks yet of meeting the Johnny Rebs.

• • •

## A SECESH BRAVE

The grand soldiers are not comprised in those of one side, any more than the other. Here is a sample of an unknown southerner, a lad of seventeen. At the War department, a few days ago, I witness'd a presentation of captured flags to the Secretary. Among others a soldier named Gant, of the 104th Ohio volunteers, presented a rebel battle-flag, which one of the officers stated to me was borne to the mouth of our cannon and planted there by a boy but seventeen years of age, actually endeavor'd to stop the muzzle of the gun wit with fence-rails. He was kill'd in the effort, and the flag-staff was sever'd by a shot from one of our men.

## THE WOUNDED FROM CHANCELLORSVILLE

*May, '63.*—As I write this, the wounded have begun to arrive from Hooker's command from bloody Chancellorsville. I was down among the first arrivals. The men in charge told me the bad cases were yet to come. If that is so I pity them, for these are bad enough. You ought to see the scene of the wounded arriving at the landing here at the foot of Sixth street, at night. Two boat loads came about half-past seven last night. A little after eight it rain'd a long and violent shower. The pale, helpless soldiers had been debark'd, and lay around on the wharf and neighborhood anywhere. The rain was, probably, grateful to them; at any rate they were exposed to it. The few torches light up the spectacle. All around—on the wharf, on the ground, out on side places—the men are lying on blankets, old quilts, &c., with bloody rags bound round heads, arms, and legs. The attendants are few, and at night few outsiders also—only a few hard-work'd transportation men and drivers. (The wounded are getting to be common, and people grow callous.) The men, whatever their condition, lie there, and patiently wait till their turn comes to be taken up. Near by, the ambulances are now arriving in clusters and one after another is call'd to back up and take its load. Extreme cases are sent off on stretchers. The men generally make little or no ado, whatever their sufferings. A few groans that cannot be suppress'd, and occasionally a scream of pain as they lift a man into the ambulance. Today, as I write, hundreds more are expected, and tomorrow and the next day more, and so on for many days. Quite often they arrive at the rate of 1000 a day.

### UNNAMED REMAINS THE BRAVEST SOLDIER

Of scenes like these, I say, who writes—whoe'er can write the story? Of many a score—aye, thousands, north and south, of unwrit heroes, unknown heroisms, incredible, impromptu, first-class desperations—who tells? No history ever—no poem sings, no music sounds, those bravest men of all—those deeds. No formal general's report, nor book in the library, nor column in the paper, embalms the bravest, north or south, east or west. Unnamed, unknown, remain, and still remain, the bravest soldiers. Our manliest—our boys—our hardy darlings; no picture gives them. Likely, the typic one of them (standing, no doubt, for hundreds, thousands) crawls aside to some bushclump, or ferny tuft, on receiving his death-shot—there sheltering a little while, soaking roots, grass, and soil, with red blood—the battle advances, retreats, flits from the scene, sweeps by—and there, haply with pain and suffering (yet less, far less, than is supposed,) the last lethargy winds like a serpent round him—the eyes glaze in death—none recks—perhaps the burial-squads, in truce, a week afterwards, search not the secluded spot—and there, at last, the Bravest Soldier crumbles in mother earth, unburied and unknown.

### SOME SPECIMEN CASES

*June 18th.*—In one of the hospitals I find Thomas Haley, company M, 4th New York cavalry—a regular Irish boy, a fine specimen of youthful physical manliness—shot through the lungs—inevitably dying—came over to this country from Ireland to enlist—has not a single friend or acquaintance here—Is sleeping soundly at this moment, (but it is the sleep of death)—has a bullet-hole straight through the lung. I saw Tom when first brought here, three days since, and didn't suppose he could live twelve hours—(yet he looks well enough in the face to a casual observer.) He lies there with his frame exposed above the waist, all naked, for coolness, a fine built man, the tan not yet bleach'd from his cheeks and neck. It is useless to talk to him, as with his sad hurt, and the stimulants they give him, and the utter strangeness of every object, face, furniture, &c., the poor fellow, even when awake, is like some frighten'd, shy animal. Much of the time he sleeps, or half sleeps. (Sometimes I thought he knew more than he show'd.) I often come and sit by him in perfect silence; he will breathe for ten minutes as softly and evenly as a young babe asleep. Poor youth, so handsome, athletic, with profuse beautiful shining hair. One time as I sat looking at him while he lay asleep, he suddenly, without the least start, awaken'd, open'd his eyes, gave me a long steady look, turning his face very slightly to gaze easier—one long, clear, silent look—a slight sigh—then turn'd back and went into his doze again. Little he knew, poor death-stricken boy, the heart of the stranger that hover'd near.

*W. H. E., Co. F., 2d N.J.*—His disease is pneumonia. He lay sick at the wretched hospital below Aquia creek, for seven or eight days before brought here. He was detail'd from his regiment to go there and help as nurse, but was soon taken down himself. Is an elderly, sallow-faced, rather gaunt, gray-hair'd man, a widower, with children. He express'd a great desire for good, strong green tea. An excellent lady, Mrs. W., of Washington, soon sent him a package; also a small sum of money. The doctor said give him the tea at pleasure; it lay on the table by his side, and he used it every day. He slept a great deal; could not talk much, as he grew deaf. Occupied bed 15, ward I, Armory. (The same lady above, Mrs. W., sent the men a large package of tobacco.)

J. G. lies in bed 52, ward I; is of company B, 7th Pennsylvania. I gave him a small sum of money, some tobacco, and envelopes. To a man adjoining also gave twenty-five cents; he flush'd in the face when I offer'd it—refused at first, but as I found he had not a cent, and was very fond of having the daily papers to read, I prest it on him. He was evidently very grateful but said little.

J. T. L., of company F., 9th New Hampshire, lies in bed 37, ward I. Is very fond of tobacco. I furnish him some; also with a little money. Has gangrene of the feet; a pretty bad case; will surely have to lose three toes. Is a regular specimen of an old-fashion'd, rude, hearty, New England countryman, impressing me with his likeness to that celebrated singed cat, who was better than she look'd.

Bed 3, ward E, Armory, has a great hankering for pickles, something pungent. After consulting the doctor, I gave him a small bottle of horse-radish; also some apples; also a book. Some of the nurses are excellent. The woman-nurse in this ward I like very much. (Mrs. Wright—a year afterwards I found her in Mansion house hospital, Alexandria—she is a perfect nurse.)

In one bed a young man, Marcus Small, company K, 7th Maine—sick with dysentery and typhoid fever—pretty critical case—I talk with him often—he thinks he will die—looks like it indeed. I write a letter for him home to East Livermore, Maine—I let him talk to me a little, but not much, advise him to keep very quiet—do most of the talking myself—stay quite a while with him, as he holds on to my hand—talk to him in a cheering, but slow, low and measured manner—talk about his furlough, and going home as soon as he is able to travel.

Thomas Lindly, 1st Pennsylvania cavalry, shot very badly through the foot—poor young man, he suffers horribly, has to be constantly dosed with morphine, his face ashy and glazed, bright young eyes—I give him a large handsome apple, lay it in sight, tell him to have it roasted in the morning, as he generally feels easier then, and can eat a little breakfast, I write two letters for him.

Opposite, an old Quaker lady is sitting by the side of her son, Amer Moore, 2d U.S. artillery—shot in the head two weeks since, very low, quite rational—from hips down paralyzed—he will surely die. I speak a very few words to him every day and evening—he answers pleasantly—wants nothing—(he told me soon after he came about his home affairs, his mother had been an invalid, and he fear'd to let her know his condition.) He died soon after she came.

MY PREPARATIONS FOR VISITS

In my visits to the hospitals I found it was in the simple matter of personal presence, and emanating ordinary cheer and magnetism, that

I succeeded and help'd more than by medical nursing, or delicacies, or gifts of money, or anything else. During the war I possess'd the perfection of physical health. My habit, when practicable, was to prepare for starting out on one of those daily or nightly tours of from a couple to four or five hours, by fortifying myself with previous rest, the bath, clean clothes, a good meal, and as cheerful an a appearance as possible.

## AMBULANCE PROCESSIONS

*June 25, Sundown.*—As I sit writing this paragraph I see a train of about thirty huge four-horse wagons, used as ambulances, fill'd with wounded, passing up Fourteenth street, on their way, probably, to Columbian, Carver, and mount Pleasant hospitals. This is the way the men come in now, seldom in small numbers, but almost always in these long, sad processions. Through the past winter, while our army lay opposite Fredericksburgh, the like strings of ambulances were of frequent occurrence along Seventh street, passing slowly up from the steamboat wharf, with loads from Aquia creek.

## BAD WOUNDS—THE YOUNG

The soldiers are nearly all young men, and far more American than is generally supposed—I should say nine-tenths are native-born. Among the arrivals from Chancellorsville I find a large proportion of Ohio, Indiana, and Illinois men. As usual, there are all sorts of wounds. Some of the men fearfully burnt from the explosions of artillery caissons. One ward has a long row of officers, some with ugly hurts. Yesterday was perhaps worse than usual. Amputations are going on—the attendants are dressing wounds. As you pass by, you must be on your guard where you look. I saw the other day a gentleman, a visitor apparently from curiosity, in one of the wards, stop and turn a moment to look at an awful wound they were probing. He turn'd pale, and in a moment more he had fainted away and fallen on the floor.

## ABRAHAM LINCOLN

*August 12th.*—I see the President almost every day, as I happen to live where he passes to or from his lodgings out of town. He never sleeps at the White House during the hot season, but has quarters at a healthy location some three miles north of the city, the Soldiers' home, a United States military establishment. I saw him this morning about 8½ coming to business, riding on Vermont avenue, near L street. He always has a company of twenty-five or thirty cavalry, with sabres drawn and held upright over their shoulders. They say this guard was against his personal wish, but he let his counselors have their way. The party makes no great show in uniform or horses. Mr. Lincoln on the saddle generally rides a good-sized, easy-going gray horse, is dress'd in plain black, somewhat rusty and dusty, wears a black stiff hat, and looks about as ordinary in attire, &c., as the commonest man. A lieutenant, with yellow straps, rides at his left, and following behind, two by two, come the cavalry men, in their yellow-striped jackets. They are generally going at a slow trot, as that is the pace set them by the one they wait upon. The sabres and accoutrements clank, and the entirely unornamental *cortége* as it trots towards Lafayette square arouses no sensation) only some curious stranger stops and gazes. I see very plainly Abraham Lincoln's dark brown face, with the deep-cut lines, the eyes, always to me with a deep latent sadness in the expression. We have got so that we exchange bows, and very cordial ones. Sometimes the President goes and comes in an open barouche. The cavalry always accompany him, with drawn sabres. Often I notice as he goes out evenings—and sometimes in the morning, when he returns early—he turns off and halts at the large and handsome residence of the Secretary of War, on K street, and holds conference there. If in his barouche I can see from my window he does not alight, but sits in his vehicle, and Mr. Stanton comes out to attend him. Sometimes one of his sons, a boy of ten or twelve, accompanies him, riding at his right on a pony. Earlier in the summer I occasionally saw the President and his wife, toward the latter part of the afternoon, out in a barouche, on a pleasure ride through the city. Mrs. Lincoln was dress'd in complete black, with a long crape veil. The equipage is of the plainest kind, only two horses, and they nothing extra. They pass'd me once very close, and I saw the

President in the face fully, as they were moving slowly, and his look, though abstracted, happen'd to be directed steadily in my eye. He bow'd and smiled, but far beneath his smile I noticed well the expression I have alluded to. None of the artists or pictures has caught the deep, though subtle and in direct expression of this man's face. There is something else there. One of the great portrait painters of two or three centuries ago is needed.

## HOSPITALS ENSEMBLE

*Aug., Sep., and Oct., '63.*—I am in the habit of going to all and to Fairfax seminary, Alexandria, and over Long bridge to the great Convalescent camp. The journals publish a regular directory of them— a long list. As a specimen of almost any one of the larger of these hospitals, fancy to yourself a space of three to twenty acres of ground, on which are group'd ten or twelve very large wooden barracks, with, perhaps, a dozen or twenty, and sometimes more than that number, small buildings, capable altogether of accommodating from five hundred to a thousand or fifteen hundred persons. Sometimes these wooden barracks or wards, each of them perhaps from a hundred to a hundred and fifty feet long, are rang'd in a straight row, evenly fronting the street; others are plann'd so as to form an immense V; and others again are ranged around a hollow square. They make altogether a huge cluster, with the additional tents, extra wards for contagious diseases, guardhouses, sutler's stores, chaplain's house; in the middle will probably be an edifice devoted to the offices of the surgeon in charge and the ward surgeons, principal attaches, clerks, &c. The wards are either letter'd alphabetically, ward G, ward K, or else numerically, 1, 2, 3, &c. Each has its ward surgeon and corps of nurses. Of course, there is, in the aggregate, quite a muster of employés, and over all the surgeon in charge. Here in Washington, when these army hospitals are all fill'd, (as they have been already several times,) they contain a population more numerous in itself than the whole of the Washington of ten or fifteen years ago. Within sight of the capitol, as I write, are some thirty or forty such collections, at times holding from fifty to seventy thousand men. Looking from any eminence and studying the topography in my rambles, I use them as landmarks. Through the rich August verdure of the trees, see that white group of buildings off yonder in the outskirts; then another cluster half a mile to the left of the first; then another a mile to the right, and another a mile beyond, and still another between us and the first. Indeed, we can hardly look in any direction but these dusters are dotting the landscape and environs. That little town as you might suppose it, off there on the brow of a hill is indeed a town, but of wounds, sickness, and death. It is Finley hospital, northeast of the city, on Kendall green, as it used to be call'd. That other is Campbell hospital. Both are large establishments. I have known these two alone to have from two thousand to twenty five hundred inmates. Then there is Carver hospital, larger still, a wall'd and military city regularly laid out, and guarded by squads of sentries. Again, off east, Lincoln hospital, a still larger one; and half a mile further Emory hospital. Still sweeping the eye around down the river toward Alexandria, we see, to the right, the locality where the Convalescent camp stands, with its five, eight, or sometimes ten thousand inmates. Even all these are but a portion. The Harewood, Mount Pleasant, Armory-square, Judiciary hospitals, are some of the rest, and all large collections.

## A SILENT NIGHT RAMBLE

*October 20th.*—Tonight, after leaving the hospital at 10 o'clock, (I had been on self-imposed duty some five hours, pretty closely confined,) I wander'd a long time around Washington. The night was sweet, very clear, sufficiently cool, a voluptuous half-moon, slightly golden, the space near it of a transparent blue-gray tinge. I walk'd up Pennsylvania avenue, and then to Seventh street, and a long while around the Patent-office. Somehow it look'd rebukefully strong, majestic, there in the delicate moonlight. The sky, the planets, the constellations all so bright, so calm, so expressively silent, so soothing, after those hospital scenes. I wander'd to and fro till the moist moon set, long after midnight.

## SPIRITUAL CHARACTERS AMONG THE SOLDIERS

Every now and then, in hospital or camp, there are beings I meet—specimens of unworldliness, disinterestedness, and animal purity and heroism—perhaps some unconscious Indianian, or from Ohio or Tennessee—on whose birth the calmness of heaven seems to have descended, and whose gradual growing up, whatever the circumstances of work-life or change, or hardship, or small or no education that attended it, the power of a strange spiritual sweetness, fibre and inward health, have also attended. Something veil'd and abstracted is often a part of the manners of these beings. I have met them, I say, not seldom in the army, in camp, and in the hospitals. The Western regiments contain many of them. They are often young men, obeying the events and occasions about them marching, soldiering, fighting, foraging, cooking, working on farms or at some trade before the war—unaware of their own nature, (as to that, who is aware of his own nature?) their companions only understanding that they are different from the rest, more silent, "something odd about them," and apt to go off and meditate and muse in solitude.

## HOSPITAL PERPLEXITY

To add to other troubles, amid the confusion of this great army of sick, it is almost impossible for a stranger to find any friend or relative, unless he has the patient's specific address to start upon. Besides the directory printed in the newspapers here, there are one or two general directories of the hospitals kept at provost's headquarters, but they are nothing like complete; they are never up to date, and, as things are, with the daily streams of coming and going and changing, cannot be. I have known cases, for instance such as a farmer coming here from northern New York to find a wounded brother, faithfully hunting round for a week, and then compell'd to leave and go home without getting any trace of him. When he got home he found a letter from the brother giving the right address.

## DOWN AT THE FRONT

CULPEPPER, VA., *Feb. '64.*—Here I am pretty well down toward the extreme front. Three or four days ago General S. who is now in chief command, (I believe Meade is absent, sick,) moved a strong force southward from camp as if intending business. They went to the Rapidan; there has since been some manœuvring and a little fighting, but nothing of consequence. The telegraphic accounts given Monday morning last, make entirely too much of it, I should say. What General S. intended we here know not, but we trust in that competent commander. We were somewhat excited, (but not so very much either,) on Sunday, during the day and night, as orders were sent out to pack up and harness, and be ready to evacuate, to fall back towards Washington. But I was very sleepy and went to bed. Some tremendous shouts arousing me during the night, I went forth and found it was from the men above mention'd, who were returning. I talk'd with some of the men; as usual I found them full of gayety, endurance, and many fine little outshows, the signs of the most excellent good manliness of the world. It was a curious sight to see those shadowy columns moving through the night. I stood unobserv'd in the darkness and watch'd them long. The mud was very deep. The men had their usual burdens, overcoats, knapsacks, guns and blankets. Along and along they filed by me, with often a laugh, a song, a cheerful word, but never once a murmur. It may have been odd, but I never before so realized the majesty and reality of the American people *en masse*. It fell upon me like a great awe. The strong ranks moved neither fast nor slow. They had march'd seven or eight miles already through the slipping unctuous mud. The brave First corps stopt here. The equally brave Third corps moved on to Brandy station. The famous Brooklyn 14th are here, guarding the town. You see their red legs actively moving everywhere. Then they have a theatre of their own here. They give musical performances, nearly everything done capitally. Of course the audience is a jam. It is good sport to attend one of these entertainments of the 14th. I like to look around at the soldiers, and the general collection in front of the curtain, more than the scene on the stage.

• • •

### PAYING THE BOUNTIES

One of the things to note here now is the arrival of the paymaster with his strong box, and the payment of bounties to veterans reenlisting. Major H. is here today, with a small mountain of greenbacks, rejoicing the hearts of the 2d division of the First corps, In the midst of a rickety shanty, behind a little table, sit the major and clerk Eldridge, with the rolls before them, and much moneys. A re-enlisted man gets in cash about $200 down, (and heavy instalments following, as the paydays arrive, one after another.) The show of the men crowding around is quite exhilarating; I like to stand and look. They feel elated, their pockets full, and the ensuing furlough, the visit home. It is a scene of sparkling eyes and flush'd cheeks. The soldier has many gloomy and harsh experiences and this makes up for some of them. Major H. is order'd to pay first all the re-enlisted men of the First corps their bounties and back pay, and then the rest. You hear the peculiar sound of the rustling of the new and crisp greenbacks by the hour, through the nimble fingers of the major and my friend clerk E.

### SUMMER OF 1864

I am back again in Washington, on my regular daily and nightly rounds. Of course there are many specialties. Dotting a ward here and there are always cases of poor fellows, long-suffering under obstinate wounds, or weak and dishearten'd from typhoid fever, or the like; mark'd cases, needing special and sympathetic nourishment. These I sit down and either talk to, or silently cheer them up. They always like it hugely, (and so do I.) Each case has its peculiarities, and needs some new adaptation. I have learnt to thus conform—learnt a good deal of hospital wisdom. Some of the poor young chaps, away from home for the first time in their lives, hunger and thirst for affection; this is sometimes the only thing that will reach their condition. The men like to have a pencil, and something to write in. I have given them cheap pocket-diaries, and almanacs for 1864, interleav'd with blank paper. For reading I generally have some old pictorial magazines or story papers—they are always acceptable. Also the morning or evening papers of the day. The best books I do not give, but lend to read through the wards, and then take them to others, and, so on; they are very punctual about returning the books. In these wards, or on the field, as I thus continue to go round, I have come to adapt myself to each emergency, after its kind or call, however trivial, however solemn, every one justified and made real under its circumstances—not only visits and cheering talk and little gifts—not only washing and dressing wounds, (I have some cases where the patient is unwilling any one should do this but me)— but passages from the Bible, expounding them, prayer at the bedside, explanations of doctrine, &c. (I think I see my friends smiling at this confession, but I was never more in earnest in my life.) In camp and everywhere, I was in the habit of reading or giving recitations to the men. They were very fond of it, and liked declamatory poetical pieces. We would gather in a large group by ourselves, after supper, and spend the time in such readings, or in talking, and occasionally by an amusing game called the game of twenty questions.

### DEATH OF A HERO

I wonder if I could ever convey to another—to you, for instance, reader dear—the tender and terrible realities of such cases, (many, many happen'd,) as the one I am now going to mention, Stewart C. Glover, company E, 5th Wisconsin—was wounded May 5, in one of those fierce tussles of the Wilderness—died May 21—aged about 20. He was a small and beardless young man—a splendid soldier—in fact almost an ideal American, of his age. He had serv'd nearly three years, and would have been entitled to his discharge in a few days. He was in Hancock's corps. The fighting had about ceas'd for the day, and the general commanding the brigade rode by and call'd for volunteers to bring in the wounded. Glover responded among the first—went out gayly—but while in the act of bearing in a wounded sergeant to our lines, was shot in the knee by a rebel sharpshooter; consequence, amputation and death. He had resided with his father, John Glover, an aged and feeble man, in Batavia, Genesee county, N. Y., but was at school in Wisconsin, after the war broke out, and there enlisted—soon took to soldier-life, liked it, was very manly, was belov'd by officers and comrades. He kept a little diary, like so many of the soldiers. On the day of his death he wrote the following in it, *to-day the doctor says I must die—all is over with me—ah, so young to die.*. On another blank leaf he pencill'd to his brother, *dear brother Thomas I have been brave but wicked—pray for me.*

## HOSPITAL SCENES.—INCIDENTS

It is Sunday afternoon, middle of summer, hot and oppressive, and very silent through the ward. I am taking care of a critical case, now lying in a half lethargy. Near where I sit is a suffering rebel, from the 8th Louisiana; his name is Irving. He has been here a long time, badly wounded, and lately had his leg amputated; it is not doing very well. Right opposite me is a sick soldier-boy, laid down with his clothes on, sleeping, looking much wasted, his pallid face on his arm. I see by the yellow trimming on his jacket that he is a cavalry boy. I step softly over and find by his card that he is named William Cone, of the 1st Maine cavalry, and his folks live in Skowhegan.

*Ice Cream Treat.*—One hot day toward the middle of June, I gave the inmates of Carver hospital a general ice cream treat, purchasing a large quantity, and, under convoy of the doctor or head nurse, going around personally through the wards to see to its distribution.

*An Incident.*—In one of the fights before Atlanta, a rebel soldier, of large size, evidently a young man, was mortally wounded top of the head, so that the brains partially exuded. He lived three days, lying on his back on the spot where he first dropt. He dug with his heel in the ground during that time a hole big enough to put in a couple of ordinary knapsacks. He just lay there in the open air, and with little intermission kept his heel going night and day. Some of our soldiers then moved him to a house, but he died in a few minutes.

*Another.*—After the battles at Columbia, Tennessee, where we repuls'd about a score of vehement rebel charges, they left a great many wounded on the ground, mostly within our range. Whenever any of these wounded attempted to move away by any means, generally by crawling off, our men without exception brought them down by a bullet. They let none crawl away, no matter what his condition.

### UNION PRISONERS SOUTH

Michael Stansbury, 48 years of age, a sea-faring man, a southerner by birth and raising, formerly captain of U. S. fight ship Long Shoal, station'd at Long Shoal point, Pamlico sound—though a southerner, a firm Union man—was captur'd Feb. 17, 1863, and has been nearly two years in the Confederate prisons; was at one time order'd releas'd by Governor Vance, but a rebel officer rearrested him; then sent on to Richmond for exchange—but instead of being exchanged was sent down (as a southern citizen, not a soldier,) to Salisbury, N. C., where he remain'd until lately, when he escap'd among the exchang'd by assuming the name of a dead soldier, and coming up via Wilmington with the rest. Was about sixteen months in Salisbury. Subsequent to October, '64 there were about 11,000 Union prisoners in the stockade; about 100 of them southern unionists, 200 U. S. deserters. During the past winter 1500 of the prisoners, to save their lives, join'd the confederacy, on condition of being assign'd merely to guard duty. Out of the 11,000 not more than 2500 came out; 500 of these were pitiable, helpless wretches—the rest were in a condition to travel. There were often 60 dead bodies to be buried in the morning; the daily average would be about 40. The regular food was a meal of corn, the cob and husk ground together, and sometimes once a week a ration of sorghum molasses. A diminutive ration of meat might possibly come once a month, not oftener. In the stockade, containing the 11,000 men, there was a partial show of tents, not enough for 2000. A large proportion of the men lived in holes in the ground, in the utmost wretchedness. Some froze to death, others had their hands and feet frozen. The rebel guards would occasionally, and on the least pretence, fire into the prison from mere demonism and wantonness. All the horrors that can be named, starvation, lassitude, filth, vermin, despair, swift loss of self-respect, idiocy, insanity, and frequent murder, were there. Stansbury has a wife and child living in Newbern—has written to them from here—is in the U. S. lighthouse employ still—(had been home to Newbern to see his family, and on his return to the ship was captured in his boat.) Has seen men brought there to Salisbury as hearty as you ever see in your life—in a few weeks completely dead gone, much of it from thinking on their condition—hope all gone. Has himself a hard, sad, strangely deaden'd kind of look, as of one chill'd for years in the cold and dark, where his good manly nature had no room to exercise itself.

### A GLIMPSE OF WAR'S HELL-SCENES

In one of the late movements of our troops in the valley, (near Upperville, I think,) a strong force of Moseby's mounted guerillas attack'd a train of wounded, and the guard of cavalry convoying them. The ambulances contain'd about 60 wounded, quite a number of them officers of rank. The rebels were in strength, and the capture of the train and its partial guard after a short snap was effectually accomplish'd. No sooner had our men surrender'd, the rebels instantly commenced robbing the train and murdering their prisoners, even the wounded. Here is the scene or a sample of it, ten minutes after. Among the wounded officers in the ambulances were one, a lieutenant of regulars, and another of higher rank. These two were dragg'd out on the ground on their backs, and were now surrounded by the guerillas, a demoniac crowd, each member of which was stabbing them in different parts of their bodies. One of the officers had his feet pinn'd firmly to the ground by bayonets stuck through them and thrust into the ground. These two officers, as afterwards found on examination, had receiv'd about twenty such thrusts, some of them through the mouth, face, &c. The wounded had all been dragg'd (to give a better chance also for plunder,) out of their wagons; some had been effectually dispatch'd, and their bodies were lying there lifeless and bloody. Others, not yet dead, but horribly mutilated, were moaning or groaning. Of our men who surrender'd, most had been thus maim'd or slaughter'd.

At this instant a force of our cavalry, who had been following the train at some interval, charged suddenly upon the secesh captors, who proceeded at once to make the best escape they could. Most of them got away, but we gobbled two officers and seventeen men, in the very acts just described. The sight was one which admitted of little discussion, as may be imagined. The seventeen captur'd men and two officers were put under guard for the night, but it was decided there and then that they should die. The next morning the two officers were taken in the town, separate places, put in the centre of the street, and shot. The seventeen men were taken to an open ground, a little one side. They were placed in a hollow square, half-encompass'd by two of our cavalry regiments, one of which regiments had three days before found the bloody corpses of three of their men hamstrung and hung up by the heels to limbs of trees by Moseby's guerillas, and the other had not long before had twelve men, after surrendering, shot and then hung by the neck to limbs of trees, and jeering inscriptions pinn'd to the breast of one of the corpses, who had been a sergeant. Those three, and those twelve, had been found, I say, by these environing regiments. Now, with revolvers, they form'd the grim cordon of the seventeen prisoners. The latter were placed in the midst of the hollow square, unfasten'd, and the ironical remark made to them that they were now to be given "a chance for themselves." A few ran for it. But what use? From every side the deadly pills came. In a few minutes the seventeen corpses strew'd the hollow square. I was curious to know whether some of the Union soldiers, some few (some one or two at least of the youngsters,) did not abstain from shooting on the helpless men. Not one. There was no exultation, very little said, almost nothing, yet every man there contributed his shot.

Multiply the above by scores, aye hundreds—verify it in all the forms that different circumstances, individuals, places, could afford—fight it with every lurid passion, the wolf's, the lion's lapping thirst for blood—the passionate, boiling volcanoes of human revenge for comrades, brothers slain—with the light of burning farms, and heaps of smutting, smouldering black embers—and in the human heart everywhere black, worse embers—and you have an inkling of this war.

• • •

## GIFTS—MONEY—DISCRIMINATION

As a very large proportion of the wounded came up from the front without a cent of money in their pockets, I soon discover'd that it was about the best thing I could do to raise their spirits, and show them that somebody cared for them, and practically felt a fatherly or brotherly interest in them, to give them small sums in such cases, using tact and discretion about it. I am regularly supplied with funds for this purpose by good women and men in Boston, Salem, Providence, Brooklyn, and New York. I provide myself with a quantity of bright new ten-cent and five-cent bills, and, when I think it incumbent, I give 25 or 30 cents, or perhaps 50 cents, and occasionally a stiff larger sum to some particular case. As I have started this subject, I take opportunity to ventilate the financial question. My supplies, altogether voluntary, mostly confidential, often seeming quite Providential, were numerous and varied. For instance, there were two distant and wealthy ladies, sisters, who sent regularly, for two years, quite heavy sums, enjoining that their names should be kept secret. The same delicacy was indeed a frequent condition. From several I had *carte blanche.* Many were entire strangers. From these sources, during from two to three years, in the manner described, in the hospitals, I bestowed, as almoner for others, many, many thousands of dollars. I learn'd one thing conclusively— that beneath all the ostensible greed and heartlessness of our times there is no end to the generous benevolence of men and women in the United States, when once sure of their object. Another thing became clear to me—while *cash* is not amiss to bring up the rear, tact and magnetic sympathy and unction are, and ever will be, sovereign still.

## ITEMS FROM MY NOTE BOOKS

Some of the half-eras'd, and not over-legible when made, memoranda of things wanted by one patient or another will convey quite a fair idea. D. S. G., bed 52, wants a good book; has a sore, weak throat; would like some horehound candy; is from New Jersey, 28th regiment. C, H. L., 145th Pennsylvania, lies in bed 6, with jaundice and erysipelas; also wounded; stomach easily nauseated; bring him some oranges, also a little tart jelly; hearty, full-blooded young fellow—(he got better in a few days, and is now home on a furlough.) J. H. G., bed 24, wants an undershirt, drawers, and socks; has not had a change for quite a while; is evidently a neat, clean boy from New England—(I supplied him; also with a comb, toothbrush, and some soap and towels; I noticed afterward he was the cleanest of the whole ward.) Mrs. G., lady-nurse, ward F, wants a bottle of brandy—has two patients imperatively requiring stimulus—low with wounds and exhaustion. (I supplied her with a bottle of first-rate brandy from the Christian commission rooms.)

## A CASE FROM SECOND BULL RUN

Well, poor John Mahay is dead. He died yesterday. His was a painful and long-lingering case, I have been with him at times for the past fifteen months. He belonged to company A, 101st New York, and was shot through the lower region of the abdomen at second Bull Run, August, '62. One scene at his bedside will suffice for the agonies of nearly two years. The bladder had been perforated by a bullet going entirely through him. Not long since I sat a good part of the morning by his bedside, ward E, Armory-square. The water ran out of his eyes from the intense pain, and the muscles of his face were distorted, but he utter'd nothing except a low groan now and then. Hot moist cloths were applied, and reliev'd him somewhat. Poor Mahay, a mere boy in age, but old in misfortune. He never knew the love of parents, was placed in infancy in one of the New York charitable institutions, and subsequently bound out to a tyrannical master in Sullivan county, (the scars of whose cowhide and club remain'd yet on his back.) His wound here was a most disagreeable one, for he was a gentle, cleanly, and affectionate boy. He found friends in his hospital fife, and, indeed, was a universal favorite. He had quite a funeral ceremony.

## ARMY SURGEONS—AID DEFICIENCIES

I must bear my most emphatic testimony to the zeal, manliness, and professional spirit and capacity, generally prevailing among the surgeons, many of them young men, in the hospitals and the army. I will not say much about the exceptions, for they are few; (but I have met some of those few, and very incompetent and airish they were.) I never ceas'd to find the best men, and the hardest and most disinterested workers, among the surgeons in the hospitals. They are full of genius, too. I have seen many hundreds of them and this is my testimony. There are, however, serious deficiencies, wastes, sad want of system, in the commissions, contributions, and in all the voluntary, and, a great part of the governmental nursing, edibles, medicines, stores, &c. (I do not say surgical attendance, because the surgeons cannot do more than human endurance permits.) Whatever puffing accounts there may be in the papers of the North, this is the actual fact. No thorough previous preparation, no system, no foresight, no genius. Always plenty of stores, no doubt, but never where they are needed, and never the proper application. Of all harrowing experiences, none is greater than that of the days following a heavy battle. Scores, hundreds of the noblest men on earth, uncomplaining, lie helpless, mangled, faint, alone, and so bleed to death, or die from exhaustion, either actually untouch'd at all, or merely the laying of them down and leaving them, when there ought to be means provided to save them.

### THE BLUE EVERYWHERE

This city, its suburbs, the capitol, the front of the White House, the places of amusement, the Avenue, and all the main streets, swarm with soldiers this winter, more than ever before. Some are out from the hospitals, some from the neighboring camps, &c. One source or another, they pour plenteously, and make, I should say, the mark'd feature in the human movement and costume-appearance of our national city. Their blue pants and overcoats are everywhere. The dump of crutches is heard up the stairs of the paymasters' offices, and there are characteristic groups around the doors of the same, often waiting long and wearily in the cold. Toward the latter part of the afternoon, you see the furlough'd men, sometimes singly, sometimes in small squads, making their way to the Baltimore depot. At all times, except early in the morning, the patrol detachments are moving around, especially during the earlier hours of evening, examining passes, and arresting all soldiers without them. They do not question the one-legged, or men badly disabled or maim'd, but all others are stopt. They also go around evenings through the auditoriums of the theatres, and make officers and all show their passes, or other authority, for being there.

## A MODEL HOSPITAL

*Sunday, January 29th, 1865.*—Have been in Armory-square this afternoon. The wards are very comfortable, new floors and plaster walls, and models of neatness. I am not sure but this is a model hospital after all, in important respects. I found several sad cases of old lingering wounds. One Delaware soldier, William H. Millis, from Bridgeville, whom I had been with after the battles of the Wilderness, last May, where he receiv'd a very bad wound in the chest, with another in the left arm, and whose case was serious (pneumonia had set in) all last June and July, I now find well enough to do light duty. For three weeks at the time mention'd he just hovered between life and death.

## BOYS IN THE ARMY

As I walk'd home about sunset, I saw in Fourteenth street a very young soldier, thinly clad, standing near the house I was about to enter. I stopt a moment in front of the door and call him to me. I knew that an old Tennessee regiment, and also an Indiana regiment, were temporarily stopping in new barracks, near Fourteenth street. This boy I found belonged to the Tennessee regiment. But I could hardly believe he carried a musket. He was but 15 years old, yet had been twelve months a soldier, and had borne his part in several battles, even historic ones. I ask'd him if he did not suffer from the cold, and if he had no overcoat. No, he did not suffer from cold, and had no overcoat, but could draw one whenever he wish'd. His father was dead, and his mother living in some part of East Tennessee; all the men were from that part of the country. The next forenoon I saw the Tennessee and Indiana regiments marching down the Avenue. My boy was with the former, stepping along with the rest. There were many other boys no older. I stood and watch'd them as they tramp'd along with slow, strong, heavy, regular steps. There did not appear to be a man over 30 years of age, and a large proportion were from 15 to perhaps 22 or 23. They had all the look of veterans, worn, stain'd, impassive, and a certain unbent, lounging gait, carrying in addition to their regular arms and knapsacks, frequently a frying-pan, broom, &c. They were all of pleasant physiognomy; no refinement, nor blanch'd with intellect, but as my eye pick'd them, moving along, rank by rank, there did not seem to be a single repulsive, brutal or markedly stupid face among them.

### BURIAL OF A LADY NURSE

Here is an incident just occurr'd in one of the hospitals, A lady named Miss or Mrs. Billings, who has long been a practical friend of soldiers, and nurse in the army, and had become attached to it in a way that no one can realize but him or her who has had experience, was taken sick, early this winter, linger'd some time, and finally died in the hospital. It was her request that she should be buried among the soldiers, and after the military method. This request was fully carried out. Her coffin was carried to the grave by soldiers, with the usual was at escort, buried, and a salute fired over the grave. This was at Annapolis a few days since.

### FEMALE NURSES FOR SOLDIERS

There are many women in one position or another, among the hospitals, mostly as nurses here in Washington, and, among the military stations; quite a number of them young ladies acting as volunteers. They are a help in certain ways, and deserve to be mention'd with respect. Then it remains to be distinctly said that few or no young ladies, under the resistible conventions of society, answer the practical requirements of nurses for soldiers. Middle-aged or healthy and good condition'd elderly women, mothers of children, are always best. Many of the wounded must be handled. A hundred things which cannot be gainsay'd, must occur and must be done. The presence of a good middle-aged or elderly woman, the magnetic touch of hands, the expressive features of the mother, the silent soothing of her presence, her words, her knowledge and privileges arrived at only through having had children, are precious and final qualifications. It is a natural faculty that is required; it is not merely having a genteel young woman at a table in a ward. One of the finest nurses I met was a red-faced illiterate old Irish woman; I have seen her take the poor wasted naked boys so tenderly up in her arms. There are plenty of excellent clean old black women that would make tip-top nurses.

### SOUTHERN ESCAPEES

*Feb. 23, '65.*—I saw a large procession of young men from the rebel army, (deserters they are call'd, but the usual meaning of the word does not apply to them,) passing the Avenue today. There were nearly 200, come up yesterday by boat from James river. I stood and watch'd them as they shuffled along, in a slow, tired, worn sort of way; a large proportion of light-hair'd, blonde, light gray-eyed young men among them, Their costumes had a dirt-stain'd uniformity; most had been originally gray; some had articles of our uniform, pants on one, vest or coat on another; I think they were mostly Georgia and North Carolina boys. They excited little or no attention. As I stood quite close to them, several good looking enough youths, (but O what a tale of misery their appearance told,) nodded or just spoke to me, without doubt divining pity and fatherliness out of my face, for my heart was full enough of it. Several of the couples trudg'd along with their arms about each other, some probably brothers, as if they were afraid they might somehow get separated. They nearly all look'd what one might call simple, yet intelligent, too. Some had pieces of old carpet, some blankets, and others old bags around their shoulders. Some of them here and there had faces, still it was a procession of misery. The two hundred had with them about half a dozen arm'd guards. Along this week I saw some such procession, more or less in numbers, every day, as they were brought up by the boat. The government does what it can for them, and sends them north and west.

*Feb. 27.*—Some three or four hundred more escapees from confederate army came up on the boat. As the day has been very pleasant indeed, (after a long spell of bad weather,) have been wandering around a good deal, without any other object than to be out-doors and enjoy it; have met these escaped men in all directions. Their apparel is the same ragged, long-worn motley as before described. I talk'd with a number of the men. Some are quite bright and stylish, for all their poor clothes—walking with an air, wearing their old head-coverings on one side, quite saucily. I find the old, unquestionable proofs, as all along the past four years, of the unscrupulous tyranny exercised by the secession government in conscripting the common people by absolute force everywhere, and paying no attention whatever to the men's time being up—keeping them in military service just the same. One gigantic young fellow, a Georgian, at least six feet three inches high, broad-sized in proportion, attired in the dirtiest, drab, well-smear'd rags, tied with strings, his trousers at the knees, all strips and streamers, was complacently standing eating. some bread and meat. He appear'd contented enough. Then a few minutes after I saw him slowly walking along. It was plain he did not take anything to heart.

*Feb. 28.*—As I pass'd the military headquarters of the city, not far from the President's house, I stopt to interview some of the crowd of escapees who were lounging there. In appearance they were the same as previously mention'd. Two of them, one about 17, and the other perhaps 25 or '6 I talk'd with some time. They were from North Carolina, born and rais'd there, and had folks there. The elder had been in the rebel service four years. He was first conscripted for two years. He was then kept arbitrarily in the ranks. This is the case with a large proportion of the secession army. There was nothing downcast in these young men's manners; the younger had been soldiering about a year; he was conscripted there were six brothers (all the boys of the family) in the army, part of them as conscripts, part as volunteers; three had been kill'd; one had escaped about four months ago, and now this one had got away; he was a pleasant and well-talking lad, with the peculiar North Carolina idiom (not at all disagreeable to my cars.) He and the elder one were of the same company, and escaped together—and wish'd to remain together. They thought of getting transportation away to Missouri, and working there; but were not sure it was judicious. I advised them rather to go to some of the directly northern States, and get farm work for the present. The younger had made six dollars on the boat, with some tobacco he brought; he had three and a half left. The elder had nothing; I gave him a trifle. Soon after, met John Wormley, 9th Alabama, a West Tennessee rais'd boy, parents both dead—had the look of one for a long time on short allowance—said very little—chew'd tobacco at a fearful rate, spitting in proportion—large clear dark-brown eyes, very fine—didn't know what to make of me—told me at last he wanted much to get some clean underclothes, and a pair of decent pants. Didn't care about coat or hat fixings. Wanted a chance to wash himself well, and put on the underclothes. I had the very great pleasure of helping him to accomplish all those wholesome designs.

*March 1st.*—Plenty more butternut or clay-color'd escapees every day. About 160 came in today, a large portion South Carolinians. They generally take the oath of allegiance, and are sent north, west, or extreme southwest if they wish. Several of them told me that the desertions in their army, of men going home, leave or no leave, are far more numerous than their desertions to our side. I saw a very forlorn-looking squad of about a hundred, late this afternoon, on their way to the Baltimore depot.

## THE CAPITOL BY GAS-LIGHT

Tonight I have been wandering awhile in the capitol, which is all lit up. The illuminated rotunda looks fine. I like to stand aside and look a long, long while, up at the dome; it comforts me somehow. The House and Senate were both in session till very late. I look'd in upon them, but only a few moments; they were hard at work on tax and appropriation bills. I wander'd through the long and rich corridors and apartments under the Senate; an old habit of mine, former winters, and now more satisfaction than ever. Not many persons down there, occasionally a flitting figure in the distance.

## THE INAUGURATION

*March 4.*—The President very quietly rode down to the capitol in his own carriage, by himself, on a sharp trot, about noon, either because he wish'd to be on hand to sign bills, or to get rid of marching in line with the absurd procession, the muslin temple of liberty, and pasteboard monitor. I saw him on his return, at three o'clock, after the performance was over. He was in his plain two-horse barouche, and look'd very much worn and tired; the lines, indeed, of vast responsibilities, intricate questions, and demands of life and death, cut deeper than ever upon his dark brown face; yet all the old goodness, tenderness, sadness, and canny shrewdness, underneath the furrows. (I never see that man without feeling that he is one to become personally attach'd to, for his combination of purest, heartiest tenderness, and native western form of manliness.) By his side sat his little boy, of ten years. There were no soldiers, only a lot of civilians on horse-back, with huge yellow scarfs over their shoulders, riding around the carriage. (At the inauguration four years ago, he rode down and back again surrounded by a dense mass of arm'd cavalrymen eight deep, with drawn sabres; and there were sharpshooters station'd at every corner on the route.) I ought to make mention of the closing levee of Saturday night last. Never before was such a compact jam in front of the White House—all the grounds fill'd, and away out to the spacious sidewalks. I was there, as I took a notion to go—was in the rush inside with the crowd—surged along the passageways, the blue and other rooms, and through the great east room. Crowds of country people, some very funny. Fine music from the Marine band, off in a side place. I saw Mr. Lincoln, drest all in black, with white kid gloves and a claw-hammer coat, receiving, as in duty bound, shaking hands, looking very disconsolate, and as if he would give anything to be somewhere else.

## INAUGURATION BALL

*March 6.*—I have been up to look at the dance and supper-rooms, for the inauguration ball at the Patent-office; and I could not help thinking, what a different scene they presented to my view a while since, fill'd with a crowded mass of the worst wounded of the war, brought in from second Bull Run, Antietam, and Fredericksburgh. To-night, beautiful women, perfumes, the violins' sweetness, the polka and the waltz; then the amputation, the blue face, the groan, the glassy eye of the dying, the clotted rag, the odor of wounds and blood, and many a mother's son amid stranger, passing away untended there, (for the crowd of the badly hurt was great, and much for nurse to do, and much for surgeon.)

### SCENE AT THE CAPITOL

I must mention a strange scene at the capitol, the hall of Representatives, the morning of Saturday last, (March 4th.) The day just dawn'd, but in half-darkness, everything dim, leaden, and soaking. In that dim light, the members nervous from the long drawn duty, exhausted, some asleep, and many half asleep. The gas-light, mix'd with the dingy day-break, produced an unearthly effect. The poor little sleepy, stumbling pages, the smell of the hall, the members with heads leaning on their desks, the sounds of the voices speaking, with unusual intonations—the general moral atmosphere also of the close of this important session—the strong hope that the war is approaching its close—the tantalizing dread lest the hope may be a false one—the grandeur of the hall itself, with its effect of vast shadows up toward the panels and spaces over the galleries—all made a mark'd combination.

In the midst of this, with the suddenness of a thunderbolt, burst one of the most angry and crashing storms of rain and hail ever heard. It beat like a deluge on the heavy glass roof of the hall, and the wind literally howl'd and roar'd. For a moment, (and no wonder,) the nervous and sleeping Representatives were thrown into confusion. The slumberers awaked with fear, some started for the doors, some look'd up with blanch'd cheeks and lips to the roof, and the little pages began to cry; it was a scene. But it was over almost as soon as the drowsied men were actually awake. They recover'd themselves, the storm raged on, beating, dashing, and with loud noises at times. But the House went ahead with its business then, I think, as calmly and with as much deliberation as at any time in its career. Perhaps the shock did it good. (One Congress, of both the Houses, that if the flat routine of their duties should ever be broken in upon by some great emergency involving real danger, and calling for first-class personal qualities, those qualities would be found generally forthcoming, and from men not now credited with them.)

## A YANKEE ANTIQUE

*March 27, 1865.*—Sergeant Calvin F. Harlowe, company C, 29th Massachusetts, 3d brigade, 1st division, Ninth corps—a mark'd sample of heroism and death, (some may say bravado, but I say *heroism*, of grandest, oldest order)—in the late attack by the rebel troops, and temporary capture by them, of fort Steadman, at night. The fort was surprised at dead of night. Suddenly awaken'd from their sleep, and rushing from their tents. Harlowe, with others, found himself in the hands of the secesh—they demanded his surrender—he answer'd, *Never while I live.* (Of course it was useless. The others surrender'd; the odds were too great.) Again he was ask'd to yield, this time by a rebel captain. Though surrounded, and quite calm, he again refused, call'd sternly to his comrades to fight on, and himself attempted to do so. the rebel captain then shot him—but at the same instant he shot the captain. Both fell together mortally wounded. Harlowe died almost instantly. The rebels were driven out in a very short time. The body was buried next day, but soon taken up and sent home, (Plymouth county, Mass.) Harlowe was only 22 years of age—was a tall, slim, dark-hair'd, blue-eyed young man—had come out originally with the 29th; and that is the way he met his death, after four years' campaign. He was in the Seven Days fight before Richmond, in second Bull Run, Antietam, first Fredericksburgh, Vicksburgh, Jackson, Wilderness, and the campaigns following—was as good a soldier as ever wore the blue, and every old officer in the regiment will bear that testimony. Though so young, and in a common rank, he had a spirit as resolute and brave as any hero in the books, ancient or modern—It was too great to say the words "I surrender"—and so he died. (When I think of such things, knowing them well, all the vast and complicated events of the war, on which history dwells and make its volumes, fall aside, and for the moment at any rate I see nothing but young Calvin Harlowe's figure in the night, disdaining to surrender.)

## WOUNDS AND DISEASES

The war is over, but the hospitals are fuller than ever, from former and current cases. A large majority of the wounds are in the arms and legs. But there is every kind of wound, in every part of the body. I should say of the sick, from my observation, that the prevailing maladies are typhoid fever and the camp fevers generally, diarrhœa, catarrhal affections and bronchitis, rheumatism, and pneumonia. These forms of sickness lead; all the rest follow. There are twice as many sick as there are wounded. The deaths range from seven to ten per cent of those under treatment.

## DEATH OF PRESIDENT LINCOLN

*April 16, '65.*—I find in my notes of the time, this passage on the death of Abraham Lincoln: He leaves for America's history and biography, so far, not only its most dramatic reminiscence—he leaves, in my opinion, the greatest, best, most characteristic, artistic, moral personality. Not but that he had faults, and show'd them in the Presidency, but honesty, goodness, shrewdness, conscience, and (a new virtue, unknown to other lands, and hardly yet known here, but the foundation and tie of all, as the future will grandly develop,) UNIONISM, in its truest and amplest sense, form'd the hard-pan of his character. These he seal'd with his life. The tragic splendor of his death, purging, illuminating all, throws round his form, his head, an aureole that will remain and will grow brighter through time, while history lives, and love of country lasts. By many has this Union been help'd; but if one name, one man, must be pick'd out, he, most of all, is the conservator of it, to the future. He was assassinated—but the Union is not assassinated—*ça ira!* One falls, and another falls. The soldier drops, sinks like a wave—but the ranks of the ocean eternally press on. Death does its work, obliterates a hundred, a thousand—President, general, captain, private—but the Nation is immortal.

### RELEAS'D UNION PRISONERS FROM SOUTH

The releas'd prisoners of war are now coming up from the southern prisons. I have seen a number of them. The sight is worse than any sight of battle-fields, or any collection of wounded, even the bloodiest. There was, (as a sample,) one large boat load, of several hundreds, brought about the 25th, to Annapolis; and out of the whole number only three individuals were able to walk from the boat. The rest were carried ashore and laid down in one place or another. Can those be *men*—those little livid brown, ash-streak'd monkey-looking dwarfs?— are they really not mummied, dwindled corpses? They lay there, most of them, quite still, but with a horrible look in their eyes and skinny lips (often with not enough flesh on the lips to cover their teeth.) Probably no more appalling sight was ever seen on this earth. (There are deeds, crimes, that may be forgiven; but this is not among them. It steeps its perpetrators in blackest, escapeless, endless damnation. Over 50,000 have been compell'd to die the death of starvation—reader, did you ever try to realize what *starvation* actually is?—in those prisons— and in a land of plenty.) An indescribable meanness, tyranny, aggra- vating course of insults, almost incredible—was evidently the rule of treatment through all the southern military prisons. The dead there are not to be pitied as much as some of the living that come from there— if they can be call'd living—many of them are mentally imbecile, and will never recuperate.

### DEATH OF A PENNSYLVANIA SOLDIER

*Frank H. Irwin, company E, 93d Pennsylvania—died May 1, '65—My letter to his mother.*—No doubt you and Frank's friend have heard the sad fact of his death in hospital here, through his uncle, or the lady from Baltimore, who took his things. (I have not seen them, only heard of them visiting Frank.) I will write you a few lines—as a casual friend that sat by his death-bed. Your son, corporal Frank H. Irwin, was

wounded near fort Fisher, Virginia, March 25th, 1865—the wound was
in the left knee, pretty bad. He was sent up to Washington, was receiv'd
in ward C, Armory-square hospital, March 28th—the wound became
worse, and on the 4th of April the leg was amputated a little above the
knee—the operation was perform'd by Dr. Bliss, one of the best surgeons in the army—he did the whole operation himself—there was a
good deal of bad matter gather'd—the bullet was found in the knee.
For a couple of weeks afterwards he was doing pretty well. I visited
and sat by him frequently, as he was fond of having me. The last ten
or twelve days of April I saw that his case was critical. He previously
had some fever, with cold spells. The last week in April he was much
of the time flighty—but always mild and gentle. He died first of May.
The actual cause of death was pyæmia (the absorption of the matter in
the system instead of its discharge.) Frank, as far as I saw, had everything requisite in surgical treatment, nursing &c. He had watches much
of the time. He was so good and well-behaved and affectionate, I
myself liked him very much. I was in the habit of coming in afternoons
and sitting by him, and soothing him, and he liked to have me—liked
to put his arm out and lay his hand on my knee—would keep it so a
long while. Toward the last he was more restless and flighty at night—
often fancied himself with his regiment—by his talk sometimes seem'd
as if his feelings were hurt by being blamed by his officers for something he was entirely innocent of—said, "I never in my life was though
capable of such a thing, and never was." At other times he would fancy
himself talking as it seem'd to children or such like, his relatives I suppose, and giving them good advice; would talk to them a long while.
All the time he was out of his head not one single bad word or idea
escaped him. It was remark'd that many a man's conversation in his
senses was not half as good as Frank's delirium. He seem'd quite willing to die—he had become very weak and had suffer'd a good deal, and
was perfectly resign'd, poor boy. I do not know his past life, but I feel
as if it must have been good. At any rate what I saw of him here, under
the most trying circumstances, with a painful wound, and among
strangers. I can say that he behaved so brave, so composed, and so

sweet and affectionate, it could be surpass'd. And now like many other noble and good men, after serving his country as a soldier, he has yielded up his young life at the very outset in her service. Such things are gloomy—yet there is a text, "God doeth all things well"—the meaning of which, after due time, appears to the soul.

I thought perhaps a few words, though from a stranger, about your son, from one who was with him at the last, might be worth while— for I loved the young man, though I but saw him immediately to lose him. I am merely a friend visiting the hospitals occasionally to cheer the wounded and sick.

W.W.

### THE ARMIES RETURNING

*May 7.—Sunday.*—To-day as I was walking a mile or tow south of Alexandria, I fell in with several large squads of the returning Western army (*Sherman's men* as they call'd themselves) about a thousand in all, the largest portion of them half sick, some convalescents, on their way to a hospital camp. These fragmentary excerpts, with the unmistakable Western physiognomy and idioms, crawling along slowly— after a great campaign, blown this way, as it were, out of their latitude—I mark'd with curiosity, and talk'd with off and on for over an hour. Here and there was one very sick; but all were able to walk, except some of the last, who had given out and were seated on the ground, faint and despondent. These I tried to cheer, told them the camp they were to reach was only a little way further over the hill, and so got them up and started, accompanying some of the worst a little way, and helping them, or putting them under the support of strongest comrades.

*May 21.*—Saw General Sheridan and his cavalry to-day; a strong, attractive sight; the men were mostly young, (a few middle-aged) superb-looking fellows, brown, spare, keen, with well-worn clothing, many with pieces of water-proof cloth around their shoulders, hanging down. They dash'd along pretty fast, in wide close ranks, all spatter'd with mud; no holiday soldiers; brigade after brigade. I could have watch'd for a week. Sheridan stood on a balcony, under a big tree, coolly smoking a cigar. His looks and manner impress'd me favorably.

*May 22.*—Have been taking a walk along Pennsylvania avenue and Seventh street north. The city is full of soldiers, running around loose. Officers everywhere, of all grades. All have the weather-beaten look of practical service. It is a sight I never tire of. All the armies are now here (or portions of them,) for to-morrow's review. You see them swarming like bees everywhere.

### THE GRAND REVIEW

For two days now the broad spaces of Pennsylvania avenue along the Treasury hill, and so by detour around to the President's house, and so up to Georgetown, and across the aqueduct bridge, have been alive with a magnificent sight, the returning armies. In their wide ranks stretching clear across the Avenue, I watch them march or ride along, at a brisk pace, through two whole days—infantry, cavalry, artillery— some 200,000 men. Some days afterwards one or two other corps; and then, still afterwards, a good part of Sherman's immense army, brought up from Charleston, Savannah, etc.

### WESTERN SOLDIERS

*May 26-7.*—The streets, the public buildings and grounds of Washington, still swarm with soldiers from Illinois, Indiana, Ohio, Missouri, Iowa, and all the Western States. I am continually meeting and talking with them. They often speak to me first, and always show great sociability, and glad to have a good interchange of chat. These Western soldiers are more slow in their movements, and in their intellectual quality also; have no extreme alertness. They are larger in size, have a more serious physiognomy, are continually looking at you as they pass in the street. They are largely animal, and handsomely so. During the war I have been at times with the Fourteenth, Fifteenth, Seventeenth, and Twentieth Corps. I always feel drawn toward the men, and like their personal contact when we are crowded close together, as frequently these days in the street-cars. They all think the world of General Sherman, call him "old Bill," or sometimes "uncle Billy."

## A SOLDIER OF LINCOLN

*May 28.*—As I sat by the bedside of a sick Michigan soldier in hospital to-day, a convalescent from the adjoining bed rose and came to me, and presently we began talking. He was a middle-aged man, belonged to the 2d Virginia regiment, but lived in Racine, Ohio, and had a family there. He spoke of President Lincoln, and said: "The war is over, and many are lost. And now we have lost the best, the fairest, the truest man in America. Take him altogether, he was the best man this country ever produced. It was quite a while I thought very different; but some time before the murder, that's the way I have seen it." There was deep earnestness in the soldier. (I found upon further talk he had known Mr. Lincoln personally, and quite closely, years before.) He was a veteran; was now in the fifth year of his service; was a cavalry man, and had been in a good deal of hard fighting.

## TWO BROTHERS, ONE SOUTH, ONE NORTH

*May 28-9.*—I staid to-night a long time beside of a new patient, a young Baltimorean, aged about 19 years, W.S.P., (2d Maryland, southern,) very feeble, right leg amputated, can't sleep hardly at all—has taken a great deal of morphine, which, as usual, is costing more than it comes to. Evidently very intelligent and well bred—very affectionate—held on to my hand, and put it by his face, not willing to let me leave. As I was lingering, soothing him in his pain, he says to me suddenly, "I hardly think you know who I am—I don't wish to impose upon you— I am a rebel soldier." I said I did not know that, but it made no difference. Visiting him daily for about two weeks after that, while he lived, (death had mark'd him, and he was quite alone,) I loved him much, always kiss'd him, and he did me. In an adjoining ward I found his brother, an officer of rank, a Union soldier, a brave and religious man, (Col. Clifton K. Prentiss, sixth Maryland infantry, Sixth corps, wounded in one of the engagements at Petersburgh, April 2—linger'd, suffer'd much, died in Brooklyn, Aug. 20, '65.) It was in the same battle both were hit. One was a strong Unionist, the other Secesh; both fought on their respective sides, both badly wounded, and both brought together here after a separation of four years. Each died for his cause.

from Berry Benson's Civil War Book
by Berry Benson

*Having served in the Confederate Army from Fort Sumter to Appomattox, Berry Benson (1843–1923) brought a wide perspective to his memoirs. Mustered as an eighteen-year-old private, he fought under Jackson, and later became a scout and sharpshooter. Benson was captured and imprisoned twice by Federal troops, and twice he escaped. In this piece, Benson describes the ordeal—and adventure—of his first dash out of Union clutches.*

On the evening of May 16, 1864, the Brigade took position on the breastwork at Spottsylvania. A picket being put out, the sharpshooters were allowed to sleep. Some pines had been felled and the boughs piled, and on these we spread our blankets, the ground being wet. Soon after failing asleep, I was awakened by the sound of talking. Captain Dunlop was asking for volunteers to go scouting. I rose, offering my services.

"You are just the man I want," the Captain said. "Take three men and report to Captain Langdon Haskell (brother of our lamented Captain William Haskell) at Brigade Headquarters."

Saying that two would do, I took Norton and Russell, who volunteered. At Headquarters, Captain Haskell told us that General Lee suspected the enemy of being about to move on the Telegraph Road from Fredericksburg to Richmond. He had therefore ordered every Brigade Commander to learn what the enemy was doing in his immediate front.

I asked whether I should go directly out front or go around and try to get in the enemy's rear. He replied that I might do as I chose. Preferring the latter course, I fixed an hour next day by which I would return with information. Captain Haskell replied that I must be back—not next day—but within two hours!

I told him that it would be impossible, then, to circle around the enemy's lines; but that I doubted my ability to learn anything of consequence in front.

"If you can't get the information *outside* the lines, then you must go *inside*," Captain Haskell replied.

Knowing that to penetrate the enemy lines directly in front and escape observation would be extremely difficult, I decided to draw as near as possible to their pickets and listen for the sound of troops moving. But here we heard nothing of any significance. So instructing my two men to keep fifty yards behind me, and whenever they heard me halted or talking to anybody, to wait a while, and if I did not return, to go back and report to Captain Haskell, I proceeded toward the enemy picket line. I had got pretty close, and was hoping that amongst the pine bushes I might creep through unnoticed, when I had to cross a wet place, and my foot made a slight noise.

"Who comes there?" cried a sentinel.

"A friend," I answered.

"Come in, then," was the reply.

If by this time I had discovered anything worth reporting, I would have gone back. But having gained no information, it only remained to me to get inside, learn what I could, then attempt to escape. I walked quietly up to the pickets, the color of my uniform concealed by the darkness.

"What are you doing out there?" a sentinel demanded.

"I've been scouting down the Rebel lines."

"Where did you go out?"

"Lower down to the left; I belong to Hancock's corps."

Having posted myself from prisoners, I knew that corps was there, and could answer satisfactorily the questions as to division, brigade, and regiment, even naming some of the officers. I went on to say that I was making a short cut through the camp to report, instead of returning by the roundabout way I had come.

"Well, it may be all right," said the officer, "but I'll have to send you up to Brigade Headquarters."

"All right," I agreed casually.

Two men were detailed to go with me, but I was allowed to carry my own gun. Passing through a good deal of camp, my guards halted at the door of a large tent, and announced to the occupant that they had a man in custody who claimed to be a Federal scout.

From the darkened tent came a voice demanding, "What regiment do you belong to?"

"Sixth New York."

"You are a Southern soldier."

"You are altogether mistaken, sir."

"You are a Southern soldier. Come in here!"

I heard a match struck; a candle was lit. It was all up. I lifted the flap of the tent and stepped inside, rifle and all.

"Aha!" he said as he cast his eyes on me. "What state are you from?" "South Carolina, sir."

"Aha!" He broke out in a laugh, and I followed suit.

He was Colonel Sweitzer, commanding a brigade. He told me he had lived in the South and had known I was a Southerner, the first word I spoke. He talked right pleasantly with me for some time and asked me a good many general questions, amongst other things how our army fared for food. Luckily when I knew I was going out to scout, I had gone to our commissary, "promptly," and inveigled from him a loaf of fresh-baked bread. This I handed to the colonel, inviting him to try it, saying we had plenty more like it. (Everything being fair in war, I hope that fib was pardonable.) He broke off a piece and ate it, pronouncing it excellent.

After a little more light, cheerful talk, the Colonel bade me a good night and a speedy exchange, for which I thanked him, intending to exchange myself before daylight if possible. Before I left, he ordered the guard to take my gun; but at my request allowed me to keep my belt, a very nice one which I had bought in South Carolina. Hanging to the belt was a short bowie knife, on the white handle of which was cut "Z. Benson." Zack had lent it to me at the opening of the campaign, and it was for the sake of the knife that I had asked to keep the belt.

As the guard conducted me through the camp, I continued on the alert for any signs or sounds of movement, but discovered nothing. Arrived at a little cluster of tents, my guards delivered me over to a sergeant, asking of him a certificate. This he gave, writing with a pencil, by the light of a candle. I was now conducted to a cluster of fly tents on the edge of a pine thicket, beyond which heavier woods loomed up. Outside was a low fire by which sat a guard, rifle in hand. To him I was delivered.

I decided that my best plan was to pump this guard as to troop movements, if I could, then with any information I had gained, to make a run for the big woods, and trust to fortune for the rest. I thought the best way to draw him out would be to start bragging for my own side; this would set him bragging for his, and I hoped he would let some cats out of the bag. It worked to a charm. He told me a good deal, including a movement of the Corcoran Legion, and of heavy artillery men who had been manning the defenses of Washington being brought to the front, giving numbers, and more.

And now a thought struck me. Remembering that inside camp our men often kept guard with unloaded guns, I thought that if I could satisfy myself that his was unloaded, I could make the break with greater confidence. Leaning against a little pine just at my left hand was a rifle, belonging to another of the guards. If one of these guns was kept unloaded, all were apt to be. So I went on bragging on the prowess of our men, and presently I said, "Why, we can beat you at drilling—that's been proved. I don't claim to be one of our best, but I dare say I can go through the manual of arms better than you can."

With these words, I picked up the gun—he looking at me and saying little. Briskly obeying the commands as I gave them to myself, I came to the order, "Load in nine times—Load!" The gun passed to my left side; the butt dropped to the ground; my right hand went back as tho' to the cartridge box; I bit off the end of an imaginary cartridge; placed it in the muzzle; drew the ramrod; passed it down the barrel— the gun was empty! I replaced the ramrod; brought the gun to the right side; cocked it; drew a cap out of my vest pocket, and capped the gun. Setting the gun back against the tree, I asked, "There! Can you beat that?" And I just had it on my tongue to add, "Good-bye, old fellow," when the corporal of the guard appeared from nowhere, and posted another man in the old guard's place.

The new guard, a corporal, a tall well-made fellow, leaned his gun against the tree right beside the one I had just placed there, and stood by the fire warming himself as the other two men walked away. Then, picking up a gun, he ordered me to come with him. We started off, he in front, along a line of wagons parked, the horses eating. Just beyond the wagons, ten yards or so to my right lay the edge of an oak woods, and I saw no tents in it. The corporal walked about a step in front of me, a little to my left, his rifle over his right shoulder. My left hand fell heavily on the gun barrel, which thudded to the ground, as I turned and sprang among the horses.

"Halt! Halt!" shouted the corporal. There was a second's silence, and then a cap snapped behind me.

"Stop that man! Stop that man!" I heard the corporal's voice as I darted amongst the trees, and I heard his feet, too, following close, as I struggled through the strip of woods; and he was not far behind when I broke into an open field where I was in full view. "Stop that man! Stop that man!" he continued to shout, hot at my heels as I pelted down a hill, jumped a ditch, and turned obliquely to the left heading for some pine woods. Running as I had never run before, I gained the woods a few paces ahead of my pursuer, but almost exhausted, when sharp upon my left came a party of armed men running, who caught me and held me fast.

The corporal came up and took charge of me, the whole party accompanying me back to where they had me before. On the way I suffered

a great deal of abuse from the corporal, who called me all kinds of vil-
lainous names, and when I dared remonstrate, he spitefully thrust the
point of his bayonet into my leg—a hurt only temporary physical, but
to my feelings it lasted a long time. I appealed to the men, asking what
crime it was in a prisoner to attempt to escape, and one or two took my
part. Their expostulations had a good effect upon the corporal's behav-
ior; he cooled down to calling me no worse names than "d——d rebel"
and such.

Arrived back at the guard's quarters, the corporal said, "I'll fix you so
you won't run any more." Whereupon he got out a small hempen rope,
tied my hands behind my back, and tied me to a tree. He had been
cursing not only me, but the gun also, for missing fire. He swore that
it had never served him such a trick before, and that I owed my life to
its defection, as he had dead aim on me not ten steps off when he
pulled the trigger. Now when he came to the light he held up the gun
to look at it, and discovered that it was not his own. His own loaded
gun leaned against the tree where he had placed it; he had taken
instead the unloaded gun which I had capped.

I now realized the perilous position I was in. Having represented
myself to the pickets as a Union scout, persisting in this assertion when
brought before the commanding officer; having pumped the guard for
information and then attempted to get away with it, I began to see that
a strong case might be made against me as a spy. The talk that I over-
heard, such as, "The d——d spy! I thought it mighty strange his asking
so many questions," added to my disquietude.

At length the compression of the ropes on my wrists became so
painful that I asked if they would be so good as to change my position
some way. Most of them paid no attention, but a sergeant came forward, and untying the ropes, tied me again, with my hands over my
head, to a low limb. This relieved me for a time, but the new position
soon began to be as painful. My hat, which had fallen off, was kindly
placed on my head. My pockets were searched, and my purse containing only stamps and a little Confederate money was returned to me.
But my diary was kept.

When day came (Tuesday, May 17, 1864) I was untied and taken to the Headquarters of General Patrick, Provost Marshall—at the same house where on the night of May 11th, I had leaned against the fence looking at the artillery and the horses and talking to the Federal soldiers. Thence I was taken to General Meade's Headquarters, at Anderson House, where Bookman and I had seen the cavalry picket on the 9th. An officer came out of the house and addressed me, opening his speech by accusing me of being a spy. I asked him what ground he had for making such a charge, which I denied.

For answer he produced my diary, asking, "Is this yours?"

"Yes, sir."

"Is this your writing?"

" It is, sir."

"Are you detached from your regular company?"

"Yes, sir."

"As what?"

"In a corps of sharpshooters, sir."

"Are these sharpshooters mounted?"

It flashed through my mind that I might somewhere have made mention of my captured mare in the book, and that he had read it. So I said, "Not as a general thing, sir. A few have horses that they use sometimes in scouting. I have one, now in charge of my Quartermaster."

Handing me a small strip of paper, he asked, "What were you doing with this in your book?"

I took it and read: "In the field, May 10, 1864—Received of Corporal Edward White, one Rebel Prisoner. (Signed) Thomas Black, Sgt. of Provost Guard."

(The names as here given are fictitious; I have forgotten the true ones).

I replied, "I never saw this paper before. It could not have been found in my book."

"But it *was* found in your book and sent me as part of your property."

"Colonel, there is some mistake here. You call me a rebel. How could I receive a rebel prisoner?"

"That's just what we don't understand," replied the Colonel. "*You* explain it."

Racking my brains, I suddenly remembered that the picket guard the night before had asked for and received a receipt for me, upon turning me over to the sergeant of the Provost Guard. This might well have been turned in along with my diary. When I offered this explanation to the Colonel, he took back the paper, scrutinized it and said, "Then how do you explain this discrepancy? You were captured last night, May 16th, and a receipt issued. But this paper is dated May 10th."

Peering at the paper extended in the Colonel's hand, I saw that this was so. But the zero was not fully joined and might conceivably have been intended for a six.

Evidently not satisfied with this explanation, the Colonel continued his interrogation: "What were you doing when captured?"

"Scouting, sir."

"For what purpose?"

"I was ordered to learn whether you were moving, sir," I answered frankly, knowing that this admission could do no harm to the Confederacy.

"Then, upon being hailed, why did you claim to be a Union scout?"

"I hoped, sir, that they would not order me in, but would let me remain outside the picket lines."

"But upon being brought in you represented yourself to Colonel Sweitzer also as a Union scout."

"True, sir. But I had to be consistent. I hoped there was a chance *he* might let me go."

The Colonel stood thinking a moment. So far he had not mentioned my attempt to escape from the guard; and I never knew whether he was aware of it. Presently he continued, "Inside a Federal camp, you misrepresented yourself as a Union scout. Was not that spying?"

"Colonel," I protested, "I was taken *outside* your lines, armed with my regular arms, dressed in full grey uniform. Only the darkness of the night prevented my being recognized as a Confederate. Was it wrong to make use of this accidental advantage? Wouldn't your scouts have done the same thing?" Thus I argued with him for some time, and I think I was more eloquent than I ever have been before or since. He listened patiently, and seemed to feel interested.

Finally he told me that in all probability, I would be tried as a spy by court-martial in a few hours; but that I would not be condemned without a hearing. He added that he felt kindly toward me, would do all he could for me, and that he hoped I would come out safe. I thanked him, and he went back in the house.

That I now felt a good deal of alarm, I cannot deny. A trial by drum-head court-martial is a terrible ordeal. I realized that the case against me would be aggravated by certain suspicious circumstances which were likely to be brought out. The question about horses had aroused a fear that there were clues connecting me with the capture of the Colonel's mare five days before on this very ground. And it might be that knowing his carelessness had afforded the opportunity, the guard had not reported that I had pumped him for information, then attempted to escape with it. But these facts were almost certain to come out in the trial; and they would be much against me.

I was now taken across the fields to a place beside the big road where two or three Confederates and several Yankee soldiers had been assembled in a fence corner under guard. Regarding my situation as so critical, I determined not to let pass the least opportunity of escape. If by any chance the court-martial were deferred till night, I would make a run for the woods, there being quite a forest on the other side of the road. I was tortured with anxiety, for I considered the chances of my being freed by the court of the charge of spying were but small.

In the party of Confederates was one whom I saw looking at his silver watch, and I asked the hour. Then as time dragged so heavily for me, longing as I was for darkness to come on, I found myself asking the time so often that in apology for the trouble I caused, I told him the cause of my anxiety. He told me that his name was Ferneyhough, and that he belonged to the Fredericksburg Artillery.

The number of prisoners gradually increased, until now it was pretty large. About three o'clock they brought in a young Confederate, who took his seat apart from the rest, and appeared wrapped in thought. Soon after, we were placed in a column, two abreast, and marched along the big road, the newcomer and Ferneyhough being the couple just ahead of me. I saw them conversing together, and presently the stranger turned around and asked, "Is your name Benson?"

I said, "Yes."

"Well," he went on, "you needn't feel any apprehension about that case of yours. You will be regarded as a prisoner of war."

"How do you know?" I asked eagerly.

He changed places with my companion and replied, "I was brought up before them this morning, and after getting through with me, they asked if I knew a man named Benson. When I said no, they told me the circumstances of your capture and asked me what motive you could have in claiming to be a Union scout. I told them that I supposed you were some greenhorn, so scared at being hailed that you hardly knew what you were saying. I listened as they talked amongst themselves, and gathered that you would be considered a prisoner of war."

I thanked him, feeling that probably he had saved my life. I still feel so, for if he had not thus relieved my apprehension of being hanged as a spy, I might have made some reckless attempt to escape, which might well have been my last act on earth.

Marching along under escort of cavalry, my companion now told me about himself. He was Sergeant Ellison of Company E Third Alabama Regiment, a scout of General Ewell's. After listening to some of his scouting exploits, I proposed to him that we attempt to escape together. He agreed, but said that there would be little opportunity before reaching Fredericksburg, because of all the woods having been cut down for fuel during the campaigns.

We met the Washington Heavy Artillery coming to the front, as my guard the night before had said. They were dressed in span new clothes, with guns and equipments of all kinds fresh as though just out of a bandbox, and even wore *white cotton gloves.* How our boys did jeer! Even our Union guards shelled them hot with ridicule, saying "Oh, yes, Johnny Reb'll have them white gloves and them fat knapsacks too!"

(Blackwood afterwards told me what a fine time they had plundering the knapsacks of the Washington Heavy Artillery!) I saw also that day another body of troops fresh arrived in the field, which my guard had said would come—the Corcoran Legion.

Being marched thro' the camps, I was continually hailed on all sides with "Hello, Johnny!" Johnny Reb being a national name they had given us. In being first thrown among them, I was surprised at the immense amount of cursing and blackguarding I heard going on everywhere. There was nothing like it in our camps. I heard oaths that I had never heard before in my life, and a man would, in mere sport, call another the vilest names—a style of language that would have brought a fight on his hands in Confederate camps, fifty times a day.

We were kept at Fredericksburg two or three days. Our prison was simply a small bare hill—knoll rather—at the foot of which was a spring, and was surrounded (spring and all) by a guard. There were a few Federal prisoners among us. While here, it rained, and as I had no tent, no blanket, oilcloth, or overcoat, I lay on the bare, cold, wet ground, not even leaves under me, and slept in the rain. I shall never forget walking about in the little enclosure as tho' walking would give me blanket or shelter, or make the ground dry or stop the rain, and finally lying down just so, with my head on my arm, while the rain kept failing. But I slept.

Our next move was to Belle Plain. Under a guard of the same number, twenty-five of us were taken, the distance being eight miles. We crossed the Rappahannock at F—— on a pontoon bridge. The country was still all open, the trees on this side of the river having been cut down by the enemy for fuel in the winter of 1862–1863, as on the other side had been done by our army.

Belle Plain was a landing on the Potomac. Monday afternoon, May 23, 1864, about five hundred prisoners were put on board a steamer and carried down to Point Lookout Prison, arriving about 4 p.m. There we were drawn up in ranks sixteen deep, and answered to our names.

The prison was a rectangular enclosure of about ten acres, and was said to contain at that time about ten thousand prisoners. The soil, inside and outside, was white sea sand, and this with the white tents and whitewashed houses and fence, made in the sunshine a strong glare. Some men, I was told, lost their eyesight in consequence. They say that many, amongst both prisoners and guards, became afflicted with night blindness—that is, inability to see at all by night. I have seen soldiers on the march who could see as well as anybody in the daytime, being led by a comrade at night, unable to see a thing.

The fence around the prison was of upright planks, about ten feet high, and around the outside of it, about four feet from the top of the fence ran a raised platform for the sentries to walk on. In one end of this fence was a large gate through which went all communication with the outside world. This was kept shut. In the side of the prison fronting the Chesapeake were three smaller gates. Opposite them, out in the Chesapeake about 25 feet from shore, stood three wooden boxes or privies, with walls about waisthigh. These were elevated on piles driven in the water, and were approached on wooden plankways leading from the beach.

The prisoners were allowed to go in and out of these three gates at pleasure all day, a line of sentries being placed at each end of the open space to prevent escape that way. At sundown, the gates were locked.

Inside the fence were rows of tents with streets between, and a number of buildings of rough pine whitewashed, used as kitchens, dining rooms, hospitals, etc. Outside the prison were a good many houses occupied by the guards, or used for storage, and a hundred other purposes. The camp was separated into divisions and the divisions subdivided into companies. I was put in Company H, eighth or maybe it was ninth Division. In the tent where I was placed were fifteen others, and it may well be believed that sixteen men, even in a Sibley tent, were badly crowded. It was a difficult matter to dispose ourselves to sleep.

Between Fredericksburg and Belle Plain I had made acquaintance with a few of my fellow prisoners I had hoped to continue in company with. But we were separated, and I now found myself with strangers—

men whom I thought I could not affiliate with. I deposited my luggage—a blanket, half a blanket, and a Federal overcoat, which I had picked up, thrown away by Union soldiers. My tentmates told me that the half blanket and overcoat would be taken away from me on Sunday, inspection day. This was proper, for new prisoners would be coming in, some of them without anything, and it was no more than right that any surplus should be divided up.

It being yet some time before dark, I knocked around camp a little, wishing to survey the situation and get an idea of the prospects for escape.

Directly I was addressed by one whose face I remembered, though he had to tell me his name—Michael Duffy of Company I, my regiment. He brought up another member, who had been in prison with him since July 1863—ten months. The talk soon turned to escape, and they told me that the night before a prisoner had dug a hole under the fence and escaped. The story seemed doubtful to me, as did other stories I heard about escapes made by tunneling out. As the whole formation of Point Lookout is loose sand, I doubt if any tunnel got more than a start.

Another story was of a boat patched together of cracker boxes and stray pieces of plank. This improbable structure was said to have been kept turned upside down in a tent, disguised as a bed, where it was found during a Sunday inspection before an opportunity offered for launching it. A more likely tale was of a swimming match in which two prisoners engaged. With sentries looking on, the contestants went further out at each trial until at last, when the gates were about to be closed, two heads were seen far out, of which only one returned, the other keeping out to sea until darkness came on, when presumably he swam to shore and made good his escape. Another tale was that on the beach while swimming and washing clothes, the men took one of the big wooden tubs (half of a barrel) to play with, and that when the gates were to be shut they came in, forgetting the tub. The sentries saw it floating far out to sea, upside down, but did not suspect that a prisoner went with it, his head under the inverted tub.

It was to the sea that I turned my attention as the best avenue of escape. But to fit myself I should have to perfect my swimming. I resolved to spend much of my time in the water, thinking that thus I might be prepared to undertake the feat in three or four weeks.

Duffy told me that the prison guard consisted of three groups (three regiments, it may have been), one white, two negro. A group went on duty early in the morning and remained twenty-four hours, the sentries being relieved every two hours, as on camp duty. We were given only two meals a day, breakfast at eight, dinner at two. As I had come in after two, I went to bed hungry.

Next day, Tuesday, May 24th, at the summons the ranks were formed and the company marched to the eating house, where we had a slight breakfast given us. After breakfast, I walked out on the beach, and seeing a number of men in the water, I went in too and swam out some distance into clearer water, that next the shore being somewhat muddy from the washing of the waves on the beach. I was glad to find myself able to swim with so much greater ease than in fresh water—a fact that everybody knows. I went in several times that day.

Sitting on one of the gangways that led up to the big boxes, I entered into conversation with a man who told me he was a Louisianian, a member of Hays's brigade, that he had been in prison here all the past winter, but had been exchanged just before the battles at Spottsylvania. Then in the battle of May 12th, he had been recaptured and brought back to the same prison. That was ugly luck. He told me a good many things about the prison, its rules, etc. He said that above the prison there were stakes in the water to which were fastened wires which communicated with the guards' quarters on shore, so that if a prisoner escaped and tried to pass up along the Bay he would touch the wires and sound an alarm.

During the day, I walked about the prison also, especially noticing a small drain which led under the fence at the northeast Corner. I went into one of the buildings which was used as a chapel and schoolhouse, with Confederate preachers and teachers. I believe the ladies of Baltimore supplied the books; I remember *Caesar's Commentaries* among them. At two o'clock we had dinner, but it seemed to me very scanty. As a whole, I don't think Confederate prisoners suffered greatly for food, tho' we had none too much truly. Perhaps because I had been roughing it for so long I needed more food than quiet prisoners.

It was a curious sight to see, before many tent doors, different trades being plied, such as cobbling, perhaps some kind of small carpenter's work, and many that I don't remember now; but chief of all prisoners' work was ring making. Then there were little tables made of cracker boxes on which wares were displayed, while the seller sat behind on a stool. Many of the tables held only hardtack and tobacco cut into squares perhaps as large as a thumbnail and called "chews." Tobacco I found to be the medium of trade, the currency, and the "chew" was the unit thereof. But tobacco and hardtack had the same value—one cracker equals one chew. A user of tobacco, feeling that he *must* have a chew, saves a cracker from his dinner (ill can he spare it!), walks up to an exchange table, deposits his cracker and takes up a chew, saying never a word, likely as not, the relative value is so well established.

The next day [May 25, 1864], just before sundown, I was sitting on the beach waiting for the sergeant to come around to close the gates, when I was surprised to see the white guards around the prison being relieved by blacks. This was surprising because, as I had learned, the new guard always went on early in the morning. And the sergeant did not come to close the gates as usual, though it was now almost sundown. By sunset nearly all the prisoners had gone to their quarters. It began to grow dusk. No sergeant yet coming, my heart began to beat fast. It was still too light, but a little later perhaps—I went inside and hurried to my tent, hearing many as I passed talking about the gates' still being open. Unperceived by the new guards, the whole prison was in a low fever of excitement.

I put on my jacket and stockings and stuck my hat in my bosom inside my shirt. My shoes, being thick-soled and heavy, I was afraid to take, as I expected to have a good deal of swimming. I went to the middle gate and stood in it, waiting for it to grow dark enough. Now and then someone passed me, going inside or out. A party of six passed out and went into the central box. Directly they came back, but just as they got to the lower end of the plankway, I saw the last man of the group squat down and dart under the plankway. I had seen another get under there a little while before. I now walked out, passing over the two men.

Inside the box, I turned around and saw four negro sentinels standing above the gate. Reaching down, I caught hold of one of the wooden pillars and slid down into the water. It was breast-deep. Backing slowly, so that I might keep the box between me and the sentinels, I went into deeper and deeper water. When it came to my chin, I turned and began to wade up the Bay.

Being thirty or forty yards from shore, and the darkness having increased greatly, I believed my head would not be seen above the water. I passed the upper end of the prison; I passed the guards' quarters, the water all the time up to my neck. Then I ventured closer in toward shore, where the water was breast-deep, and later to where it was waist-deep. Passing the guards' quarters, I saw a stake in the water. Curiosity prompted me to find out whether there were really any wires as the Louisianian had said. I waded up to it, felt all around, and found there were no wires. My stockings, getting filled with water, came partly off and draggled at my feet. I pulled them off and put them in my pocket, but one getting lost out, I threw the other away.

I was now a good way past the prison. The walking so far was easy for my bare feet, being fine smooth sand or clay. Suddenly a sharp pain struck. I was no longer on sand, but stumbling over raccoon oyster beds, the shells cutting my feet like knives. It could not have been worse walking over broken bottles. Stumbling on, I passed over the first oyster bed, glad to get my wounded feet again on the sand. But soon I struck another oyster bed. Setting my lips against the pain which must be endured, I hobbled on, reaching down to break off two or three with my hands. These I ate, biting the thin edges of the shells so I could pull them apart and get at the meat.

I now drew nearer the shore where the water was only knee-deep. But I found that my legs in passing one another splashed the surface, so I went out again until it reached my hips, which seemed to be the best depth. Behind me trailed a cloud of phosphorescent light, by which I could see as low as my knees. I could see little fishes too that came playing around me, each in his own circle of light.

I looked behind me. Far away lay the white walls of the prison. Out at sea were the lights of one or two passing ships. The moon had risen, but was veiled by heavy clouds. Despite my wounded feet, how happy I was! For I was free! I had escaped those four awful white walls and with care and labor I would soon be under the red flag again, again under the Stars and Bars!

I dared not come to land yet, for I heard a dog barking on the shore, and feared guards might be there. I waded on, the water growing deeper. Seeking shallower water, I turned more in towards the shore. As it continued to deepen, I turned square in. The water rose to my breast, then to my neck. A moment later, I was swimming. A few strong strokes, and I let down my feet. No bottom! I swam quite a distance before letting my feet down again. Still no bottom! Another good, strong swim, and down went my feet. Still deep water! A thought, a fearful one, shot through me. Maybe the tide was going out and I was being drifted out to sea. I swam hard for what seemed a long time. And when next I let down my feet, the tips of my toes touched sand. I stood so for a moment resting, then pulled into shallow water, relieved and thankful.

Pretty soon I had another fright. I was walking along steadily, not thinking of sharks, when all at once one came rushing at me from deep water, churning it into foam as he came. How I sprinted! Before you could say "Jack Robinson," I stood in water not half knee-deep. And then didn't I feel cheap when the next shark came and the next, and I knew it was just the coming back of the tide, which had turned, and these were but the first waves. I made up my mind never to tell anybody about it.

Standing half leg-deep in the Chesapeake, watching the retiring monsters of the deep, I figured that I had come nearly two miles from Point Lookout Prison. Breathing the fresh, cool free air of Maryland, no bayonets, nor walls, nor obedience—only the fields and the woods, the sea and the sky, I suddenly felt proud. What I had planned and striven for nine days without ceasing, I had at last achieved. I was a free man once more, free to fight again under the Stars and Bars for the liberty of my country.

I now quit the sea. Along the beach ran a road, a fence on the other side. I crossed both and found myself in a grain field near a dwelling, which I avoided. Soon I came to a sheet of water, probably a quarter of a mile wide. I walked along its edge toward my left until it narrowed to only a marshy branch, and there crossed it. I came into another field where were a farmhouse and outbuildings. The field was strewn with broken oyster shells, which hurt my sore feet badly, and I hurried on to reach some woods which lay beyond. Before reaching them, I was stopped by a sheet of water about two or three hundred yards wide, evidently an arm of the bay. Having walked up it some distance without finding any change in its breadth, I concluded to swim it. Just as I reached my foot forward to step into the water, I was brought back with a jerk by perceiving that I was about to step off a bank ten or twelve feet high. In the darkness, it had appeared to me that I was walking along the water's edge.

Farther up, I found it narrowed to about forty feet in width. The water in midchannel was only breast-deep. But how was I disappointed when I had crossed, to find before me yet another hundred yards of water. Apparently this was an island. On it were piles of split pine, in four-foot lengths, evidently intended for fuel. I had heard in prison that details of prisoners were sometimes sent out under guard to cut wood for the prison, and I thought this was possibly prison work. Taking a stick of the four-foot light pine under each arm, I went down into the water and made the passage. By the sparks in the water I knew it to be salt.

Landing, I climbed up a bank and found stretched before me another hundred yards of water. My landing place was but a point, whether of an island or the junction of two streams, I don't know. I have thought this might be St. Mary's River. Having swum this last stretch, I found myself amongst fallen trees, cut for fuel, and had much difficulty getting thro' them, for the broken twigs were constantly piercing my feet in the fresh cuts, so that every step was exceedingly painful.

Coming out of the woods into a field, I saw two horses; and at once I coveted one, longing for the relief that riding would give my wounded feet. I tried to catch one, but not succeeding, I went towards a house that I could see on a hill. Near one of the outhouses, I found an old pair of shoes, but they were so large and hard and stiff (having lain out in sun and rain till nearly rotten) that I could not bear them on my feet. I got into a small road and continued in it until it entered a larger public road, along which ran a telegraph line—the line from Washington to Point Lookout. Afraid to travel in it, I took to the byroads and paths through the woods. Again I tried to capture a horse in a field, but after having his heels flourished around my head once or twice, I left him alone. Near daybreak, May 26th, I was walking in a lane when I came upon two horses feeding. Approaching very cautiously, I caught one. He was facing the right way, and I sprang on his back. But no sooner was I mounted than he whisked around and carried me back at a gallop the way I had come. Having no bridle, I tugged at his mane and growled, "Whoa!" But he only sped the faster. Not daring to jump off because of the condition of my feet, I reached forward and seized his ear and gave it a wrench. He stopped. So did I. But the method of my dismounting I respectfully decline to state.

Painfully retracing my steps, I had passed a little beyond where I had caught my steed, when I saw before me at some distance the masts of a schooner. I knew this must be in the Potomac, which is here about eight miles wide. So I turned off to the right, thro' a gate opening to a field, and walked a little distance. Being very tired, I sat down in a fence corner. By me lay some old, torn clothing. I picked this up, and tearing it into strips, commenced binding up my bruised and bleeding feet. Whilst I was thus engaged, a little negro boy and girl came by, and seeing me, stopped and looked all the astonishment they must have felt.

Finding that I could not adjust the rags to my feet comfortably, I threw them away, disappointed that this effort to alleviate the pain of the hurts and bruises to my feet had also failed. The cuts had become filled with grit, and were so sore and tender that every step was attended with pain.

It was now near sunrise. I went to the cowpen and started talking with the negro children, trying to learn whether there were any Southern sympathisers about. The little girl, who was the elder, told me that at first nearly everybody was for the South, but now some of them had changed sides, and that her master had.

"How do you know?" I asked.

"I hears 'em talking," replied the child.

"Does anybody around here still hold out for the South?" I asked.

"Yessir, Mr. H——."

"How do you know?"

"I hears him and my master arguing."

In response to questioning, she told me that Mr. H—— lived alone, that he was rich, and that his house was the third past something or other—I think it was past a mill. With high hopes of finding the suc- cor I sorely needed, I followed her directions until I came to "the third house" past something or other. I think it was a mill. It was old, weather beaten, in the last stages of dilapidation. Certainly no rich man lived *there*. I passed on with a heavy heart. It may be that I had misunderstood the child's directions.

It now began to rain, which was in one way a benefit—it softened the road, making it easier to my feet. As for getting wet, I was already wet through, and had been since dark the night before. Though much fatigued, I continued to plod on, not stopping to rest long at a time. I traveled thro' the woods all I could, obliged to pick my way carefully, yet despite all my caution, I often stepped on things that hurt my feet. Once I got into such a maze of calico bushes, vines, and briers that I had to get on hands and knees and crawl.

About midday, the rain ceased and the sun came out. I stopped in a fence corner, and pulling off my jacket, spreading it out to dry, I lay down and slept some. I waked in the afternoon, feeling very hungry. Out in the field I saw two small boys. I put on my jacket and going to them, asked whether they had seen a stray horse, giving a description of one that I pretended to be looking for. They had not. I shifted the conversation gradually to the war, and was told by them that three men in the neighborhood were Southern sympathisers, one especially so. His house they pointed out in the distance. I left them, going off in another direction; but out of their sight, I turned and went to the house.

A lady, I suppose his wife, being in the room with the man, I hesitated to state my case, so I made inquiry again as to the horse, saying I had followed him farther than I had expected and was hungry, and asked if he would be so kind as to give me a little something to eat. He asked the lady to get something for me, and as soon as she stepped out of the room I told the man the truth. At once he said he was a Union man, and could give me nothing. I asked him not to inform on me. He replied that there was no one nearer than the Point to inform; that he was unwell and shouldn't go there. So I left, dinnerless and disheartened. I made a firm resolve not to betray myself to anyone again. This resolution I rigidly adhered to, though I think now that I made a mistake in not having bestowed confidence somewhere.

All that day and night I continued to walk, stopping to rest and sleep only at long intervals, and then for but a short time. In the night it rained. Walking along the road in the rain, I continually cast my eyes to one side coveting this or that spot to rest and sleep in. Once I passed a thick bushy tree with low overhanging boughs like a tent. It was dripping with rain and all underneath was saturated, but the bed of leaves looked so soft and the boughs came down in such a sheltering way that I said to myself, "How I would like to lie down and sleep here!" But with a resolution which I fear I do not possess now, I plodded on.

Sometime probably early in the night of May 26th, I came to a river which I took to be the Potomac. I now think it was the St. Mary's River and the town of St. Mary's. I looked along the banks for a small boat, but found none. Getting over into a garden, I pulled up some onions and stuck them in my pocket. I was very hungry, but had no appetite for raw onions. As day was beginning to break, I entered another town—Leonardtown, I think. Throughout the town I saw but one light, at a window. I passed a church on my right hand and directly was out of the town. Just outside I met a negro riding, who appeared to regard me with curiosity. No doubt, my personal appearance, barefoot, with Confederate uniform, was sufficiently striking. About a mile farther on, a man came riding from behind and passed me, followed by a negro riding—I think the same whom I had just before met. The negro turned and eyed me several times after passing. I thought I would better leave the road as it was getting so light.

As I was very tired I went off into a pine thicket on the right, and lay down in a little dry ditch or trench about 25 yards from the road. A log also intervening, I was pretty well hidden from the road. It was now about sunrise of Friday, May 27th. Now and then a cart would go by. Feeling quite hungry, I took out my onions and looked at them. A drink of milk the little negro children had given me and a couple of raw oysters had now been the only food I had had in forty hours, and I had endured much fatigue during that time. Hungry as I was, it was with difficulty that I forced myself to eat two of the onions. The others I put back in my pocket.

Hearing a horse coming from toward the town, I looked up. There he rode, the man I had been all along on the lookout for—a Federal cavalryman! I lay low and watched. He passed and then following him at about one hundred yards came four more, two abreast. As far behind them again rode four more—nine in all. Such an unusual order of riding meant business, and that business I interpreted as pursuit. I saw that I must leave that road and keep to the woods.

My traveling now became very painful. I was always stepping on stones and dead branches, which gave me great pain. And I grew exceedingly hungry. Passing a little marsh where I saw a number of frogs, I wished I had the means of making a fire that I might catch some and broil them.

I continued to walk until about noon, when I came to a little field, in which were a negro woman and her two children hoeing near their cabin. Deciding to venture, I went to her and asked about the stray horse. Of course she hadn't seen it. I then asked whether she would give me something to eat. Inviting me into her cabin, she fried a rasher or two of bacon and placed it before me, with some cold cornbread and cold coffee. Had my eyes been shut, I might possibly have been able to tell by the feel in my mouth, which was bread and which meat. But not by the taste, for my taste was completely gone, with my forty-eight-hour fast. Altho' I ate heartily, I tasted nothing until near the end of the meal, I began to taste the bacon grease into which I was dipping my bread, having eaten all the meat.

While I ate, the woman told me that she was a Catholic, and that her husband, tho' temporarily absent, was afraid to go abroad much, his life having been threatened by a neighbor. Having finished, I thanked my black hostess and bade her goodbye, which I did very hastily, as I felt that the victuals would not rest upon my stomach. I restrained myself long enough to reach the woods (some thirty yards away) when I threw up the whole dinner, including the onions of that morning. A deathly sickness came over me. Feeling faint and weak, I managed to go a little way into the woods, where I lay down. But mosquitoes gathered on me so thick that I had to get up and move further away from the swamp. I lay down again, so completely exhausted that I did not move when I saw a big snake crawling toward me, passing right by my feet.

A faintness came over me and a sort of stupor. I never knew whether I was awake or asleep when I plainly saw three men walking toward me along a little path. I started up to run. There was the path, but no men—it was all imagination or a dream. After a little I began to feel much better. I think I had had fever, which now wearing off left my head clear. But my limbs were weak and I walked slowly, feeling no hunger now, but knowing that I must eat to regain strength.

I had walked about a mile when I came to a small house where I saw a lady with a little child. To her I told my horse tale, concluding by saying I had got lost and was very hungry. She placed before me some cold broiled bacon, cornbread, milk, and butter. Fearing that the meat might make me sick again, I made my dinner off bread and butter and a glass of milk. While I ate, an old man came in and began asking questions, to all of which I found it necessary to give evasive replies. Finally he said, "I expect you are a deserter from Lee's army."

Though it had not occurred to me before, it now struck me that this might be an excellent role for me to play. So without saying so directly (for the words stuck in my throat) I gave such a reply as led him to think I was a deserter, afraid or ashamed to acknowledge it. At once he grew frightened, and declared that if the military authorities were to know I had been fed there, he and the lady would both be put in prison, citing a parallel instance that had happened in the neighborhood. I assured him that I didn't wish to get him into any trouble, and by continued representations of my alarm for his safety I so worked upon his fears as to induce him to accede eagerly to my proposal that neither of us should mention my having been there. He then urged me to go, directing me to the County Road, and advising me earnestly to go straight to Leonardtown and take the oath of allegiance to the U.S. I seemed very willing and asked whether I should run to the right or the left when I reached the road. He said left. But alas for the unreliability of human nature—when I found the road I turned to the right, and from that day to this I have never seen Leonardtown or the man that administers the oath.

I came to a branch—probably McIntosh Run or Brooks' Run—which I crossed, rolling up my breeches as I did when a boy. After a while I came to a field, a man in it plowing. It was now near sundown; and not wanting him to see me, and there being no way to flank him, I crept into a fence corner where concealed by bushes, I lay resting till he went home. I then crossed the field to the woods where I found a road, into which I jumped from a bank five or six feet high. This was a mistake from which my feet suffered.

As it was now dark and the road led through a great forest, I kept on it until sometime in the middle of the night, feeling very tired, I went a little way off it and lay down. I was about going to sleep when I heard horses' feet, and directly a rider went by at a swift gallop, traveling in the same direction as I was. It was so dark I could only see a dim form flit past; but I decided it would be safer to keep off the road. After a short sleep, I traveled on, keeping to the woods and fields.

I think it was Saturday, May 28th, that my road led through an immense forest, probably the country north west of Hollywood. For miles I saw no fields or habitation. In the forenoon, I grew very hungry. I tried to eat a raw mushroom but could not, so I ate a few green huckleberries. None of the wild fruits were ripe. Finally I came into what appeared to be a plantation road. About noon, I stopped at a house and asked for something to eat. The lady gave me some bread and bacon. She also gave me some matches that I asked for (six) to light my pipe. These I put away to kindle a fire. Sometime during the night of the 28th, I entered a chestnut wood, and it may well be conceived that I suffered much by stepping on the fallen burrs with my wounded feet. There I lay down to sleep, kindling a little fire of dry limbs to keep me warm. Every now and then I would wake from the cold, and get up and replenish the fire.

I got up at sunrise (Sunday, May 29th) and was sitting down leaning against a tree when I saw walking thro' the woods, a man followed by a little girl. The man passed close by, but did not see me. Nor did the little girl until she got quite close. Then she stopped still and gazed at me. I kept perfectly still, hoping she would pass on, but she continued staring. And so she staid till the man was out of sight. Then she began quietly to get behind a tree. The man, missing her, now began to call her. She made no answer. Knowing now that the man would return for her, I got up and walked quickly away. The little girl must have been considerably frightened, no doubt associating me with all the giants, ogres, Bluebeards and what-nots that she'd ever heard about. I had wanted very much to try to comfort her but had dared not, fearing any move I should make would increase her fright.

In a little while I came to a house and ventured to go up and ask for something to eat. A man was sitting in the yard. He called to his little daughter to bring a chair for me, and while his wife prepared some breakfast, he questioned me. I told him that I was a deserter from Lee's army (it didn't choke much now), and that I was on my way to Washington to take the oath. He asked my reason for deserting, and now my solid loyalty to the cause fought against my denying my country even in seeming. I replied, "I quarreled with my Captain, and finally struck him. Being arrested, court-martialed, and sentenced to imprisonment, I managed to escape and deserted." This story I repeated ever after when questioned; it reflecting no blame on the Confederacy.

The lady brought me some warm cornbread, broiled fish, and plenty of milk and butter, and wrapped some food in a clean cloth and gave it to me to take with me. She also brought out a pair of socks, saying they had no shoes to spare, but maybe I could get shoes from someone else. Moved by their kindness, I was sorely tempted to tell my true history, but I kept firm. I think now that I ought to have told.

I thanked the couple heartily for their kindness and departed, but the gentleman said he would go with me to the road he advised me to take. We passed a house where a elderly gentleman was sitting on the porch, and as he appeared curious, my guide walked towards him and said something, obviously about me. I think he said that I claimed to be a deserter, but that he thought I was an escaped prisoner. Anyhow, the old gentleman called to me, "Better mind how you travel. I saw two cavalrymen pass here this morning."

Coming in sight of the road I was to take, my guide wished me good luck and left. At the fork of the road some negroes watched me attentively, and as I walked away one began to sing "Dixie." Once before in a field someone had started singing "The Bonnie Blue Flag" as I passed. A little past the fork, I met a carriage in which were two men. As I passed, I asked, "Is this the road to Washington?"

They answered, "Yes."

They had passed me about thirty yards, I suppose, when one of them put his head out and called back to me, "There are soldiers stationed up on the hill there," and drove on.

Immediately I left the road and took to the fields, more than half wishing the carriage had stopped and given me a chance to confide in the men. The country was quite hilly, and in places the fields were covered with stones and gravel. It was such torture to my feet that coming to a house, I ventured to ask for a pair of shoes. I was met by a voting man who stammered badly. Of an exceedingly obliging disposition, he began to exert himself at once to find me a pair. After a little he brought shoes which, though worn, were yet quite serviceable. Apologizing for their condition, he said he had neglected to clean them after his last fishing trip, that he was sorry he hadn't a better pair etc. etc. But I was only too glad to get these and expressed my gratitude accordingly. He gave me some directions as to traveling and I left.

Having now shoes and stockings, I stopped at the first stream I came to, and washed my feet well and long, picking the sand out from the cuts with a needle, and greasing them with some of the fat bacon the lady gave me this morning. I also washed my shoes of the mud, and greased them to make them soft. Then I put them on and they fit me nicely. Oh how proud I felt, and how comfortable! Then I washed my face and combed my hair, cocked my hat to one side, and shuffled on, no longer barefoot, though the shoes hurt my sore feet some, of course.

Traveling in the road, I met a carriage, in which were some ladies—returning from church, I suppose. As I passed they looked at me with considerable attention, which seemed to deepen into marked interest. Then as I lifted my hat with a graceful bow, they—they bowed in return! To me, a poor ragged dirty devil whose only claim to recognition from them was the grey jacket I wore. Why did I not stop and say, "Ladies, I am in trouble. I belong to Lee and am trying to get back to him. Can you not help me?"

I had said I would not ask for help. And I suppose it is true that I am obstinate. I think this happened near a little place called Charlotte Hall, and I believe it was after dark that I passed through Beantown. It was still early in the evening when I was overtaken by two little negro boys who volunteered the information that they were looking for—a horse! I was immediately suspicious. My previously practiced deception rose in judgment before me. But I kept on with the boys, until coming to a gate across the road, they found their horse and left me.

My way now lay along the Telegraph Road, which I followed by the posts. After traveling a long time, I missed the post and concluded I had taken a wrong turn somewhere. I decided to go off in the woods and sleep some. When I woke, it was after sunrise, Sunday, May 30th. I now saw why I had missed the posts. They ran thro' the field, making a short cut at a bend in the road. I ate a light breakfast out of my cloth, still keeping back a little. Then I traveled on, keeping in sight of the telegraph poles.

Learning now, by asking, that I was within twenty miles of Washington, I determined to go to the river and see how things looked. I therefore turned to the left, down a creek which must have been the Piscataway, crossed on a log to its right bank, and kept down it. Soon it began to widen rapidly, from which I judged that I was close to the river. Directly, from the top of a low hill, I saw it, with schooners and other small vessels on it, both in motion and at anchor. I kept up the river, going over many hills, high and steep.

About three p.m. I climbed a tall chestnut tree on top of one of the highest hills, to take a survey. When I reached the top, I had a fair view of the Potomac, and could see vessels of many kinds going up and down. Upriver on the opposite side I saw a city, which I knew must be Alexandria. To the right of it, and seeming to rise out of the river was a monument—the unfinished Washington monument. Farther to the right, looming above the tree tops, was a great white dome—the dome of the Capitol. Resting comfortably on a limb, I caught myself near dozing.

Before sunset I came down from the tree and ate the remainder of my provisions. Making my way up the river, I heard drums beating, and on the river bank I saw a fort, apparently built of stone, and there a band began to play. Afraid of being seen, I got into a gully lined with trees and bushes, and protected thus I walked a good distance, until I came to a place where a marsh full of weeds and water lilies barred my way upriver. I thought it would be too far to go around this marsh, so I waded across, the width being about sixty yards, and the mud in some places about knee-deep. I had to cross three or four of these marshes one after another. Then I found myself on a neck of land between the Potomac and the marshy creek I had just crossed—it must have been Swan Creek—which emptied into it. At its mouth, the creek was probably a quarter of a mile wide, and across it now below me was the fort—Fort Washington, about fifteen miles below Washington city.

Exhausted, I had lain down to rest, when a man came up to drive away two horses that were feeding near. He saw me and looked surprised, continuing to regard me attentively without speaking. I saw that I had better do or say something as an excuse for being there, so I asked if he could tell me how to get over to the fort.

"You can't get over there now," he replied. "What do you want to get over there for?"

"To get work."

"Why don't you get work from somebody over here?" he demanded, and went on to tell me that he was overseer at a nearby plantation where there was plenty of work, asking whether I could do gardening.

When I replied that I could, he offered me a job at eighteen dollars a month. I said I thought I could do better than that, whereupon he replied scoffingly that other people were offering no more than ten dollars. Replying that I should try to get more at some houses I had passed, I started off towards Washington. Once out of his sight, I turned off towards the river, and lay down within sight of it, debating with myself whether I should attempt passage here, or go up perhaps as far as Leesburg, where the Potomac was narrower and shallower and where I had a friend, Judge Gray, who would help me. Here the river was wide—a mile or more, I suppose, for the trees looked very small on the other side. But to go to Leesburg, I would have to pass around Washington, a long circuit in Maryland, passing through dangerous country between Washington and Baltimore, and I was tired and my feet were sore.

The fact that swimming the Potomac was the "short cut" to Virginia, where I would be in my own country, decided me, and I did not wait long after coming to my decision. If I had felt strong, I should probably have entered the water and made a bold, unaided swim for the opposite shore, but worn out as I was, prudence dictated that I would better take such help as I could get. It was now quite dark. I went to a fence nearby and from a short panel I took two rails some five or six feet long. Placing them on the ground, parallel to one another and about eighteen inches apart, I tied them in this position at both ends.

The cord I tied them with I had picked up on the side of the road a day or two before. I had passed it some little distance when I thought, "Benson, that string may do you some good service," and back for it I went.

Taking from my pocket the string with which the lady had tied the package of food, I tied my five remaining matches strongly in the middle of it. Placing the matches on the crown of my head, I tied the end of the cord under my chin. This way, if any inch of me landed dry on the other side, the matches would, and I would need a fire to dry and warm myself. I folded up my hat and put it in my bosom and buttoned my jacket close. I did not remove any of my clothes—not even my shoes. They were light, and I could not bear to part from them. Launching my two rails quietly, I got between them, one under each arm, and waded off from shore. In a few yards, I was swimming.

The rails were not large enough to hold me above water when I kept still, but were a great help. Having free use of my hands, I could make fair progress. Though I aimed for a point of woods on the opposite shore, I expected that the current would drift me below it. But the water seemed to be nearly still; perhaps the tide was coming in and so counteracted the current. My rails would slip forward, however, and after shifting them back several times, I let them alone, the cord across the hinder end pressing against my back, the two foremost ends coming nearly together in front.

I had not got far when the cord across my back suddenly snapped, the rails slipped from me and began to float off. A few strokes enabled me to regain them, but now, the cord being broken, I was obliged to hold onto the rails with my hands, propelling myself only with my feet. Directly I saw a schooner with all sails set coming up the river, headed right towards me. Whether it would pass in front or behind or over me, I could not tell. As I watched anxiously, I saw it would pass behind me, very close.

Near the middle of the river, a rowboat came along, going upstream, two men in it rowing. As it drew close, the men saw me and held up their oars, the boat gliding on. They began talking in a low tone, and I recognized their voices as negroes'. With my head as low as possible in the water, the ends of the two rails sticking out in front, I knew the men were regarding me closely. Keeping perfectly still, I had the great satisfaction as they passed of hearing the one word, "log," which seemed to me at that moment the sweetest word in the English language.

Soon after this adventure, cramp seized my left leg. Alarmed, I kicked hard, and the cramp left me. Not long after, I saw a steamboat coming up the river, lit from stem to stern with lights, white and red. A beautiful sight, as I knew, even when it seemed about to pass over me. But I had the satisfaction of seeing it, too, pass close behind me, while I rode up and down, up and down on the waves in its wake. This was my last danger. I soon drew near the point of woods that I had been swimming for. After one or two trials, letting down my feet, I was able to touch bottom, and my long swim was over. I was on Virginia soil— my own country! This was near Mount Vernon.

I climbed up a steep bank and went some distance into the woods to make a fire. Gathering some sticks, I tried to strike a match, but it was wet. But the second match lit, and I soon had a low, hot fire, and lay down before it, taking off some of my clothes and spreading them and my testament before it to dry. Then I slept.

When dawn came, I took up the line of march, though my clothes had not dried out much during the night. Passing a house, I took to a plantation road, but quitted it for some pine woods, to dodge a man I saw with a gun. At length I brought up in a field against a lagoon about thirty yards wide. Hunting a place to cross, I came to a boat with a paddle in it, but close by was a man plowing. He had his back to me, or he might have seen me take his boat. I was soon on the other side, where I had to resort to Jacksonian tactics, winding amongst hollows and sneaking behind bushes in an almost open field, to avoid being seen by some half dozen men plowing.

Coming out upon a high road, I passed a stately residence where I saw an elderly gentlewoman talking to a man who seemed to be the overseer, apparently giving instructions about the grounds, which were ornamented with flowers and shade trees. I passed unobserved, but had not got far when I heard horse's hoofs behind me. I jumped over the fence into some woods and lay down. The man passed—the same whom I had just seen. I staid there some time debating whether I ought not go back and tell my story to the lady. Finally deciding against it, I traveled on, and after a while encountered a lady with two children. I asked the way to Alexandria (though actually wishing to go in the opposite direction). She told me but advised me to be careful, as the citizens throughout that neighborhood arrested all strangers.

So I went into the woods and lay down in a spot of sunshine, pulling off my coat to dry. Here the ticks seemed determined to eat me up or carry me off. Both here and in Maryland they swarmed. I remained here till late in the afternoon, watching passengers and vehicles on the road, myself hidden. By their number, I thought I must be near a village. I intended keeping close till night, but chafed so at the delay that I decided to risk a little daylight, keeping to the woods and fields.

Walking thro' the woods, I came to the brow of a hill, below which lay a narrow valley, a stream thro' it. Where the stream crossed the road was a wooden and brick mill and several other houses. Deciding to circle around and cross the valley below this settlement instead of above, I was walking along a little byroad in the woods, when two boys came in sight, one about eighteen, the other about twelve. Immediately, the eldest called out, "Halt!" Knowing that it would not do to run or in any way appear to shun them, I walked towards them, apparently unconcerned.

"Where are you going?" the elder demanded.

I told him that I was looking for work, and after a little talk, he said that the miller wanted to hire someone, and that he would show me the way. In vain I urged him not to trouble himself, that I could follow his directions; he *would* go. Realizing that in my present condition, I could not outdo the two boys, either in a fight or a footrace, I saw no resource but to go with them, hoping the miller would be some old codger whom I could manage to fool.

Far from an "old codger," the miller turned out to be a big strapping fellow of about thirty-five, with a pistol buckled round his waist. In reply to his questioning, I told him I was from Alexandria, a carpenter by trade. Quickly informing me that my hands showed no signs of carpenter's work, he asked, "Who is Provost Marshal, in Alexandria?" When I had to confess that I didn't know, he said, "I thought so. Now tell who you are."

"I am a deserter from Lee's army," I said.

Not accepting this either, he put me through some sharp questioning as to how I had got here, where I had got so wet, the appearance of the Occoquan River, which I claimed to have swum, finally demanding, "Are you one of Kincheloe's men?"

"I don't even know who Kincheloe is," I answered—this time speaking the truth.

I was informed that Kincheloe was a rebel guerrilla, operating on the lower Potomac as Mosby operated on the upper. I learned that the miller was a New Jersey man named Troth, who had raised a company of home guards (he claimed three hundred in number) to resist the depredations of guerrillas. By his band he was called Captain Troth.

With a sinking heart, I realized that I had toiled and suffered so for the past six days, through the length of the partly hostile state of Maryland to reach the safety of my own country, and there I had fallen into the wrong hands!

from Andersonville: A Story
of Military Prisons
by John McElroy

*If the Confederacy held Butler's occupation of Louisiana and Sherman's march through Georgia to be extreme and uncivilized acts of aggression, then the Union held the administration of Southern military prisons to be an atrocity. Conditions at Andersonville were so harsh that 12,000 Union prisoners died there, many of starvation. John McElroy (1846–1929) spent fifteen months as, in his words, "a guest of the so-called Confederacy."*

To our minds the world now contained but two grand divisions, as widely different from each other as happiness and misery. The first—that portion over which our flag floated—was usually spoken of as "God's Country"; the other—that under the baneful shadow of the banner of rebellion—was designated by the most opprobrious epithets at the speaker's command.

To get from the latter to the former was to attain, at one bound, the highest good. Better to be a doorkeeper in the House of the Lord, under the Stars and Stripes, than to dwell in the tents of wickedness, under the hateful Southern Cross.

To take even the humblest and hardest of service in the field now would be a delightsome change. We did not ask to go home—we would be content with anything, so long as it was in that blest place—"within our lines." Only let us get back once, and there would be no more grumbling at rations or guard duty—we would willingly endure all the hardships and privations that soldier flesh is heir to.

There were two ways of getting back—escape and exchange. Exchange was like the ever receding mirage of the desert, that lures the thirsty traveler on over the parched sands, with illustrations of refreshing springs, only to leave his bones at last to whiten by the side of those of his unremembered predecessors. Every day there came something to build up the hopes that exchange was near at hand—every day brought something to extinguish the hopes of the preceding one. We took these varying phases according to our several temperaments. The sanguine built themselves up on the encouraging reports; the desponding sank down and died under the discouraging ones.

Escape was a perpetual allurement. To the actively inclined among us it seemed always possible, and daring, busy brains were indefatigable in concocting schemes for it. The only bit of Rebel brain work that I ever saw for which I did not feel contempt was the perfect precautions taken to prevent our escape. This is shown by the fact that, although, from first to last, there were nearly fifty thousand prisoners in Andersonville, and three out of every five of these were ever on the alert to take French leave of their captors, only three hundred and twenty-eight succeeded in getting so far away from Andersonville as to leave it to be presumed that they had reached our lines.

The first, and almost superhuman, difficulty was to get outside the Stockade. It was simply impossible to scale it. The guards were too close together to allow an instant's hope to the most sanguine, that he could even pass the Dead Line without being shot by some one of them. This same closeness prevented any hope of bribing them. To be successful half of those on post would have to be bribed, as every part of the Stockade was clearly visible from every other part, and there was no night so dark as not to allow a plain view to a number of guards of the dark figure outlined against the light colored logs of any Yankee who should essay to clamber towards the top of the palisades.

The gates were so carefully guarded every time they were opened as to preclude hope of slipping out through them. They were only unclosed twice or thrice a day—once to admit the men to call the roll, once to let them out again, once to let the wagons come in with rations, and once, perhaps, to admit new prisoners. At all these times every precaution was taken to prevent any one getting out surreptitiously.

This narrowed down the possibilities of passing the limits of the pen alive to tunneling. This was also surrounded by almost insuperable difficulties. First, it required not less than fifty feet of subterranean excavation to get out, which was an enormous work with our limited means. Then the logs forming the Stockade were set in the ground to a depth of five feet, and the tunnel had to go down beneath them. They had an unpleasant habit of dropping down into the burrow under them. It added much to the discouragements of tunneling to think of one of these massive timbers dropping upon a fellow as he worked his molelike way under it, and either crushing him to death outright, or pinning him there to die of suffocation or hunger.

In one instance, in a tunnel near me, but in which I was not interested, the log slipped down after the digger had got out beyond it. He immediately began digging for the surface, for life, and was fortunately able to break through before he suffocated. He got his head above the ground, and then fainted. The guard outside saw him, pulled him out of the hole, and when he recovered sensibility hurried him back into the Stockade.

In another tunnel, also near us, a broad-shouldered German, of the Second Minnesota, went in to take his turn at digging. He was so much larger than any of his predecessors that he stuck fast in a narrow part, and despite all the efforts of himself and comrades, it was found impossible to move him one way or the other. The comrades were at last reduced to the humiliation of informing the Officer of the Guard of their tunnel and the condition of their friend, and of asking assistance to release him, which was given.

The great tunneling tool was the indispensable half-canteen. The inventive genius of our people, stimulated by the war, produced nothing for the comfort and effectiveness of the soldier equal in usefulness to this humble and unrecognized utensil. It will be remembered that a canteen was composed of two pieces of tin struck up into the shape of saucers, and soldered together at the edges. After a soldier had been in the field a little while, and thrown away or lost the curious and complicated kitchen furniture he started out with, he found that by melting the halves of his canteen apart, he had a vessel much handier in every way than any he had parted with. It could be used for anything—to make soup or coffee in, bake bread, brown coffee, stew vegetables, etc., etc. A sufficient handle was made with a split stick. When the cooking was done, the handle was thrown away, and the half canteen slipped out of the road into the haversack. There seemed to be no end of the uses to which this ever-ready disk of blackened sheet iron could be turned. Several instances are on record where infantry regiments, with no other tools than this, covered themselves on the field with quite respectable rifle pits.

The starting point of a tunnel was always some tent close to the Dead Line, and sufficiently well closed to screen the operations from the sight of the guards nearby. The party engaged in the work organized by giving every man a number to secure the proper apportionment of the labor. Number One began digging, with his half canteen. After he had worked until tired, he came out, and Number Two took his place, and so on. The tunnel was simply a round, ratlike burrow, a little larger than a man's body. The digger lay on his stomach, dug ahead of him, threw the dirt under him, and worked it back with his feet till the man behind him, also lying on his stomach, could catch it and work it back to the next. As the tunnel lengthened the number of men behind each other in this way had to be increased, so that in a tunnel seventy-five feet long there would be from eight to ten men lying one behind the other. When the dirt was pushed back to the mouth of the tunnel it was taken up in improvised bags, made by tying up the bottoms of pantaloon legs, carried to the Swamp, and emptied. The work in the tunnel was very exhausting, and the digger had to be relieved every half-hour.

The greatest trouble was to carry the tunnel forward in a straight line. As nearly everybody dug most of the time with the right hand, there was an almost irresistible tendency to make the course veer to the left. The first tunnel I was connected with was a ludicrous illustration of this. About twenty of us had devoted our nights for over a week to the prolongation of a burrow. We had not yet reached the Stockade, which astonished us, as measurement with a string showed that we had gone nearly twice the distance necessary for the purpose. The thing was inexplicable, and we ceased operations to consider the matter. The next day a man walking by a tent some little distance from the one in which the hole began, was badly startled by the ground giving way under his feet, and his sinking nearly to his waist in a hole. It was very singular, but after wondering over the matter for some hours, there came a glimmer of suspicion that it might be, in some way, connected with the missing end of our tunnel. One of us started through on an exploring expedition, and confirmed the suspicions by coming out where the man had broken through. Our tunnel was shaped like a horse shoe, and the beginning and end were not fifteen feet apart. After that we practised digging with our left hand, and made certain compensations for the tendency to the sinister side.

Another trouble connected with tunneling was the number of traitors and spies among us. There were many—principally among the N'Yaarker crowd—who were always zealous to betray a tunnel, in order to curry favor with the Rebel officers. Then, again, the Rebels had numbers of their own men in the pen at night, as spies. It was hardly even necessary to dress these in our uniform, because a great many of our own men came into the prison in Rebel clothes, having been compelled to trade garments with their captors.

One day in May, quite an excitement was raised by the detection of one of these "tunnel traitors" in such a way as left no doubt of his guilt. At first everybody was in favor of killing him, and they actually started to beat him to death. This was arrested by a proposition to "have Captain Jack tattoo him," and the suggestion was immediately acted upon.

"Captain Jack" was a sailor who had been with us in the Pemberton building at Richmond. He was a very skilful tattoo artist, but, I am sure, could make the process nastier than any other that I ever saw attempt it. He chewed tobacco enormously. After pricking away for a few minutes at the design on the arm or some portion of the body, he would deluge it with a flood of tobacco spit, which, he claimed, acted as a kind of mordant. Wiping this off with a filthy rag, he would study the effect for an instant, and then go ahead with another series of prickings and tobacco juice drenchings.

The tunnel-traitor was taken to Captain Jack. That worthy decided to brand him with a great "T," the top part to extend across his forehead and the stem to run down his nose. Captain Jack got his tattooing kit ready, and the fellow was thrown upon the ground and held there. The Captain took his head between his legs, and began operations. After an instant's work with the needles, he opened his mouth, and filled the wretch's face and eyes full of the disgusting saliva.

The crowd round about yelled with delight at this new process. For an hour, that was doubtless an eternity to the rascal undergoing branding, Captain Jack continued his alternate pickings and drenchings. At the end of that time the traitor's face was disfigured with a hideous mark that he would bear to his grave. We learned afterwards that he was not one of our men, but a Rebel spy. This added much to our satisfaction with the manner of his treatment. He disappeared shortly after the operation was finished, being, I suppose, taken outside. I hardly think Captain Jack would be pleased to meet him again.

from Memoirs of
General W. T. Sherman
by William Tecumseh Sherman

*Many historians consider William Tecumseh Sherman (1820–1891) to be the greatest of the Civil War generals. His sweeps through Georgia and South Carolina were designed to break the will of the South and to deny supplies to the Confederate armies still in the field. His success was total. Reading the steely prose of this memoir, no one can deny the force of Sherman's will. But a close reading reveals that Sherman was intent on strategic destruction, not wanton killing.*

On the 12th of November the railroad and telegraph communications with the rear were broken, and the army stood detached from all friends, dependent on its own resources and supplies. No time was to be lost; all the detachments were ordered to march rapidly for Atlanta, breaking up the railroad *en route,* and generally to so damage the country as to make it untenable to the enemy. By the 14th all the troops had arrived at or near Atlanta, and were, according to orders, grouped into two wings, the right and left, commanded respectively by Major-Generals O. O. Howard and H. W. Slocum, both comparatively young men, but educated and experienced officers, fully competent to their command.

The cavalry division was held separate, subject to my own orders. It was commanded by Brigadier-General Judson Kilpatrick, and was composed of two brigades, commanded by Colonels Eli H. Murray, of Kentucky, and Smith D. Atkins, of Illinois.

The strength of the army, as officially reported shows an aggregate of fifty-five thousand three hundred and twenty-nine infantry, five thousand and sixty-three cavalry, and eighteen hundred and twelve artillery—in all, sixty-two thousand two hundred and four officers and men.

The most extraordinary efforts had been made to purge this army of non-combatants and of sick men, for we knew well that there was to be no place of safety save with the army itself; our wagons were loaded with ammunition, provisions, and forage, and we could ill afford to haul even sick men in the ambulances, so that all on this exhibit may be assumed to have been able-bodied, experienced soldiers, well armed, well equipped and provided, as far as human foresight could, with all the essentials of life, strength, and vigorous action.

The two general orders made for this march appear to me, even at this late day, so clear, emphatic, and well-digested, that no account of that historic event is perfect without them, and I give them entire, even at the seeming appearance of repetition; and, though they called for great sacrifice and labor on the part of the officers and men, I insist that these orders were obeyed as well as any similar orders ever were, by an army operating wholly in an enemy's country, and dispersed, as we necessarily were, during the subsequent period of nearly six months.

[Special Field Orders, No. 119.]
HEADQUARTERS MILITARY DIVISION OF THE MISSISSIPPI, IN THE FIELD, KINGSTON, GEORGIA, *November* 8, 1864.

The general commanding deems it proper at this time to inform the officers and men of the Fourteenth, Fifteenth, Seventeenth, and Twentieth Corps, that he has organized them into an army for a special purpose, well known to the War Department and to General Grant. It is sufficient for you to know that it involves a departure from our present base, and a long and difficult march to a new one. All the chances of war have been considered and provided for, as far as human sagacity can. All he asks of you is to maintain that discipline, patience, and courage, which have characterized you in the past; and he hopes, through you, to strike a blow at our enemy that will have a material effect in producing what we all so much desire, his complete over-throw. Of all things, the most important is, that the men, during marches and in camp, keep their places and do not scatter about as stragglers or foragers, to be picked up by a hostile people in detail. It is also of the utmost importance that our wagons should not be loaded with any thing but provisions and ammunition. All surplus servants, non-combatants, and refugees, should now go to the rear, and none should be encouraged to encumber us on the march. At some future time we will be able to provide for the poor whites and blacks who seek to escape the bondage under which they are now suffering. With these few simple cautions, he hopes to lead you to achievements equal in importance to those of the past.

By order of Major-General W. T. Sherman,

L. A DAYTON, *Aide-de-Camp.*

[Special Field Orders, No. 120]
HEADQUARTERS MILITARY DIVISION OF THE MISSISSIPPI, IN THE FIELD, KINGSTON, GEORGIA, *November* 9, 1864.

1. For the purpose of military operations, this army is divided into two wings viz.:

The right wing, Major-General O. O. Howard commanding, com-posed of the Fifteenth and Seventeenth Corps; the left wing, Major-General H. W. Slocum commanding, composed of the Fourteenth and Twentieth Corps.

2. The habitual order of march will be, wherever practicable, by four roads, as nearly parallel as possible, and converging at points hereafter to be indicated in orders. The cavalry, Brigadier-General Kilpatrick commanding, will receive special orders from the commander-in-chief.

3. There will be no general train of supplies, but each corps will have

its ammunition-train and provision-train, distributed habitually as follows: Behind each regiment should follow one wagon and one ambulance; behind each brigade should follow a due proportion of ammunition-wagons, provision-wagons, and ambulances. In case of danger, each corps commander should change this order of march, by having his advance and rear brigades unencumbered by wheels. The separate columns will start habitually at 7 a.m., and make about fifteen miles per day, unless otherwise fixed in orders.

4. The army will forage liberally on the country during the march. To this end, each brigade commander will organize a good and sufficient foraging party, under the command of one or more discreet officers, who will gather, near the route traveled, corn or forage of any kind, meat of any kind, vegetables, corn-meal, or whatever is needed by the command, aiming at all times to keep in the wagons at least ten days' provisions for his command, and three days' forage. Soldiers must not enter the dwellings of the inhabitants, or commit any trespass; but, during a halt or camp, they may be permitted to gather turnips, potatoes, and other vegetables, and to drive in stock in sight of their camp. To regular foraging-parties must be intrusted the gathering of provisions and forage, at any distance from the road traveled.

5. To corps commanders alone is intrusted the power to destroy mills, houses, cotton-gins, etc.; and for them this general principle is laid down: In districts and neighborhoods where the army is unmolested, no destruction of such property should be permitted; but should guerrillas or bushwhackers molest our march, or should the inhabitants burn bridges, obstruct roads, or otherwise manifest local hostility, then army commanders should order and enforce a devastation more or less relentless, according to the measure of such hostility.

6. As for horses, mules, wagons, etc., belonging to the inhabitants, the cavalry and artillery may appropriate freely and without limit; discriminating, however, between the rich, who are usually hostile, and the poor and industrious, usually neutral or friendly. Foraging also take mules or horses, to replace the jaded animals of or to serve as pack-mules for the regiments or brigades. In all foraging, of what-

ever kind, the parties engaged will refrain from abusive or threatening language, and may, where the officer in command thinks proper, give written certificates of the facts, but no receipts; and they will endeavor to leave with each family a reasonable portion for their maintenance,

7. Negroes who are able-bodied and can be of service to the several columns may be taken along; but each army commander will bear in mind that the question of supplies is a very important one, and that his first duty is to see to those who bear arms.

8. The organization, at once, of a good pioneer battalion for each army corps, composed if possible of negroes, should be attended to This battalion should follow the advance-guard, repair roads and double them if possible, so that the columns will not be delayed after reaching bad places. Also, army commanders should practise the habit of giving the artillery and wagons the road, marching their troops on one side, and instruct their troops to assist wagons at steep hills or bad crossings of streams.

9. Captain O. M. Poe, chief-engineer, will assign to each wing of the army a pontoon-train, fully equipped and organized; and the commanders thereof will see to their being properly protected at all times.

By order of Major-General W. T. Sherman,

L. M. DAYTON, *Aide-de-Camp.*


The greatest possible attention had been given to the artillery and wagon trains. The number of guns had been reduced to sixty-five, or about one gun to each thousand men, and these were generally in batteries of four guns each.

Each gun, caisson, and forge, was drawn by four teams of horses. We had in all about twenty-five hundred wagons, with teams of six mules to each, and six hundred ambulances, with two horses to each. The loads were made comparatively light, about twenty-five hundred pounds net; each wagon carrying in addition the forage needed by its own team. Each soldier carried on his person forty rounds of ammunition, and in the wagons were enough cartridges to make up about two hundred rounds per man, and in like manner two hundred rounds of assorted ammunition were carried for each gun.

The wagon-trains were divided equally between the four corps, so that each had about eight hundred wagons, and these usually on the march occupied five miles or more of road. Each corps commander managed his own train; and habitually the artillery and wagons had the road, while the men, with the exception of the advance and rear guards, pursued paths improvised by the side of the wagons, unless they were forced to use a bridge or causeway in common.

I reached Atlanta during the afternoon of the 14th, and found that all preparations had been made—Colonel Beckwith, chief commissary, reporting one million two hundred thousand rations in possession of the troops, which was about twenty days' supply, and he had on hand a good supply of beef-cattle to be driven along on the hoof. Of forage, the supply was limited, being of oats and corn enough for five days, but I knew that within that time we would reach a country well stocked with corn, which had been gathered and stored in cribs, seemingly for our use, by Governor Brown's Militia.

Colonel Poe, United States Engineers, of my staff, had been busy in his special task of destruction. He had a large force at work, had leveled the great depot, round-house, and the machine-shops of the Georgia Railroad, and had applied fire to the wreck. One of these machine-shops had been used by the rebels as an arsenal, and in it were stored piles of shot and shell, some of which proved to be loaded, and that night was made hideous by the bursting of shells, whose fragments came uncomfortably near Judge Lyon's house, in which I was quartered. The fire also reached the block of stores near the depot, and the heart of the city was in flames all night, but the fire did not reach the parts of Atlanta where the courthouse was, or the great mass of dwelling-houses.

The march from Atlanta began on the morning of November 15th, the right wing and cavalry following the railroad southeast toward Jonesboro', and General Slocum with the Twentieth Corps leading off to the east by Decatur and Stone Mountain, toward Madison. These were divergent lines, designed to threaten both Macon and Augusta at the same time, so as to prevent a concentration at our intended destination, or "objective," Milledgeville, the capital of Georgia, distant southeast about one hundred miles. The time allowed each column for reaching Milledgeville was seven days. I remained in Atlanta during the 15th with the Fourteenth Corps, and the rear-guard of the right wing, to complete the loading of the trains, and the destruction of the buildings of Atlanta which could be converted to hostile uses, and on the morning of the 16th started with my personal staff, a company of Alabama cavalry, commanded by Lieutenant Snelling, and an infantry company, commanded by Lieutenant McCrory, which guarded our small train of wagons.

About 7 a.m. of November 16th we rode out of Atlanta by the Decatur road, filled by the marching troops and wagons of the Fourteenth Corps; and reaching the hill, just outside of the old rebel works, we naturally paused to look back upon the scenes of our past battles. We stood upon the very ground whereon was fought the bloody battle of July 22d, and could see the copse of wood where McPherson fell. Behind us lay Atlanta, smouldering and in ruins, the black smoke rising high in air, and hanging like a pall over the ruined city. Away off in the distance, on the McDonough road, was the rear of Howard's column, the gun-barrels glistening in the sun, the white-topped wagons stretching away to the south; and right before us the Fourteenth Corps, marching steadily and rapidly, with a cheery look and swinging pace, that made light of the thousand miles that lay between us and Richmond. Some band, by accident, struck up the anthem of "John Brown's soul goes marching on"; the men caught up the strain, and never before or since have I heard the chorus of "Glory, glory, hallelujah!" done with more spirit, or in better harmony of time and place.

Then we turned our horses' heads to the east, Atlanta was soon lost behind the screen of trees and became a thing of the past. Around it clings many a thought of desperate battle, of hope and fear, that now seem like the memory of a dream; and I have never seen the place since. The day was extremely beautiful, clear sunlight, with bracing air, and an unusual feeling of exhilaration seemed to pervade all minds— a feeling of something to come, vague and undefined, still full of venture and intense interest. Even the common soldiers caught the inspiration, and many a group called out to me as I worked my way past them, "Uncle Billy, I guess Grant is waiting for us at Richmond!" Indeed, the general sentiment was that we were marching for Richmond, and that there we should end the war, but how and when they seemed to care not; nor did they measure the distance, or count the cost in life, or bother their brains about the great rivers to be crossed, and the food required for man and beast, that had to be gathered by the way. There was a "devil-may-care" feeling pervading officers and men, that made me feel the full load of responsibility, for success would be accepted as a matter of course, whereas, should we fail, this "march" would be adjudged the wild adventure of a crazy fool. I had no purpose to march direct for Richmond by way of Augusta and Charlotte, but always designed to reach the sea-coast first at Savannah or Port Royal, South Carolina, and even kept in mind the alternative of Pensacola.

The first night out we camped by the roadside near Lithonia. Stone Mountain, a mass of granite, was in plain view, cut out in clear outline against the blue sky; the whole horizon was lurid with the bonfires of rail-ties, and groups of men all night were carrying the heated rails to the nearest trees, and bending them around the trunks. Colonel Poe had provided tools for ripping up the rails and twisting them when hot; but the best and easiest way is the one I have described, of heating the middle of the iron-rails on bonfires made of the cross-ties, and then winding them around a telegraph-pole or the trunk of some convenient sapling. I attached much importance to this destruction of the railroad, gave it my own personal attention, and made reiterated orders to others on the subject.

The next day we passed through the handsome town of Covington, the soldiers closing up their ranks, the color-bearers unfurling their flags, and the bands striking up patriotic airs. The white people came out of their houses to behold the sight, spite of their deep hatred of the invaders, and the negroes were simply frantic with joy. Whenever they heard my name, they clustered about my horse, shouted and prayed in their peculiar style, which had a natural eloquence that would have moved a stone. I have witnessed hundreds, if not thousands, of such scenes; and can now see a poor girl, in the very ecstasy of the Methodist "shout," hugging the banner of one of the regiments, and jumping up to the "feet of Jesus."

I remember, when riding around by a by-street in Covington, to avoid the crowd that followed the marching column, that some one brought me an invitation to dine with a sister of Sam Anderson, who was a cadet at West Point with me; but the messenger reached me after we had passed the main part of the town. I asked to be excused, and rode on to a place designated for camp, at the crossing of the Ulcofauhachee River, about four miles to the east of the town. Here we made our bivouac, and I walked up to a plantation-house close by, where were assembled many negroes, among them an old, gray-haired man, of as fine a head as I ever saw. I asked him if he understood about the war and its progress. He said he did; that he had been looking for the "angel of the Lord" ever since he was knee-high, and, though we professed to be fighting for the Union, he supposed that slavery was the cause, and that our success was to be his freedom. I asked him if all the negro slaves comprehended this fact, and he said they surely did. I then explained to him that we wanted the slaves to remain where they were, and not to load us down with useless mouths, which would eat up the food needed for our fighting-men; that our success was their assured freedom; that we could receive a few of their young, hearty men as pioneers; but that, if they followed us in swarms of old and young, feeble and helpless, it would simply load us down and cripple us in our great task. I think Major Henry Hitchcock was with me on that occasion, and made a note of the conversation, and I believe that old man spread this message to the slaves, which was carried from mouth to mouth, to the very end of our journey, and that it in part saved us from the great danger we incurred of swelling our numbers so that famine would have attended our progress. It was at this very plantation that a soldier passed me with a ham on his musket, a jug of sorghum-molasses under his arm, and a big piece of honey in his hand, from which he was eating, and, catching my eye, he remarked *sotto voce* and carelessly to a comrade, "Forage liberally on the country," quoting from my general orders. On this occasion, as on many others that fell under my personal observation, I reproved the man, explained that foraging must be limited to the regular parties properly detailed, and that all provisions thus obtained must be delivered to the regular commissaries, to be fairly distributed to the men who kept their ranks.

From Covington the Fourteenth Corps (Davis's), with which I was traveling, turned to the right for Milledgeville, *via* Shady Dale. General Slocum was ahead at Madison, with the Twentieth Corps, having torn up the railroad as far as that place, and thence had sent Geary's division on to the Oconee, to burn the bridges across that stream, when this corps turned south by Eatonton, for Milledgeville, the common "objective" for the first stage of the "march." We found abundance of corn, molasses, meal, bacon, and sweet-potatoes. We also took a good many cows and oxen, and a large number of mules. In all these the country was quite rich, never before having been visited by a hostile army; the recent crop had been excellent, had been just gathered and laid by for the winter. As a rule, we destroyed none, but kept our wagons full, and fed our teams bountifully.

The skill and success of the men in collecting forage was one of the features of this march. Each brigade commander had authority to detail a company of foragers, usually about fifty men, with one or two commissioned officers selected for their boldness and enterprise. This party would be dispatched before daylight with a knowledge of the intended day's march and camp; would proceed on foot five or six miles from the route traveled by their brigade, and then visit every plantation and farm within range. They would usually procure a wagon or family carriage, load it with bacon, cornmeal, turkeys, chickens, ducks, and every thing that could be used as food or forage, and would then regain the main road, usually in advance of their train. When this came up, they would deliver to the brigade commissary the supplies thus gathered by the way. Often would I pass these foraging-parties at the roadside, waiting for their wagons to come up, and was amused at their strange collections—mules, horses, even cattle, packed with old saddles and loaded with hams, bacon, bags of corn-meal, and poultry of every character and description. Although this foraging was attended with great danger and hard work, there seemed to be a charm about it that attracted the soldiers, and it was a privilege to be detailed on such a party. Daily they returned mounted on all sorts of beasts, which were at once taken from them and appropriated to the general use; but the next day they would start out again on foot, only to repeat the experience of the day before. No doubt, many acts of pillage, robbery, and violence, were committed by these parties of foragers, usually called "bummers"; for I have since heard of jewelry taken from women, and the plunder of articles that never reached the commissary; but these acts were exceptional and incidental. I never heard of any cases of murder or rape; and no army could have carried along sufficient food and forage for a march of three hundred miles; so that foraging in some shape was necessary. The country was sparsely settled, with no magistrates or civil authorities who could respond to requisitions, as is done in all the wars of Europe; so that this system of foraging was simply indispensable to our success. By it our men were well supplied with all the essentials of life and health, while the wagons retained enough in case of unexpected delay, and our animals were well fed. Indeed, when we reached Savannah, the trains were pronounced by experts to be the finest in flesh and appearance ever seen with any army.

In a well-ordered and well-disciplined army, these things might be deemed irregular, but I am convinced that the ingenuity of these younger officers accomplished many things far better than I could have ordered, and the marches were thus made, and the distances were accomplished, in the most admirable way. Habitually we started from camp at the earliest break of dawn, and usually reached camp soon after noon. The marches varied from ten to fifteen miles a day, though sometimes on extreme flanks it was necessary to make as much as twenty, but the rate of travel was regulated by the wagons; and, considering the nature of the roads, fifteen miles per day was deemed the limit.

On the 20th of November I was still with the Fourteenth Corps, near Eatonton Factory. . . .The afternoon was unusually raw and cold. My orderly was at hand with his invariable saddle-bags, which contained a change of under-clothing, my maps, a flask of whiskey, and bunch of cigars. Taking a drink and lighting a cigar, I walked to a row of negro-huts close by, entered one and found a soldier or two warming themselves by a woodfire. I took their place by the fire, intending to wait there till our wagons had got up, and a camp made for the night. I was talking to the old negro woman, when some one came and explained to me that, if I would come farther down the road, I could find a better place. So I started on foot, and found on the main road a good double-hewed-log house, in one room of which Colonel Poe, Dr. Moore, and others, had started a fire. I sent back orders to the "plum-bushes" to bring our horses and saddles up to this house, and an orderly to conduct our head-quarter wagons to the same place. In looking around the room, I saw a small box, like a candle-box, marked "Howell Cobb," and, on inquiring of a negro, found that we were at the plantation of General Howell Cobb, of Georgia, one of the leading rebels of the South, then a general in the Southern army, and who had been Secretary of the United States Treasury in Mr. Buchanan's time. Of course, we confiscated his property, and found it rich in corn, beans, pea-nuts, and sorghum-molasses. Extensive fields were all round the house; I sent word back to General Davis to explain whose plantation it was, and instructed him to spare nothing. That night huge bonfires consumed the fence-rails, kept our soldiers warm, and the teamsters and men, as well as the slaves, carried off an immense quantity of corn and provisions of all sorts.

Therefore, by the 23d, I was in Milledgeville with the left wing, and was in full communication with the right wing at Gordon. The people of Milledgeville remained at home, except the Governor (Brown), the State officers, and Legislature, who had ignominiously fled, in the utmost disorder and confusion; standing not on the order of their going, but going at once—some by rail, some by carriages, and many on foot. Some of the citizens who remained behind described this flight of the "brave and patriotic" Governor Brown. He had occupied a public building known as the "Governor's Mansion," and had hastily stripped it of carpets, curtains, and furniture of all sorts, which were removed to a train of freight-cars, which carried away these things— even the cabbages and vegetables from his kitchen and cellar—leaving behind muskets, ammunition, and the public archives. On arrival at Milledgeville I occupied the same public mansion, and was soon overwhelmed with appeals for protection. General Slocum had previously arrived with the Twentieth Corps, had taken up his quarters at the Milledgeville Hotel, established a good provost-guard, and excellent order was maintained. The most frantic appeals had been made by the Governor and Legislature for help from every quarter, and the people of the State had been called out *en masse* to resist and destroy the invaders of their homes and firesides. Even the prisoners and convicts of the penitentiary were released on condition of serving as soldiers, and the cadets were taken from their military college for the same purpose. These constituted a small battalion, under General Harry Wayne, a former officer of the United States Army, and son of the then Justice Wayne of the Supreme Court. But these hastily retreated east across the Oconee River, leaving us a good bridge, which we promptly secured.

At Milledgeville we found newspapers from all the South, and learned the consternation which had filled the Southern mind at our temerity; many charging that we were actually fleeing for our lives and seeking safety at the hands of our fleet on the seacoast. All demanded that we should be assailed, "front, flank, and rear;" that provisions should be destroyed in advance, so that we would starve; that bridges should be burned, roads obstructed, and no mercy shown us. Judging from the tone of the Southern press of that day, the outside world must have supposed us ruined and lost. I give a few of these appeals as samples, which today must sound strange to the parties who made them:

CORINTH, MISSISSIPPI, *November* 18, 1864.
*To the People of Georgia:*
Arise for the defense of your native soil! Rally around your patriotic Governor and gallant soldiers! Obstruct and destroy all the roads in Sherman's front, flank, and rear, and his army will soon starve in your midst. Be confident. Be resolute. Trust in an overruling Providence, and success will soon crown your efforts. I hasten to join you in the defense of your homes and firesides.

G. T. BEAUREGARD.

RICHMOND, *November* 18, 1864.
*To the People of Georgia:*
You have now the best opportunity ever yet presented to destroy the enemy. Put every thing at the disposal of our generals; remove all provisions from the path of the invader, and put all obstructions in his path.

Every citizen with his gun, and every negro, with his spade and axe, can do the work of a soldier. You can destroy the enemy by retarding his march.

Georgians, be firm! Act promptly, and fear not!
B. H. HILL, *Senator.*
I most cordially approve the above.

JAMES A. SEDDON, *Secretary of War.*

RICHMOND, *November* 19, 1864.

*To the People of Georgia:*

We have had a special conference with President Davis and the Secretary of War, and are able to assure you that they have done and are still doing all that can be done to meet the emergency that presses upon you. Let every man fly to arms! Remove your negroes, horses, cattle, and provisions from Sherman's army, and burn what you cannot carry. Burn all bridges, and block up the roads in his route. Assail the invader in front, flank, and rear, by night and by day. Let him have no rest.

JULIAN HARTRIDGE, MARK BLANDFORD
J. H. ECHOLS, GEO. N. LESTER,
JOHN T. SHUEMAKE, JAS. M. SMITH,
*Members of Congress,*

Of course, we were rather amused than alarmed at these threats, and made light of the feeble opposition offered to our progress. Some of the officers (in the spirit of mischief) gathered together in the vacant hall of Representatives, elected a Speaker, and constituted themselves the Legislature of the State of Georgia! A proposition was made to repeal the ordinance of secession, which was well debated, and resulted in its repeal by a fair vote! I was not present at these frolics, but heard of them at the time, and enjoyed the joke.

Meantime orders were made for the total destruction of the arsenal and its contents, and of such public buildings as could be easily converted to hostile uses. But little or no damage was done to private property, and General Slocum, with my approval, spared several mills, and many thousands of bales of cotton, taking what he knew to be worthless bonds, that the cotton should not be used for the Confederacy. Meantime the right wing continued its movement along the railroad toward Savannah, tearing up the track and destroying its iron.

from Before Freedom,
When I Just Can Remember
by Adeline Grey,
interviewed by Phoebe Faucette

*Adeline Grey's account of the day the Yankees
descended on the farm of her "Missus" conveys
something of the hardships slaves endured during the war that eventually freed them. Grey's
matter-of-fact recollections also include refer-
ences to the family's post-War poverty—a
reminder that further suffering awaited former
slaves in the post-war South.*

I remember when the Yankees come through. I was right to the old
boss' place. It was on the river side. Miss Jane Warner, she was the
missus. My ma used to belong to Old Man Dave Warner. I remember how she used to wash and iron and cook for the white folks
during slavery time. The place here now, where all the chillun raise. Mr.
Rhodes got a turpentine still there now, just after you pass the house.

I remember when my ma saw the Yankees coming that morning.
She grab the sweet potatoes that been in that oven and throw 'em in
the barrel of feathers that stayed by the kitchen fireplace. Just a barrel
to hold chicken feathers when you pick 'em. That's all we had to eat
that day.

They went into the company room where the old missus was stay-
ing and start tearing up the bed. Then, the captain come and the old
missus say to him, "Please don't let them tear up my bed," and the captain went in there and tell them, "Come out!"

The old missus wasn't scared. But young Miss May was sure scared.

She was courting at the time. She went off and shut herself up in a room. The old missus ask the captain, "Please go in and talk to the missus, she so scared." So he went in and soon he bring her out.

We chillun wasn't scared. But my brother run under the house. The soldiers went under there a-poking the bayonets into the ground to try to find where the silver buried, and they ran across him. "What you doing under here?" they say.

"I's just running the chickens out, sir." he say.

"Well, you can go on out," they say. "We ain't going to hurt you."

They choked my ma. They went to her and they say, "Where is all the white people's gold and silver?" My ma say she don't know.

"You does know," they say, and choke her till she couldn't talk.

I remember she had a red striped shawl. One of the Yankees take that and start to put it under his saddle for a saddle cloth. My brother go up to him and say, "Please sir, don't carry my ma's shawl. That the only one she got." So he give it back to him.

They burn the ginhouse, the shop, the buggyhouse, the turkey-house, and the fowlhouse. Start to set the cornhouse afire, but my ma say, "Please sir, don't burn the cornhouse. Give it to me and my chillun." So, they put the fire out. I don't know why they didn't burn the house. Must have been 'cause the captain was along. The house there now. One of the chimney down. I don't think they ever put it up again. Colored folks are in it now.

I remember when they started to break down the smokehouse door, and Old Missus come out and say, "Please don't break the door open; I got the key." So they quit.

I remember when they shoot down the hog. I remember when they shoot the two geese in the yard. I remember when they kill the hog and cook 'em. Cook on the fire, where the little shop been. Cook 'em and eat 'em. Why didn't they cook 'em on the stove in the house? Didn't have no stoves. Just had to cook on the fireplace. Had an oven to fit in the fireplace.

Old Missus had give my ma a good moss mattress. But the Yankees had carry that off. Rip it up, throw out the moss, and put meat in it.

Fill it full of meat. Them Yankees put the meat in the sack and go on off. It was late then, about dusk. I remember how the missus bring us all round the fire. It was dark then.

"Well, chillun," she say, "I is sorry to tell you, but the Yankees has carry off your ma. I don't know if you'll ever see her anymore."

Then, we chillun all start crying. We still a-sitting there when my ma come back. She say she slip behind, and slip behind, and slip behind, and when she come to a little pine thicket by the side of the road, she dart into it, drop the sock of meat they had her carrying, and start out for home. When we had all make over her, we say to her then, "Well, why didn't you bring the sack of meat along with you?"

They took the top off Old Marster John carriage, put meat in it, and made him pull it same as a horse. Carry him way down to Lawtonville, had to pull it through the branch and all. Got the rockaway back, though—and the old man. I remember that well.

Had to mend up the old rockaway. And it made the old man sick. He keep on sick, sick, until he died. I remember how he'd say, "Don't you all worry." And he'd go out in the orchard. They'd say, "Don't bother him. Just let him be. He want to pray." After a while he died and they buried him. His name was John Stafford. They marster wasn't there. I guess he was off to the war.

I was a girl when Freedom was declared, and I can remember about the times. But, after Freedom, was the time when they suffered more than before. These chillun don't know how they blessed. To keep warm at night, they had to make their pallet down by the fire. When all wood burn out, put on another piece. Didn't have nothing on the bed to sleep on.

My ma cooked for the white folks for one year after Freedom. I remember they cook bread, and they ain't have nothing to eat on it. Was thankful for a cornbread hoecake baked in the fireplace.

But they had some things. Had buried some meat, and some syrup. And they had some corn. My ma had saved the cornhouse. The rice burn up in the ginhouse.

I remember when the old missus used to have to make soap, out of these red oaks. Burn the wood, and catches the ashes. Put the ashes in a barrel with a trough under it, and pour the water through the ashes. If the lyewater that come out could cut a feather, it was strong.

Used to weave cloth after Freedom. Used to give a broach [a measurement of yarn] or two to weave at night. I's sometimes thread the needle for my ma, or pick the seed out the cotton, and make it into rolls to spin. Sometimes I'd work the foot pedal for my ma. Then they'd warp the thread.

If she want to dye it, she'd get indigo—you know that bush—and boil it. It was kinder blue. It would make good cloth. Sometimes, the cloth was kinder striped, one stripe of white, and one of blue. I remember how they'd warp the thread across the yarn after it was dyed, and I remember seeing my ma throw that shuttle through and weave that cloth.

I never did know my pa. He was sold off to Texas when I was young. My mother would say, "Well, chillun, you ain't never known your pa. Joe Smart carry him off to Texas when he went. I don't guess you'll ever see him."

My father was named Charles Smart. He never did come back. Joe Smart come back once, and say that our father is dead. He say our pa had three horses and he want one of them to be sent to us children here, but no arrangements had been made to get it to us. You see, he had chillun out there, too.

After Freedom, my ma plow many a day, same as a man, for us chillun. She work for Old Man Bill Mars. Then, she marry again. Part of the time they work for Mr. Benny Lawton, the one-arm man, what lost his arm in the war. These chillun don't know what hard times is. They don't know how to 'preciate our blessings.

from Memoirs and Selected Letters
by Ulysses S. Grant

*Ulysses S. Grant (1822–1885) accepted Lee's surrender at Appomattox, and recalled that event in his memoirs, widely considered an American masterpiece. Grant's graceful and understated prose conveys the strength of his character and the depth of his respect for his opponent. The dignity that Grant here bestows on Lee ultimately reflects upon himself.*

Here I met Dr. Smith, a Virginian and an officer of the regular army, who told me that in a conversation with General Ewell, one of the prisoners and a relative of his, Ewell had said that when we had got across the James River he knew their cause was lost, and it was the duty of their authorities to make the best terms they could while they still had a right to claim concessions. The authorities thought differently, however. Now the cause was lost and they had no right to claim anything. He said further, that for every man that was killed after this in the war somebody is responsible, and it would be but very little better than murder. He was not sure that Lee would consent to surrender his army without being able to consult with the President, but he hoped he would.

I rode in to Farmville on the seventh, arriving there early in the day. Sheridan and Ord were pushing through, away to the south. Meade was back towards the High Bridge, and Humphreys confronting Lee as before stated. After having gone into bivouac at Prince Edward's Court

House, Sheridan learned that seven trains of provisions and forage were at Appomattox, and determined to start at once and capture them; and a forced march was necessary in order to get there before Lee's army could secure them. He wrote me a note telling me this. This fact, together with the incident related the night before by Dr. Smith, gave me the idea of opening correspondence with General Lee the subject of the surrender of his army. I therefore wrote to him on this day, as follows:

> HEADQUARTERS ARMIES OF THE U. S.,
> April 7, 1865, 5 p.m.

GENERAL R. E. LEE,
Commanding C. S. A.

The results of the last week must convince you of the hopelessness of further resistance on the part of the Army of Northern Virginia in this struggle. I feel that it is so, and regard it as my duty to shift from myself the responsibility of any further effusion of blood, by asking of you the surrender of that portion of the Confederate States army known as the Army of Northern Virginia.

U. S. GRANT,
Lieutenant-General.

Lee replied on the evening of the same day as follows:

> April 7, 1865.

GENERAL:—I have received your note of this day. Though not entertaining the opinion you express on the hopelessness of further resistance on the part of the Army of Northern Virginia, I reciprocate your desire to avoid useless effusion of blood, and therefore before considering your proposition, ask the terms you will offer on condition of its surrender.

R. E. LEE,
General.

• • •

This was not satisfactory, but I regarded it as deserving another letter and wrote him as follows:

April 8, 1865.

GENERAL R. E. LEE,
Commanding C. S. A.

Your note of last evening in reply to mine of same date, asking the condition on which I will accept the surrender of the Army of Northern Virginia is just received. In reply I would say that, peace being my great desire, there is but one condition I would insist upon, namely: that the men and officers surrendered shall be disqualified for taking up arms again against the Government of the United States until properly exchanged. I will meet you, or will designate officers to meet any officers you may name for the same purpose, at any point agreeable to you, for the purpose of arranging definitely the terms upon which the surrender of the Army of Northern Virginia will be received.

U.S. GRANT,
Lieutenant General.

Lee's army was rapidly crumbling. Many of his soldiers had enlisted from that part of the State where they now were, and were continually dropping out of the ranks and going to their homes. I know that I occupied a hotel almost destitute of furniture at Farmville, which had probably been used as a Confederate hospital. The next morning when I came out I found a Confederate colonel there, who reported to me and said that he was the proprietor of that house, and that he was a colonel of a regiment that had been raised in that neighborhood. He said that when he came along past home, he found that he was the only man of the regiment remaining with Lee's army, so he just dropped out, and now wanted to surrender himself. I told him to stay there and he would not be molested. That was one regiment which had been eliminated from Lee's force by this crumbling process.

Although Sheridan had been marching all day, his troops moved with alacrity and without any straggling. They began to see the end of what they had been fighting four years for. Nothing seemed to fatigue them. They were ready to move without rations and travel without rest until the end. Straggling had entirely ceased, and every man was now a rival for the front. The infantry marched about as rapidly as the cavalry could.

Sheridan sent Custer with his division to move south of Appomattox Station, which is about five miles southwest of the Court House, to get west of the trains and destroy the roads to the rear. They got there the night of the 8th, and succeeded partially; but some of the train men had just discovered the movement of our troops and succeeded in running off three of the trains. The other four were held by Custer.

The head of Lee's column came marching up there on the morning of the ninth, not dreaming, I suppose, that there were any Union soldiers near. The Confederates were surprised to find our cavalry had possession of the trains. However, they were desperate and at once assaulted, hoping to recover them. In the melée that ensued they succeeded in burning one of the trains, but not in getting anything from it. Custer then ordered the other trains run back on the road towards Farmville, and the fight continued.

So far, only our cavalry and the advance of Lee's army were engaged. Soon, however, Lee's men were brought up from the rear, no doubt expecting they had nothing to meet but our cavalry. But our infantry had pushed forward so rapidly that by the time the enemy got up they found Griffin's corps and the Army of the James confronting them. A sharp engagement ensued, but Lee quickly set up a white flag.

On the eighth I had followed the Army of the Potomac in rear of Lee. I was suffering very severely with a sick headache, and stopped at a farmhouse on the road some distance in rear of the main body of the army. I spent the night in bathing my feet in hot water and mustard, and putting mustard plasters on my wrists and the back part of my neck, hoping to be cured by morning. During the night I received Lee's answer to my letter of the 8th, inviting an interview between the lines on the following morning. But it was for a different purpose from that of surrendering his army, and I answered him as follows:

> HEADQUARTERS ARMIES OF THE U. S.,
> April 9, 1865.
>
> GENERAL R. E. LEE,
> Commanding C. S. A.
>
> Your note of yesterday is received. As I have no authority to treat on the subject of peace, the meeting proposed for ten a.m. today could lead to no good. I will state, however, General, that I am equally anxious for peace with yourself, and the whole North entertains the same feeling. The terms upon which peace can be had are well understood. By the South laying down their arms they will hasten that most desirable event, save thousands of human lives, and hundreds of millions of property not yet destroyed. Sincerely hoping that all our difficulties may be settled without the loss of another life I subscribe myself, etc.,
>
> U. S. GRANT,
> Lieutenant-General.

I proceeded at an early hour in the morning, still suffering with the headache, to get to the head of the column. I was not more than two or three miles from Appomattox Court House at the time, but to go direct I would have to pass through Lee's army, or a portion of it. I had therefore to move south in order to get upon a road coming up from another direction.

When the white flag was put out by Lee, as already described, I was in this way moving towards Appomattox Court House, and consequently could not be communicated with immediately, and be informed of what Lee had done. Lee, therefore, sent a flag to the rear to advise Meade and one to the front to Sheridan, saying that he had sent a message to me for the purpose of having a meeting to consult about the surrender of his army, and asked for a suspension of hostilities until I could be communicated with. As they had heard nothing of this until the fighting had got to be severe and all going against Lee, both of these commanders hesitated very considerably about suspending hostilities at all. They were afraid it was not in good faith, and we had the Army of Northern Virginia where it could not escape except by some deception. They, however, finally consented to a suspension of hostilities for two hours to give an opportunity of communicating with me in that time, if possible. It was found that, from the route I had taken, they would probably not be able to communicate with me and get an answer back within the time fixed unless the messenger should pass through the rebel lines.

Lee, therefore, sent an escort with the officer bearing this message through his lines to me.

April 9, 1865.

GENERAL:—I received your note of this morning on the picketing whither I had come to meet you and ascertain definitely what terms were embraced in your proposal of yesterday with reference to the sur-render of this army. I now request an interview in accordance with the offer contained in your letter of yesterday for that purpose.

R. E. LEE,
General.

LIEUTENANT-GENERAL U. S. GRANT,
Commanding U. S. Armies.

When the officer reached me I was still suffering with the sick headache; but the instant I saw the contents of the note I was cured. I wrote the following note in reply and hastened on:

April 9, 1865.

GENERAL R. E. LEE,
Commanding C. S. Armies.

Your note of this date is but this moment (11:50 a.m.) received, in consequence of my having passed from the Richmond and Lynchburg road to the Farmville and Lynchburg road. I am at this writing about four miles west of Walker's Church and will push forward to the front for the purpose of meeting you. Notice sent to me on this road where you wish the interview to take place will meet me.

U. S. GRANT,

Lieutenant-General.

I was conducted at once to where Sheridan was located with his troops drawn up in line of battle facing the Confederate army near by. They were very much excited, and expressed their view that this was all a ruse employed to enable the Confederates to get away. They said they believed that Johnston was marching up from North Carolina now, and Lee was moving to join him; and they would whip the rebels where they now were in five minutes if I would only let them go in. But I had no doubt about the good faith of Lee, and pretty soon was conducted to where he was. I found him at the house of a Mr. McLean, at Appomattox Court House with Colonel Marshall, one of his staff officers, awaiting my arrival. The head of his column was occupying a hill, on a portion of which was an apple orchard, beyond a little valley which separated it from that on the crest of which Sheridan's forces were drawn up in line of battle to the south.

Before stating what took place between General Lee and myself, I will give all there is of the story of the famous apple tree.

Wars produce many stories of fiction, some of which are told until they are believed to be true. The war of the rebellion was no exception to this rule, and the story of the apple tree is one of those fictions based on a slight foundation of fact. As I have said, there was an apple orchard on the side of the hill occupied by the Confederate forces. Running diagonally up the hill was a wagon road, which, at one point, ran very near one of the trees, so that the wheels of vehicles had on that side, cut off the roots of this tree, leaving a little embankment. General Babcock, of my staff, reported to me that when he first met General Lee he was sitting upon this embankment with his feet in the road below and his back resting against the tree. The story had no other foundation than that. Like many other stories, it would be very good if it was only true.

I had known General Lee in the old army, and had served with him in the Mexican War; but did not suppose, owing to the difference in our age and rank, that he would remember me; while I would more naturally remember him distinctly, because he was the chief of staff of General Scott in the Mexican War.

When I had left camp that morning I had not expected so soon the result that was then taking place, and consequently was in rough garb. I was without a sword, as I usually was when on horseback on the field, and wore a soldier's blouse for a coat, with the shoulder straps of my rank to indicate to the army who I was. When I went into the house I found General Lee. We greeted each other, and after shaking hands took our seats. I had my staff with me, a good portion of whom were in the room during the whole of the interview.

What General Lee's feelings were I do not know. As he was a man of much dignity, with an impassible face, it was impossible to say whether he felt inwardly glad that the end had finally come, or felt sad over the result, and was too manly to show it. Whatever his feelings, they were entirely concealed from my observation; but my own feelings, which had been quite jubilant on the receipt of his letter, were sad and depressed. I felt like anything rather than rejoicing at the downfall of a foe who had fought so long and valiantly, and had suffered so much for a cause, though that cause was, I believe, one of the worst for which a people ever fought, and one for which there was the least excuse. I do not question, however, the sincerity of the great mass of those who were opposed to us.

General Lee was dressed in a full uniform which was entirely new, and was wearing a sword of considerable value, very likely the sword which had been presented by the State of Virginia; at all events, it was an entirely different sword from the one that would ordinarily be worn in the field. In my rough traveling suit, the uniform of a private with the straps of a lieutenant-general, I must have contrasted very strangely with a man so handsomely dressed, six feet high and of faultless form. But this was not a matter that I thought of until afterwards.

We soon fell into a conversation about old army times. He remarked that he remembered me very well in the old army; and I told him that as a matter of course I remembered him perfectly, but from the difference in our rank and years (there being about sixteen years' difference in our ages), I had thought it very likely that I had not attracted his attention sufficiently to be remembered by him after such a long interval. Our conversation grew so pleasant that I almost forgot the object of our meeting. After the conversation had run on in this style for some time, General Lee called my attention to the object of our meeting, and said that he had asked for this interview for the purpose of getting from me the terms I proposed to give his army. I said that I meant merely that his army should lay down their arms, not to take them up again during the continuance of the war unless duly and properly exchanged. He said that he had so understood my letter.

Then we gradually fell off again into conversation about matters foreign to the subject which had brought us together. This continued for some little time, when General Lee again interrupted the course of the conversation by suggesting that the terms I proposed to give his army ought to be written out. I called to General Parker, secretary on my staff, for writing materials, and commenced writing out the following terms:

APPOMATTOX C. H., VA.,
April 19th 1865.

GEN. R. E. LEE,
Comd'g C. S. A.

GEN: In accordance with the substance of my letter to you of the 8th inst., I propose to receive the surrender of the Army of N. Va. on the following terms, to wit: Rolls of all the officers and men to be made in duplicate. One copy to be given to an officer designated by me, the other to be retained by such officer or officers as you may designate. The officers to give their individual paroles not to take up arms against the Government of the United States until properly exchanged, and each company or regimental commander sign a like parole for the men of their commands. The arms, artillery and public property to be parked and stacked, and turned over to the officer appointed by me to receive them. This will not embrace the side arms of the officers, nor their private horses or baggage. This done, each officer and man will be allowed to return to their homes, not to be disturbed by United States authority so long as they observe their paroles and the laws in force where they may reside.

Very respectfully,

U. S. GRANT,

Lt. Gen.

When I put my pen to the paper I did not know the first word that I should make use of in writing the terms. I only knew what was in my mind, and I wished to express it clearly, so that there could be no mistaking it. As I wrote on, the thought occurred to me that the officers had their own private horses and effects, which were important to them, but of no value to us; also that it would be an unnecessary humiliation to call upon them to deliver their side arms.

No conversation, not one word, passed between General Lee and myself, either about private property, side arms, or kindred subjects. He appeared to have no objections to the terms first proposed; or if he had a point to make against them he wished to wait until they were in writing to make it. When he read over that part of the terms about side arms, horses and private property of the officers, he remarked, with some feeling, I thought, that this would have a happy effect upon his army.

Then, after a little further conversation, General Lee remarked to me again that their army was organized a little differently from the army of the United States (still maintaining by implication that we were two countries); that in their army the cavalrymen and artillerists owned their own horses; and he asked if he was to understand that the men who so owned their horses were to be permitted to retain them. I told him that as the terms were written they would not; that only the officers were permitted to take their private property. He then, after reading over the terms a second time, remarked that that was clear.

I then said to him that I thought this would be about the last battle of the war—I sincerely hoped so; and I said further I took it that most of the men in the ranks were small farmers. The whole country had been so raided by the two armies that it was doubtful whether they would be able to put in a crop to carry themselves and their families through the next winter without the aid of the horses they were then riding. The United States did not want them and I would, therefore, instruct the officers I left behind to receive the paroles of his troops to let every man of the Confederate army who claimed to own a horse or mule take the animal to his home. Lee remarked again that this would have a happy effect.

He then sat down and wrote out the following letter:

HEADQUARTERS ARMY OF NORTHERN VIRGINIA,
April 9, 1865.

GENERAL:—I received your letter of this date containing the terms of the surrender of the Army of Northern Virginia as proposed by you. As they are substantially the same as those expressed in your letter of the 8th inst., they are accepted. I will proceed to designate the proper officers to carry the stipulations into effect.

R. E. LEE,
General.

While duplicates of the two letters were being made, the Union generals present were severally presented to General Lee.

The much talked of surrendering of Lee's sword and my handing it back, this and much more that has been said about it is the purest romance. The word *sword* or *side arms* was not mentioned by either of us until I wrote it in the terms. There was no premeditation, and it did not occur to me until the moment I wrote it down. If I had happened to omit it, and General Lee had called my attention to it, I should have put it in the terms precisely as I acceded to the provision about the soldiers retaining their horses.

General Lee, after all was completed and before taking his leave, remarked that his army was in a very bad condition for want of food, and that they were without forage; that his men had been living for some days on parched corn exclusively and that he would have to ask me for rations and forage. I told him "certainly," and asked for how many men he wanted rations. His answer was "about twenty-five thousand:" and I authorized him to send his own commissary and quartermaster to Appomattox Station, two or three miles away, where he could have, out of the trains we had stopped, all the provisions wanted. As for forage, we had ourselves depended almost entirely upon the country for that.

Generals Gibbon, Griffin and Merritt were designated by me to carry into effect the paroling of Lee's troops before they should start for their homes—General Lee leaving Generals Longstreet, Gordon and Pendleton for them to confer with in order to facilitate this work. Lee and I then separated as cordially as we had met, he returning to his own lines, and all went into bivouac for the night at Appomattox.

Soon after Lee's departure I telegraphed to Washington as follows:

> HEADQUARTERS APPOMATTOX C. H., VA.,
> April 9th 1865, 4.30 p.m.

HON. E. M. STANTON, Secretary of War,
Washington.

General Lee surrendered the Army of Northern Virginia this afternoon on terms proposed by myself. The accompanying additional correspondence will show the conditions fully.

U. S. GRANT,
Lieutenant-General.

When news of the surrender first reached our lines our men commenced firing a salute of a hundred guns in honor of the victory. I at once sent word, however, to have it stopped. The Confederates were now our prisoners, and we did not want to exult over their downfall.

I determined to return to Washington at once, with a view to putting a stop to the purchase of supplies, and what I now deemed other useless outlay of money. Before leaving, however, I thought I would like to see General Lee again; so next morning I rode out beyond our lines towards his headquarters, preceded by a bugler and a staff-officer carrying a white flag.

Lee soon mounted his horse, seeing who it was, and met me. We had there between the lines, sitting on horseback, a very pleasant conversation of over half an hour, in the course of which Lee said to me that the South was a big country and that we might have to march over it three or four times before the war entirely ended, but that we would now be able to do it as they could no longer resist us. He expressed it as his earnest hope, however, that we would not be called upon to cause more loss and sacrifice of life; but he could not foretell the result. I then suggested to General Lee that there was not a man in the Confederacy whose influence with the soldiery and the whole people was as great as his, and that if he would now advise the surrender of all the armies I had no doubt his advice would be followed with alacrity. But Lee said that he could not do that without consulting the President first. I knew there was no use to urge him to do anything against his ideas of what was right.

I was accompanied by my staff and other officers, some of whom seemed to have a great desire to go inside the Confederate lines. They finally asked permission of Lee to do so for the purpose of seeing some of their old army friends, and the permission was granted. They went over, had a very pleasant time with their old friends, and brought some of them back with them when they returned.

When Lee and I separated he went back to his lines and I returned to the house of Mr. McLean. Here the officers of both armies came in great numbers, and seemed to enjoy the meeting as much as though they had been friends separated for a long time while fighting battles under the same flag. For the time being it looked very much as if all thought of the war had escaped their minds. After an hour pleasantly passed in this way I set out on horseback, accompanied by my staff and a small escort, for Burkesville Junction, up to which point the railroad had by this time been repaired.

# acknowledgments

I have a number of debts—indirect and direct—to acknowledge. First thanks go to my parents, Peter and Anna Kadzis, who stocked our house in Dorchester, Massachussetts, with a judicious selection of books published by American Heritage. These well-thumbed volumes kindled a life-long love of history and an early fascination with the Civil War. Later, two teachers at Boston Latin, Dan Leary and Aaron Gordon, helped me to understand that history was more than a series of true-life stories; that it was a way of looking at the past so that we could better understand the present. Professor Thomas Brown of the University of Massachussetts at Boston, in his vivid lectures on American History at the University of Massachusetts, dramatically demonstrated that history can inspire enduring literary forms, and is often best animated by the voices of those who made it. Edmund Wilson's *Patriotic Gore: Studies in the Literature of the American Civil War* started me 30 years ago on a journey that has led to this book. Daniel Aaron's *The Unwritten War: American Writers and the Civil War*, which I read 20 years later, also helped shape my thinking. My editors, Clint Willis and Tom Dyja, helped shape what at one point was an amorphous manuscript into what I hope is now a coherent collection. Their dedication to the arts of writing, editing and publishing is inspiring and instructive. Learned biographer and historian Douglass Shand-Tucci on innumerable occasions offered sage and subtle counsel. Shawn Hachey managed the permissions process with impressive efficiency. This book would not have been possible without the active and enthusiastic assistance of the research staffs at the Boston Public

Library and the Boston Athenaeum. My greatest debt is to my wife, Susan Kelley, who encouraged me to undertake this project; supported me when balancing the book with my other professional responsibilities threatened to tip me over the edge; and shouldered an at times unfair responsibility for caring for our three young sons so that I could get on with this work. All of the people I mention here contributed to whatever virtues this book manifests. Any shortcomings are my own.

—Peter Kadzis

We would like to thank Ron Hussey at Simon & Schuster for his help on rights issues, as well as Carolyn Parsons of the Museum of the Confederacy and Nicole Wells of The New-York Historical Society for their good offices in securing imagery. Mike Miliard in Peter Kadzis's office also came through with some clutch help at the end.

—Balliett & Fitzgerald Inc.

# b i b l i o g r a p h y

The selections used in this anthology were taken from the editions listed below. In some cases, other editions may be easier to find. Hard to find or out-of-print titles often can be acquired through inter-library loan services. Internet sources also may be able to locate these books.

*Before Freedom, When I Just Can Remember: Twenty-seven Oral Histories of Former South Carolina Slaves.* Belinda Hurmence, editor. Winston-Salem, North Carolina: John F. Blair, 1999.

Benson, Berry. *Berry Benson's Civil War Book.* (Susan Williams Benson, editor). Athens, GA: The University of Georgia Press, 1991.

Blackford, Lieut. Colonel W. W. *War Years With Jeb Stuart.* New York: Charles Scribner's Sons, 1945.

Callaway, Joshua K. *The Civil War Letters of Joshua K. Callaway.* (Judith Lee Hallock, editor). Athens, GA: The University of Georgia Press, 1997.

Dawson, Sarah Morgan. *A Confederate Girl's Diary.* New York: Houghton Mifflin, 1913.

Douglas, Henry Kid. *I Rode with Stonewall.* Chapel Hill, North Carolina: The University of North Carolina Press, 1940.

Foote, Shelby. *Shiloh: A Novel.* New York: The Dial Press, 1952.

Grant, Ulysses S. *Memoirs and Selected Letters (Personal Memoirs of U.S. Grant Selected Letters, 1839-1865).* New York: The Library of America, 1990.

Higginson, Thomas Wentworth. *Army Life in a Black Regiment.* New York: Penguin Books, 1997.

Lincoln, Abraham. *Abraham Lincoln: Speeches & Writings, 1859-1865.* New York: The Library of America, 1989.

McElroy, John. *Andersonville: A Story of Rebel Military Prisons, Fifteen Months a Guest of the So-called Southern Confederacy.* Toledo: D.R. Locke, 1879.

Pickett, George Edward. *Soldier of the South: General Pickett's War Letters to His Wife*. (Arthur Crew Inman, editor). New York: Houghton Mifflin, 1928.

Seabury, Caroline. *Diary of Caroline Seabury, 1854-1863*. (Suzanne Bunkers, editor). Madison, Wisconsin: University of Wisconsin, 1991.

Shaara, Michael. *The Killer Angels: A Novel About the Four Days of Gettysburg*. New York: David McKay Company, 1974.

Sherman, William Tecumseh. *Memoirs of General W. T. Sherman*. New York: The Library of America, 1990.

*Short Shorts: An Anthology of the Shortest Stories*. Irving Howe and Ilana Wiener Howe, editors. New York: Bantam Books, 1983 (for "An Episode of War" by Stephen Crane).

Stevens, George T. *Three Years in the Sixth Corps*. Albany, NY: SR Gray, 1866.

Strong, George Templeton. *The Diary of George Templeton Strong*. New York: The MacMillan Company, 1952.

Watkins, Samuel R. *"Co. Aytch": A Side Show of the Big Show*. New York: Touchstone Books, 1997.

Whitman, Walt. *Complete Poetry and Collected Prose*. New York: The Library of America, 1982.

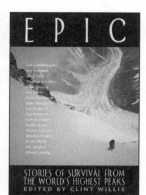

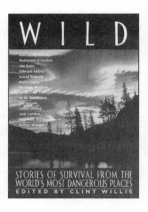
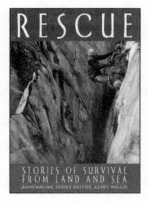

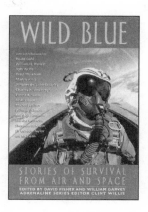
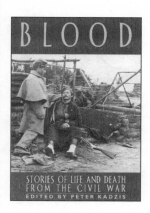
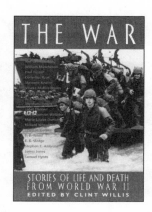

# adrenaline™